The Nightly Missive
A COVID Memoir
March 14, 2020-March 14, 2021

by
Mary K. Rossi
with contributions from
the **Campfire Girls** and the **College Angels**

To request permissions, contact the publisher at:
publishing@villagebooks.com

ISBN: 9798218214272
LCCN: 2023909918

Cover art by Owen Paznokas
Layout by Owen Paznokas
Printed in the USA by Village Books

Village Books
1200 11th St
Bellingham WA,
98225
villagebooks.com

This memoir is dedicated to all the beings of Planet Earth who persisted in finding ways to prevail during the COVID-19 Global Pandemic. I'd like to Remember all those who were lost; Thank all those who helped save the rest of us; and Encourage everyone to move forward with new knowledge and understanding. We can choose to care for one another.

Introduction

What's a Nightly Missive anyway?

Do you remember where you were when the World Health Organization (WHO) declared a Global Pandemic? It was a Wednesday; March 11, 2020, to be exact. I had returned home to Washington State (then, Ground Zero in the U.S.) the Saturday before around midnight after visiting my folks, as my Dad was battling inoperable prostate cancer. Leading up to my return trip, I had been watching the news with growing concern and texting my spouse with increasing frequency as she continued her work in the local school district. I doubled those texting efforts upon my return. What was the school district thinking? They needed to send everyone in that petri dish home ASAP. On Friday, March 13, they did just that, and districts across the country followed suit.

Saturday, March 14 dawned on a new era: COVID lockdown. What to do, what to do? Like so many, my friends and I took to our text strings with a vengeance. The world was scary and dangerous (even your groceries could kill you), and the stay-at-home orders were unprecedented. Would we all get COVID? Would there ever be a cure? How long would the lockdowns last (and would our toilet paper supplies last that long)? As in any situation, humor - even (especially?) the black kind - proved a helpful coping mechanism.

Sharing of COVID memes became a popular pastime. I still laugh at them!

As that first day (which, like most days in March 2020, felt like it lasted an entire year) drew to a close, I reached out to my friends with some profound (haha…humor again) observations and ended with "Congrats on making it through Day #…1."

Over the next week or so, the nightly texts caught on. To my surprise, since I worried I might be taking up much more than my fair share of the text strings, my friends told me they had started looking forward to them. Over a few more days, the "Nightly Missive," as it (some say "she") became known, developed a style and rhythm of its own. At one point, I wrote a few haiku, and soon, those were requested, as well. I didn't promise nightly haiku, but I sure ended up writing a lot of them! At other points, I "read" kids' books of wisdom and encouragement, complete with selfies of me flashing the illustrations at them, just like story time at school.

Soon, I realized I might need to keep this going for a while. Things were still scary and uncertain, and no one knew how long it would last. If my friends were getting a little relief from the Missive, I would keep her going. I was not going to let them down when everything else seemed to be crumbling.

Whenever I doubt my memory of their importance to others (because I know how valuable they were to me), I just remind myself what my friends said in their own words as we neared that one-year mark:

"They have helped more than just a little bit. They have been a constant in the storm. They've made me laugh, made me think, made me cry, gave me comfort, gave me motivation - and brought me closer to all of you" (Margaret).

"Thank you, Mary, for 100 pages and 51 weeks of grounding in this otherwise splintered, shifting year. It strikes me that the missive takes the tiny pieces of each and gives them a kaleidoscopic twist so that patterns and pictures and beauty emerge. Thank you for your dedication and imagination! Happy almost-birthday, Missive!" (Leslie).

That, dear reader, is how you have come to be holding an entire year's worth of Nightly Missives. I can't believe it either.

As with all great (more humor) pursuits, I did not last an entire year without plenty of help. Two groups of friends, each with their own text string, motivated (and were subjected to) the Nightly Missives: the Campfire Girls (Laura, Spicoli, and Stephenie) and the College Angels (Cameron, Catherine, Cathy, Elizabeth, Leslie, Margaret, and Mel). Not only did they receive, read (I assume), and respond to them, they wrote their own original "Guest Missives" when I needed a break, and they helped research the newspaper headlines provided at the beginning of each week for historical context. I owe them a huge Thank You, for no Missives would exist without their friendship, interest, and support.

As you embark on your own reading journey, I offer a new haiku in your honor:

The Nightly Missive
took on a life of its own.
I hope you like them.

~Mary Rossi, March 2022

A Year of Missives

WEEK #1
Saturday, March 14, 2020 – Friday, March 20, 2020

"Stocking Up for the Unknown: Store Shelves Are Plucked Bare" (Corina Knoll, *The New York Times*, March 14, 2020)

"Scarcity of Testing Continues to Stymie State as Disease Spreads" (Lewis Kamb and Patrick Malone, *The Seattle Times*, March 14, 2020)

"Whatcom County Schools Set to Close Through April 24" (David Rasback, *The Bellingham Herald*, March 14, 2020)

Campfire Girls' Quarantine String (Or, What the Hell, Man)
Day #1 Saturday March 14, 2020: As the sun sinks ever lower, I'd like to congratulate everyone on a successful Day#...1.

College Angels' Quarantine String (Or, It's Too Bad We Needed This)
Day #1 Saturday March 14, 2020. I'm back from long dog walk in sun & dinner of MREs (not really). Just had to thank Mel for her offer of help for my parents (talk about a disaster brewing) & Catherine for her suggestion of a visit. I have some time on my hands, so sounds great! I'll book tonight. Also, I'd like to congratulate everyone on a successful Day#...1.

Campfire Girls
As the sun sets on Day 2, I tip my hat to my fellow Campfire Girls and wish them delicious cocktails, fresh bread, and fellow humans who will immediately realize we must all inconvenience ourselves for a while for the good of the order. (I mean, we've all seen the movies!) Hang in there, stay safe, and start thinking about how virtual Camp will work. Until tomorrow....

Angels
Day #2 (Cathy's birthday): I started the day with, "GEEZ, I'm not still asleep, I'm catching up on 60+ texts (yay!!)" What I've learned: 1) I might actually be Typhoid Mary; 2) Happy B'day, Cathy!! 3) I am Loving the response to Molly & Mary's Super-Fantastic Self-Quarantine Daily Routine; 4) dogs, cats, kids, & wine rule; 5) Margaret & Molly target the same great news articles for which I'm very grateful; 6) we all survived Day #1 (I'm counting from when Bellingham Schools finally sent Molly home [Friday, March 13, 2020]).

Molly later said, "I'm going to take a nap. Wake me up in 6 weeks."

As the sun sets on Day 3, I present to you Campers a sign of Hope [photo of promising tulip buds]. General Leia would want us to hold on to Hope. Sleep well and restoratively, Friends.

As the sun sets on Day 4 [St. Patrick's Day], I realize...I'm kinda drunk! Just kidding, but I was a wee bit silly earlier. And it was fun. So, be sure to be silly at some point today! Or, maybe at multiple points! (Or, maybe all day!)

As the sun sets on Day 5, look what Molly found for me on Instagram:
https://www.instagram.com/p/B95M4kNhbzz/?hl=en   [Gal Gadot "Imagine" for the Wonder Woman fanatic]

As the sun sets on Day 6, I tip my hat to my fellow Campers who find special ways to spend a little time together (apart). While the days have begun merge together, don't forget to TGIF. May we never lose the sense of excitement that is a Friday afternoon. Buona Notte!

Campfire Girls
As the sun sets on Day 7, I tip my hat to neighbors clinging to the TGIF spirit & to Campers working to stay informed to keep their families safe. I tip my hat a second time to eccentric Southern relatives, which we all have, no matter where we're from originally. Sleep well, my Friday warriors.

Angels
As the sun sets on Day 7, I tip my hat to funny memes, Lego robots, solid social distancing choices, silver tresses, & brave friends making the best of a strange, strange week & world. TGIF & sleep soundly, Pioneers.

Week #2

Saturday, March 21, 2020 – Friday, March 27, 2020

"Pressure on Trump as Millions Are Kept Home: Mixed Signals From President Sow Confusion" (Katie Rogers, Maggie Haberman, and Ana Swanson, *The New York Times*, March 21, 2020)

"'It Will Not Be Pretty': State Could Face Life-or-Death Choices – 'Crisis Standard of Care' Looks at Possible Health System Crash" (Mike Carter, *The Seattle Times*, March 21, 2020)

"Man in 60s is First Whatcom County Coronavirus Patient to Die" (Kie Relyea, *The Bellingham Herald*, March 21, 2020)

Campfire Girls

As the sun sets on Day 8, I tip my hat to baby animals because... well, duh...and to all the Roners because...well, that's all of us now. Sleep well & according to your own circadian rhythms, my Courageous Campers.

Angels

As the sun sets on Day 8, I tip my hat to those tackling coronaprojects, like bridges and victory gardens and, yes, even sanitizing and staying informed. I'm grateful for the inspiration & reminder to Just Keep Swimming. Sleep well & dream a little dream of the Obamas, my project people.

As the sun sets on Day 9, I reflect on the suggestion by the Archbishop of Canterbury to light a candle tonight for Hope. Here is my Hope for you, brave shut-ins [photo of candle].

As the sun sets on Day 10, I tip my hat to my Governor & my fellow Washingtonians scurrying to finish preparing to Stay Home, Stay Safe. I miss my faraway Angels, but I recognize that mysterious & all-powerful thread that still connects us. What is it, exactly? I dunno, but it's there. Enjoy your snoozes, Stalwart Sleepers.

As the sun sets on Day 11, I tip my hat to my fellow Campers as they navigate work challenges (considerable), grocery shopping (challenging), and dry hands (chapped). I send each of you a reminder of simple pleasures, like the smell of banana bread baking and the sight of cute little sparrows chattering away in the hedge without a single thought of microbiology, PPE, or Cheetos. My hope is that you can channel some of your favorite simple things when the other thing threatens to take over. It pleases me that the former are still there, even with the latter. We can still choose which one gets our attention. Sleep soundly for now, my little sparrows, and we'll try again tomorrow.

Campfire Girls

As the sun sets on Day 12, I tip my hat to Lemurs (on foot), Lookers (on Zoom), and Laughter (on point). I treasure the creativity and support shared on this string (infinity), and I marvel at and admire the attempts at the everyday while still remaining vigilant, as well as the courage it takes to Keep Calm and Carry On. At that, I tip my hat a second time to the Queen. May she, like my fellow Campers, sleep peacefully and wake to fight another day.

Angels

As the sun sets on Day 12, I tip my hat to far-flung Angels trying to make the best of a very unexpected situation, from loaded banana bread to Yoga ball chairs, from sleep aids to games made for friends far away. I marvel at and admire the attempts at the everyday while still remaining vigilant and acknowledge the courage it takes to Keep Calm and Carry On (a second tip of the hat to Prince Charles...and the Queen and the U.K. for good measure). From this morning's anonymous nod to Dr. Seuss: "People did realize they'd all be ok, They don't need so much to get through the day. Maybe this virus that caused so much stress Showed the whole world that more can mean less." Sleep peacefully and wake to fight another day.

As the sun sets on Day 13 (like Summit 13) and the cherry blossoms, I tip my hat to you brave Angels who continue to look to the Future. Rest assured, it is still out there, though it may be a bit more mysterious than before. I admire your concern for one another, your families, and your quarantine diets. I tip my hat a second time to Technology, specifically the magical Zoom app that will allow me to see my Yoga teacher tomorrow morning for the first time in weeks. I send you my wishes for your peace and health, both mental and physical. Sleep deeply, sweet sapiens, and I will speak with thee tomorrow

As the sun sets on Day 14, I tip my hat to the realization that, while we cannot be together geographically right now, it is a comfort to know that you are out there pursuing and enjoying some of your interests. Puppies and kitties, kids and comedy, gardening and cooking. Some might say simple, but that's probably the point...basic but nourishing, just like comfort chili. And straight tequila. Sleep soundly, inquisitive souls, and we will explore again tomorrow.

WEEK #3
Saturday, March 28, 2020 – Friday, April 3, 2020

"'We Have Lost It All': Millions Reel From Sudden Unemployment" (Sabrina Tavernise, Audra D. S. Burch, Sarah Mervosh, and Campbell Robertson, *The New York Times*, March 28, 2020)

"Coronavirus-Era Funeral Ban Makes Tough Time Even Tougher" (Brendan Kiley, *The Seattle Times*, March 28, 2020)

"How Can $2.2 Trillion Coronavirus Aid Package Help You?" (Christopher Rugaber, Alexandra Olson, and Sarah Sell, *The Bellingham Herald*, March 28, 2020)

As the sun sets on Day 15, I ponder with my puzzler how I can be this tired when I've only been up for 12 hours and was still in my jammies at 3pm (or was it 4?) I choose to think that I am, indeed, practicing taking things slow(ly). Enjoying coffee and memes till late in the day and then doing some simple quarantine chores and Zooming and cleaning out the DVR in the evening. Laughing and talking and prepping and zoning. These are the things that will get us through until we can laugh and talk together again. Sleep restfully, dear puzzlers, and we shall wake to another Sunday.

As the sun sets on Day 16 and the Federal guidelines are extended to April 30, I reflect on Patience and Choices. While I am not surprised at the extension, it is a bit sobering all the same. Doubts creep in. Can I remain patient? Will the curve be flattened? When will this end? Am I short of breath? (Yes, but it's anxiety for now.) At the same time, though, I remember with gratitude that I do still have Choices. I can choose to get up in the morning. I can choose to do the best I can at my job, at home, in my relationships, on my dog walks, and with my memes. And I can choose to give myself a break when my "best" isn't as great as I'd like it to be. Because, hey, there's literally a pandemic on, and I'm doing OK. Rest, my Angels, with the assurance that we can choose the kind of day we have tomorrow.

As the sun sets on Day 17, I tip my hat to online ordering and curbside pickup (at places like BevMo, for example). Because, Campers, I think this is going to take a while. Which reminds me to practice Letting Go. Letting go of how things used to be; letting go of my old daily routine; letting go of how I wish things were; letting go of intermittent impatience and frustration with the way things are now. Because, Campers, this is the way things are now. Which reminds me about Acceptance. The sooner I accept the way things are now, the sooner I can let go and get living. It's OK. We can learn to do this. Sleep restoratively, Campers, and we shall learn new skills tomorrow.

As the sun sets on Day 18, I offer you Angels a pictorial take on our current situation [photo from Day #3 and photo of same – now larger - tulip buds from today]. Let the tenacious Tulip remind you that Spring still arrived & life is rolling on all around us. Don't miss out! There are beautiful things to experience. Be one of them. Sleep soundly, weary Angels, and we will spring into action again tomorrow.

As the sun sets on Day 19, the beginning of the second calendar month of our trials, I am filled with deep Gratitude for all those keeping us safe. Know that this includes each and every one of you, too, Campers. I feel Gratitude for your memes, for your homeschooling, for your safe shopping practices, for your care for your families/co-workers/teens/neighbors/animals, for your humor, for your candor, for your bravery, for your love for each another. I am grateful, too, for finding this Chris Mann song (not a parody), as it seems he's been pondering a similar theme: https://www.youtube.com/watch?v=xGKFVMgjrPc. Enjoy your sleep, enjoy the song, enjoy your new day, and channel some of that all-powerful Gratitude, Campers.

As the sun sets on Day 20 and my Governor, in his wisdom (truly), extends the 'tine to May the 4th (be with you), I tip my hat to Alcohol. Since I am fortunate to have the very best of friends, I have hap-hap-happy hours tomorrow and Saturday, so suck it, SARS-CoV-2! We've got this! Between the alcohol in our hand sanitizers and the alcohol in our bloodstreams, we will overcome! And here I thought I might write tonight about the human dignity and tender care and concern depicted in *Call the Midwife*. But then, I turned on the news. So...alcohol. Sweet dreams, Angels, and gird your loins because we are going to need one another...and those happy hours.

As the sun sets on Day 21, I tip my hat to monkeys and bananas [emojis]. What's that you say? You didn't think that's what I'd write about today? OK, so that's more Seuss-ian. What I'm referencing is the sweet book *Keep Curious and Carry a Banana: Wisdom from the World of Curious George* by H. A. Rey (2016). You may recall a pre-corona conversation about said book. Well, Molly found it (of course), and I had a nice time sharing it with my Dad a mere 4-5.5 weeks ago. Ah, the good ol' days! If only we'd known it then. But I digress! I have enjoyed seeing "story time" on the interwebs, so I thought I might try it with you, Kind Kampers. So, for the next few nights, I'll turn to 3 pages at random and "read" them to you as a night-night story (there are 39 pearls of wisdom, so this will get us to the middle of the month!) Here goes: 1) Take the road less traveled. 2) Use all your frequent flyer miles (some restrictions may apply). 3) Bring home the bacon...and the donuts, too! Your job now, Korona Kampers, is to apply these pearls to your Saturday. And what a day it will be!! Use your Imagination. It is one of your greatest tools right now (and I happen to know that you all have some of the best ones around!) Sleep deeply and wake to dream another day.

WEEK #4

Saturday, April 4, 2020 – Friday, April 10, 2020

"As Deaths Mount, New York Pleads For Outside Help: Under-cutting C.D.C., President Says He Won't Wear Mask" (Michael D. Shear and Sheila Kaplan, *The New York Times*, April 4, 2020)

"Americans Are Urged To Wear Face Masks – But It's Voluntary" (Michael D. Shear and Sheila Kaplan, *The Seattle Times*, April 4, 2020)

"(Governor) Inslee Extends Stay-Home Order, Business Closures Through May 4" (James Drew, *The Bellingham Herald*, April 4, 2020)

As the sun sets on Day 22, I tip my tiara to Group FaceTime, alcohol, and food. This pandemic does have its moments. Thanks for enjoying a few with me this evening! As we lean into our fourth week, I send you a little more Patience and Acceptance. Do not worry. We can do it! Together (apart). Slow down; one day at a time; go plant a garden; mimic the plants...they know how to do this. And now...story time! 1) Life can be a high-wire act - the trick is keeping your balance. 2) There will be bumps in the road. The trick is to get right back on your bike and pop a wheelie! 3) Sure, life can be a circus. Get in the center ring! Well, now...those seem pretty appropriate! The monkey strikes again. Sleep soundly, Campers, and wake to a new adventure!

As the sun sets on Day 23, I tip my hat to the Queen…again! [See https://www.youtube.com/watch?v=2klmuggOElE if you missed her.] Crikey, that was a bloody good address!! Eloquence, strength, grace, determination, compassion. Let's channel a little of that tomorrow, Angels, and get our week off to a solid start. And now…story time! 1) Don't just stand there on the sidelines. Get in the game! 2) Expand the parameters of your job. 3) Stay on top of technology. (But don't let it own you.) Sleep peacefully, Angels, and greet the sunrise with optimism!

As the sun sets on Day 24, I tip my hat to my Mom and Dad and the great start they gave me. How else would I be able to sustain myself through the COVIDtine in such grand style?? High-speed Internet access for all the meme-forwarding, YouTube watching, online shopping, and Zoom/FaceTime happy hours; near-daily deliveries from a wide variety of food and product companies (arranged during the aforementioned online shopping sessions); Yoga classes in the sunroom and Boxing workouts in the Pop Shop. As important as the "things" are, so are the pearls of wisdom imparted, such as "One day at a time" and "Keep it between the ditches." I mean, what CAN'T we do with such an attitude?? So, thanks, Mom and Dad. I'm going to be OK. We're all going to be OK. And now…story time! 1) Always have an exit plan. 2) Just say yes! Sign up for some serious monkey business. 3) Don't forget to look back. History has much to teach us. Rest up, Campers...the monkey indicates we have a busy day ahead!

As the sun sets on Day 25, I tip my hat to Cameron because I (we) make up the rules here, and who says we can't shine a light on a friend when they need a (virtual) pat on the back?? I hope Cameron and all you Angels are sleeping soundly right now. A little sleep can provide a lot of perspective. It can be just the breather needed for slowing down and checking in with yourself. There's a Buddhist teaching that helps me when the big wave threatens to crash down: Everything you need is already inside you. So, stretch. Deep breath. Today's another opportunity. Get up and take it. And…how about a story first to get you started?? 1) If someone says "Go fly a kite!" take their advice. 2) Give free hugs. 3) Begin each day ready to monkey around! Whoa. The wisdom of the monkey is uncanny. Coffee up, Angels, hug your monkeys, and let's get going!

As the sun sets on Day 26, I tip my hat to musical hero John Prine. Rest easy, vaunted wordsmith. Campers, no one said life was going to be easy, but life is better together (apart), even when it's sad. Lean on each other! And don't forget to have some shortbread and scones along the way (guess we'd better tip our hats to butter, too). Tonight's story is dedicated to all our heroes out there, with us and not: 1) Hang loose! 2) Read everything you can get your paws on. 3) Always stay one step ahead of the crowd. Dream broadly, Campers, and be glad for the day ahead.

As the sun sets on Day 27, I reflect upon some of the things we are all enjoying during this truly kooky and bewildering time. Baking, pets, memes, Zoom, walks, drinking, texting, sleeping, televisioning, kid creativity, painting, studying, horses, Lego challenges, drinking, donating, gardening, farm chores, online shopping, mulling, celebrating, sowing, writing, sewing, drinking. While there is much to sadden, frustrate, and worry us, Angels, there is also much to enjoy. The eye of the beholder is sharp. Focus yours on the good around you. It is still there. And to help you focus…story time! 1) Be the wind beneath your own wings. 2) Remember, there's more than one way to catch a fish. 3) Let them eat cake. But save a slice for yourself, too. My, my, my…how does the monkey know that we also enjoy cake? Wise little monkey. Rest sweetly, my Angels, and wake to a Good Friday!

As the sun sets on Day 28, I tip my hat to Friends. As you well know (since you are one of them), I am lucky to have the best friends around. I'm amazed that today, in the middle of a lock-down, I participated in a Birthday Parade for an 8-year-old neighbor, a Zoom happy hour with college friends, and an appropriately socially-distanced happy hour with my neighbors. Quite the busy day for one in quarantine. I also tip my hat to Puppies. Because… puppies!!! And to all those who love and care for puppies, both young and old, both here and gone. All this action has made me sleepy and, therefore, in need of a bedtime story! 1) Take time to smell the roses (or eat a banana). 2) Keep curious. 3) If you hit a wall, don't be discouraged. Up and over! Snoozle away, dear Campers, for tomorrow is another day for curiosity!

WEEK #5

Saturday, April 11, 2020 – Friday, April 17, 2020

"Braced for Apocalyptic Surge, New York Avoids Worst, So Far" (Alan Feuer and Jesse McKinley, *The New York Times*, April 11, 2020)

"Early Data In King County Hints People Of Color Hard Hit By Virus" (Heidi Groover, *The Seattle Times*, April 11, 2020)

"COVID-19 Deaths Exceed 100K Globally" (Matt Sedensky and Jim Mustian, *The Bellingham Herald*, April 11, 2020)

As the sun sets on Day 29, I tip my hat to the Universe. Too deep on a Saturday night? Allow me to explain: we watched the Amazon original movie *Troop Zero* tonight (highly recommended!) in which the young heroine dreams of going into outer space. What does she need to start working towards her dream? Her friends, of course! (see previous entry) There are some lovely shots of the cosmos and a magnificent final scene that made me think about our place in the Universe during this oh-so-uncertain time, a time when I feel like we are just a piece of dirt on a bigger piece of dirt (that's actually a movie reference and it's not meant to be depressing…I've always felt a certain comfort when thinking about how small I am in the grand scheme of things). See, I told you it wasn't really deep…just some Amazon Studios musings on a Pandemic Saturday night. What's that? You'd rather have a story? No problem! Here goes: 1) Clothes make the mammal. Be bold in your fashion choices. 2) Wisdom begins with being puzzled. With a little help from your friends, the pieces will fall into place. 3) Rainy day? Who cares! Your friends will get you through. So, that's one reference to mammals and two to friends. Coincidence? I think not! Dream fiercely, Campers, and wake to another chance at the journey!

As the sun sets on Day 30, I think to myself, "30? Really??" Yes, 30. I shall decide to look at it as 3 of my favorite number (10). Because I still have choices. Also, 3 is a significant number in many religions. And it is Easter, which comes 3 days after the Crucifixion. So, once again, it's all about how you choose to look at it. Wait, what were we talking about? Oh, yeah…30. Two thoughts for tonight: 1) Sacrifice. Blame it on Easter and the outbreak, but this word is on my mind tonight. Discuss. 2) Pillsbury Doughboy. I swear, that meme has delighted me all the livelong day (and the scores of people to whom I forwarded it; you're welcome, scores of people). Thank you, "Meme Master" Mel! I am still laughing. Now, a story: 1) A blank canvas is a brilliant opportunity. 2) Respect differences in others. It's much more interesting that way! 3)

Imagine the best! Prepare to be pleasantly surprised. There it is, Angels...prepare to be surprised tomorrow. Sleep soundly now so that you are ready!

As the sun sets on Day 31, I'm noticing the Quiet. Fewer cars, fewer planes, fewer people. They're still there...I called out to some neighbors while assembling my first raised bed (for our Victory Garden!), and the kids were out riding their bikes in the afternoon sunshine. However, tonight (well, this morning) it is Quiet. And I like it. I mean, the reasons for it are unfortunate, to say the least, but there are benefits, too. I can think straight; I can breathe deeper. This is like so much in life: double-edged swords, unintended consequences, contradictions. All a reminder to seek Balance. Too much Yoga stuff? OK, then...a story! 1) It's a zoo out there. So keep your sense of humor. 2) Life is a bowl of pasta – make sure to noodle around. 3) Make the most of a messed-up situation. The monkey knows! In these messed-up times, lean on laughter. And some nice shelf-stable pasta. Dream of laughing lasagnas, Campers, and we will giggle in the morrow!

As the sun sets on Day 32, I'm reflecting on the word Optimism. While one door is closing, at least temporarily (I'm looking at you, "Lucky" 13th Summit), another is opening (I'm looking at you, work friend), and I am grateful and excited, as with my other quarantine projects, such as cooking, gardening, stationary cycling in the Pop Shop, Zoom Yoga, online grocery ordering, and those sorts of isolationist pursuits. I feel like I'm learning some new skills, and that always feels good. Look for the silver linings! They're usually there. Now, how about a story? 1) Unlock the potential in others. 2) Grab a great seat. You don't want to miss a thing. 3) Multitask, multitask, multitask! Oh, that cheeky monkey...I am going to have to work on that last one. Sleep peacefully, Angels, and pull up a great seat to another great day!

As the sun sets on Day 33, I find myself thinking about Endings. Nothing too drastic, mind you. In fact, I've started thinking of Endings as more of a brief pause before a New Beginning. As you get older (the rate of which surely increases during lockdowns), you realize that, while there might be a pause, things just keep rolling on. That's a wise way for things to unfold, don't you think? However, if Endings make you a bit sad or wistful or even depressed, as they are sometimes wont to do, then perhaps a story would help! 1) Be wildly creative! Sometimes you need to really turn things on their head. 2) Create the world you want to inhabit. 3) Remember that every ending is a bright new beginning. The End. The monkey knows, Campers; the monkey knows. I had forgotten that's how this particular story Ends. But it is also the Beginning of Yours! Dream fiercely, Campers, for tomorrow is a New Beginning!

As the sun sets on Day 34, I tip my hat to my friend's cat, Marcus, who we lost today and to all those experiencing hard times, tragedy, and loss during the time of COVID. It's hard enough dealing with these things during "normal" times; it seems especially unfair, painful, and draining right now. Work stressors, family/friend tensions, health issues. All part of life but just particularly painful and draining at this time. All there is to do is move through it and lean on your friends. Don't be afraid to get a little messy. Or maybe a lot. Sit in the sun and just take some time to do nothing. The universe is telling us (screaming at us?) that it's OK to do that right now. And eventually, after a while, you will feel like getting up again. And whenever that is is when it is. Sleep soundly, Angels, and we'll see what tomorrow brings.

As the sun sets on Day 35, I tip my hat to Symbol and the wonderful book she gave us at Roaring '20s/Groundhog Day Camp way back in our former lifetimes: *A Drinkable Feast: A Cocktail Companion to 1920s Paris* by Philip Greene (2018). What a marvelous addition to my Friday evening. Perhaps it's the dry gin, but tonight, I am reflecting on Being Satisfied. Very early on in the

Time of COVID, I remarked to Molly that I suspected some of the people that would do the best during lockdown would be those who can Be Satisfied with what they have. How we fight and flail when things aren't the way we want them to be, or when we don't have what we want, or when we can't do what we want to do. Well, Campers, who ever said things would always be the way we want them to be, or that we'd get everything we want, or that we'd always be able to do what we want, all the time, world without COVID, amen? No one, that's who. But don't fight and flail about it. You know what I'm starting to suspect? Maybe I don't know what's best – even for me – all the time, world without viruses, amen. Maybe while I'm fighting and flailing, I'm missing what's right in front of me. Might take a little pressure off me, too, to quit thrashing about all the time and close my mouth and open my eyes and fists. Yeah, that's sounds pretty good, actually. Sleep calmly, Campers, and dream of a world you haven't even considered…Yet.

WEEK #6
Saturday, April 18, 2020 – Friday, April 24, 2020

"Death Toll Spikes at Nursing Homes as Defenses Crack: A Fifth of U.S. Virus Fatalities Are Now Tied to Struggling Care Facilities" (Farah Stockman, Matt Richtel, Danielle Ivory, and Mitch Smith, *The New York Times*, April 18, 2020)

"Long-term Care Facilities May Finally See Widespread Testing" (Asia Fields and Paige Cornwell, *The Seattle Times*, April 18, 2020)

"Challenging (Governor) Inslee, GOP Lawmakers Release Plan For a Restart" (James Drew, *The Bellingham Herald*, April 18, 2020)

As the sun sets on Day 36, I tip my hat to sunshine and dirt. I spent some time today working on my first raised bed. I have big plans to be a vegetable farmer! Well, maybe not big plans so much as delayed plans that I've had for years and are finally turning into action (remember, silver linings!) While I worked, the sun shone, the breeze breezed, neighbors called over from their yards, birds sang, bees buzzed, kids biked, friends texted, songs played, dogs were groomed, and worms wormed. For a few blissful, healthy hours, the simple things eclipsed the stressful things. So, get out in the sunshine and get some dirt on your hands, literally or just figuratively if you prefer. You are worth it! Dream peacefully, Campers, and greet that morning sun (or rain…those veggies need some rain, too!)

As the sun sets on Day 37, I grin as I listen to Walter snore beside me on the couch. Turns out weekend sunshine and dirt and grooming are good for dogs, too! It is true what they say…we should all try to be more like our animals. Live in the moment. Enjoy your food and your play and your sleep. Give others the benefit of the doubt. Expect each day to be the best day. Find and exploit every sunbeam possible. Find joy in your exercise. Be curious and inquisitive. Let others know when you're unhappy with them… and then forgive them within 3 seconds and ask them to play with you again. Who knew the snoring fur ball beside me was so wise? Sleep soundly, Angels, and set your clocks forward to Day 39 for the next nightly missive…we are officially postponing the Summit tomorrow, and I'm going to lie about like a dog and pretend it isn't happening. Practice your animal attitudes in the meantime!

[Day 38 – no message due to Summit mourning]

As the sun sets on Day 39, I tip my hat to my Campers who seemed to miss me last night and to continue to appreciate these nightly missives. I am flattered and grateful and pleased because hey, I'm only human! I try not to complain too much or ask for too much (yes, I realize others may have a different take on that), but it can be awfully nice to be noticed. So, Thank You all right back, and I want to let you know that I miss and appreciate each and every one of you, too!! I've realized during the lockdown with no small amount of surprise that I am even more of an introvert than I already thought I was. I'm pretty happy sticking close to my home base, just working and doing projects I haven't made time for in the past (the Past being defined as 39 days ago) and cooking and on-line shopping and dog walking and writing to you fine folks. I don't really miss how harried I felt trying to cover all that, plus errands and play dates and house chores, not to mention the scheduling it takes to do all of the above. One thing I really do miss, though, is dreaming of Camp and enjoying the anticipation of being with my Campers for a whole weekend of laughing and eating and drinking and movies and drinks in my ear and laughing and drinking, all in my Camp shirt and sweats (although, the Camp outfit has just become my Everyday Quarantine outfit, even more so than before). So, I guess what I'm saying is Thank You for missing me last night, and I miss and appreciate you tonight and every night. But I'm gonna try to focus on Future Camp because Campers, we just gotta believe. I do think we will be together again some day. Do I want to venture a guess as to when that will be? Heck no! I'm no oracle. But let's Dream and Believe because there's comfort and optimism in that, and really our only job right now is to stay healthy and try to imagine a Future. So, sleep tranquilly, Campers, and I will see you again tomorrow (and by "see" I mean "communicate with you virtually" because that is our Present, at least for now).

As the sun sets on Day 40, I tip my hat to the Earth because… Earth Day!! The 50th Anniversary of Earth Day, no less. Can you believe the myriad lessons available to us as Earth Day coincides with Day 40 of the COVID quarantine if we will just open our eyes and our minds?? It's a bit mind-boggling, actually. And yes, it is admittedly a challenge to open one's eyes and minds right now, seeing as they are rather preoccupied with a myriad of other concerns.

But I think it's important that we try. Try it for yourself; try it for your family and friends; try it for the animals; try it for the Earth, the wind, and the fire; try it because it's a nice break from Zoom meetings, homeschooling, and washing your groceries. We've got one Earth, people (at least that I know of or can get to), so let's take care of it. Look at those Sheep roaming the Welsh streets and the Lions sunning themselves on the streets of South Africa! Look at the Air quality improve in the Northeast United States and in Europe and in Delhi! Look at the Water quality improve in the canals of Venice! Will these stunning improvements last? No! Will they be temporary and limited to our time of confinement? Yes!! Why? Because we're humans, and we like to drive our cars (or sit and eat in them while stuck in traffic) and fly in metal tubes through the sky (I still have no idea how that works) and order things from Amazon Prime that will arrive in only two days unless your name is Mel (courtesy of big rigs or flying metal tubes, of course) and do absolutely whatever we want whenever and wherever we want. And I mean "NOW!" mister! Whew!! [mop brow; take deep breath] But today, Angels, while we are confined to our home bases, let's take a moment, however brief, to tip our caps to this beautiful blue planet that we call home and to all the beings riding on it alongside us. We've got this. We have to. We will!! Sleep well, Angels, because those of Kingdom Animalia need it, and wake to another beautiful day on the third rock from the sun.

As the sun sets on Day 41, I am reflecting on the tendency of some (many?) of us to Blame Ourselves. What prompted this, you may ask? (Spoiler Alert: if you didn't ask, I'm about to offer it up unsolicited.) Well, I was taking my now-customary mid-afternoon shower where I typically do all my best brainstorming (although, that has become a rather generous term for me and my Quarantine Brain), and I was wondering, once again, how it could already be Fill-In-The-Blank P.M. and I could be this far behind on my To-Do List. To which, my brain, in a now all-too-infrequent moment of wisdom, said, "You have no one to blame but yourself." "Now, wait a minute, brain," I says, "I was just about to blame Quarantine Brain for my suspect time-management of late. I'm sure it can't be Me!" "Sorry," said my brain, "no can do. It's You." And you know what really got me? My stupid brain was right. HOWEVER...that also got me to noodling about all the times we Blame Ourselves when it really isn't merited, or at least it isn't very kind. Because while I value Honesty and Taking Responsibility above just about everything else, Kindness is way up there, too, and it is often ignored or at least devalued. (Psssst...especially in Women, I might propose. Yeah, you know to whom I'm whispering. Quit squirming. It's OK. We just have to get better.) I'll venture you may be Blaming Yourselves for even more than usual during the Time of COVID: Why can't you balance work, homeschooling, housework, information-gathering, and sanitizing the living heck out of your entire home universe every single damn day, virus without end? Why can't you be more productive as you are trying to do the aforementioned, every damn day? Why don't you love Zoom meetings? Why don't you exercise more? Why don't you eat and drink less? Well, hell, folks...why did this virus have to show up, huh? It's truly crazy times we're in, Campers, so why don't you give yourself a break? Save the blame for something you are fully responsible for, and maybe stop blaming and just take responsibility (our next lesson will be Then Do Something About It). Oh, look...here we are back at Kindness. If it's a struggle to be kind to yourself right off the bat, because it does take practice, then practice by extending some kindness to someone else. Then, maybe you can turn it around on yourself. Because I bet you could use a little kindness right about now...or a lot. Sleep deliciously, Campers, because you deserve it!

As the sun sets on Day 42, I realize I've subjected you to some rather lengthy missives this week. I think my Quarantine Brain has been racing a bit. Well, Angels, even this Night Owl gets tired eventually. I'm looking forward to clean sheets and my head on my pillow. So, for the very first time this Quarantine String, I present...a haiku (just for you)! I rather enjoy the occasional haiku and hope you do, too. And now, without further ado: Thinking of you from / my home base, because where else / would I be right now? Dream of poetry that is actually good, Angels, and wake to the promise of the weekend!

WEEK #7
Saturday, April 25, 2020 – Friday, May 1, 2020

"Dire Warnings as President Pushes Sham Cures: Uproar at a Suggestion Disinfectants May Heal the Sick" (Katie Rogers, Christine Hauser, Alan Yuhas, and Maggie Haberman, *The New York Times*, April 25, 2020)

"As States Ease Up On Closures U.S. Virus Death Toll at 50,000" (The Associated Press and *The New York Times*, *The Seattle Times*, April 25, 2020)

"Ruling by High Court Means No Early Release for Inmates" (James Drew, *The Bellingham Herald*, April 25, 2020)

As the sun sets on Day 43, I tip my hat to Prime Numbers. I love them; I know not why. I also love Prime Video. That one should be obvious. Glad to hear some Campers were snuggled in with a movie tonight. Two things for you this evening: 1) I'm pleased to announce we have another aspiring Camp group! My college friends have become VERY interested in Camp, and we are in the process of putting together a shirt order (don't worry...Archaeology Edition will still be the only group with cool raglan tees!) Some of our future Campers were having trouble explaining Camp to their families (who are also getting tees). So, I offered to send them a Camp History that we wrote back in 2016. I would like to share that with you all, too! Check your text string or your email (in the event I can't send a PDF by text). Perhaps you will learn something about Camp Whatchamakeit that you did not know. Or the Girl Scouts. Or glow stick dancing. 2) One of my college friends asked if the haiku will be our new story. Well, I am not promising a daily haiku, but it got me thinkin', and I did come up with one for tonight: What are you trying / to do to me with this talk / of nightly haikus?? Sleep well, Campers, for tomorrow is another Sunday full of potential. What will you do with yours??

As the sun sets on Day 44, I tip my hat to Distractions. Namely, Sundays, friends, Zoom, FaceTime, dogs, cooking, and the blessed [two syllables, please] Television. Hey, I never said I was a complicated person. In fact, I think that's helping me an awful lot these days. It was so nice focusing solely on some of my favorite Distractions today instead of pretending to be functioning on other levels of modern life. Kind of a relief, actually. I hope you were able to have a break here and there, too. If you weren't, make time for it tomorrow! It's important, and you set your own priorities. And since I'm going to try to curtail my Night Owlness just a bit, here's a bedtime haiku for you Angels: Searching, searching, search- / ing; looking and discussing. / What should we watch now? Hmmmm...maybe that TV thing is more complicated than I thought. Besides sweet dreams, I send you hopes for a new binging obsession. Tomorrow is a new opportunity for Distraction! (And maybe a little work and school since it's Monday.) But mostly, Distraction! (I know it's probably mostly the other things, but I can dream.)

As the sun sets on Day 45, I realize I'm up too late again. This time, it's the all-important online grocery order, which I'm kind of into now. So many new Quarantine Skills! I suspect my spouse and my dog tire of my owl-like behavior. I will have to attempt to curtail my nighttime exploits, as I sense humans, generally, are growing weary of lockdown. I suppose I understand this to a point, but it still seems unwise to stick my head out of our warm, safe cave just yet. And groups of Corona Carriers don't sound very appealing. So, it's back to my online shopping. I mean, it's back to bed. Before that, though, thanks to my friend, my mind wanders to the poetry of Japan again…. Sitting in the dark / Only the glow of the lap- / top guides me to bed. Dream deeply, Campers; get some restorative sleep, and rise to the avian poetry that greets you!

As the sun sets on Day 46, I realize I have been thinking it was Day 45 all day. Yikes. Time has always been a perplexing concept to me, even more so as I get older and after finally reading *A Brief History of Time*, and this quarantine thing is obviously not helping. The days flow by, my hair grows longer (and grayer…like the weather today which doesn't help either), but my clothing never changes, nor does the view from my home office. My yearly benchmarks have disappeared, too (no annual archaeology conference, no Summit, no Camp, no dinner dates with friends). How am I supposed to keep 2020 straight exactly?? Well, I don't know the answer to that one yet, but I do know one thing that helps with all of this. Tonight, I tip my hat to you Angels, once again. Thank you for sharing some FaceTime together recently. It was so good to see and hear everyone. I love the printed word and the voice(s) in my head, but my eyes and ears like to play sometimes, too. Thank you for being there for me, and I am here for you. It will be weird along the way, but we will get through this…together. Just keep swimming. As a little thank-you, I dedicate tonight's haiku to you Angels. Here goes: A love letter to / my friends: you all lift me up / during this wack time. I'm sure the Japanese masters would be well pleased. Dream of the future together, Angels, and we'll see what tomorrow looks like in a few hours. Or, maybe we'll see what today looks like tomorrow. I'm still confused.

As the sun sets on Day 47 (oooh…another Prime Number!), I tip my hat to simple acts of kindness. They are not hard to do ("simple" is right there in the phrase!) They make a difference. They help others. Let's all try to do one tomorrow! And since we're all stuck at home, it still counts if it's a family member (heck, that might be even more important right now!) I like how we journeyed together today from chalk art to grief placement to small shoppers to vegetarianism. Campers, you may feel boxed in and stressed and frustrated and worried, but look what you have done today! You are learning and seeking and working to improve, even in the midst of a pandemic. I salute you and your spirits! And I am excited to see what you do tomorrow. And since I can't seem to help myself now, a haiku for you: Tiny masked shopper, / helping Dad and deliver- / ing on smiles, Thank You. Sleep soundly, Campers, and wake tomorrow ready to learn!

As the sun sets on Day 48, I tip my hat to Wes Tank. His unlikely partnership with Doctors Seuss and Dre has fascinated me to no end today. Since he is the clear master of the mic/mike and the words (all the words!), I tip my hat to his tickling of my ears (and funny bone) and offer up the following humble tribute: I tip my Cat in / the Hat to mad rhymes and mad / rapping skills. Hot Damn! Dream of new creative pursuits, Angels, and wake to unleash them!

As the sun sets on Day 49, I tip my hat to what is perhaps my favorite sitcom of all time, *Parks and Recreation* (and that's saying something because I typically don't have faves of things so subjective). I appreciated all the laughs during the recent reunion special. While our Governor had to extend our Stay Home, Stay Healthy order today for another month, no one can stop us from laughing, even if it's hysterically into our morning coffee (or our morning cocktail). I also tip my hat to Quarantine Strings like this because it allowed me to look back to Day 20 and peruse my mental state when the Governor had to extend our order the first time. Hint: alcohol was mentioned, e.g. "Between the alcohol in our hand sanitizers and the alcohol in our bloodstreams, we will overcome!" I see some themes: stay-home extensions, alcohol, and laughter, at times hysterical. Well, I say, "It's OK. Do what you gotta do to get through. Together, Campers." OK, admittedly, I added "Campers" to make it a haiku because I suspected I was getting perilously close. However, rather than haiku you tonight, I really wanted to focus on the "community poem" shared earlier (https://www.npr.org/2020/04/30/845910766/if-the-trees-can-keep-dancing-so-can-i-a-community-poem-to-cope-in-crisis). We are not alone, even though it might feel like it at times. Sleep gently, Campers, and be kind to all living things tomorrow.

WEEK #8

Saturday, May 2, 2020 – Friday, May 8, 2020

"Reopenings Expose U.S. Divisions: Risky New Phase Brings Discord and Unease" (Julie Bosman and Sarah Mervosh, *The New York Times*, May 2, 2020)

"(Governor) Inslee Extends Stay-Home Order, Details Plan For Phased Reopening" (Joseph O'Sullivan, *The Seattle Times*, May 2, 2020)

"Asian Giant Hornet: Chart Provides Way to Size Up What You Are Looking At" (Kie Relyea, *The Bellingham Herald*, May 2, 2020)

As the sun sets on Day 50, I tip my hat, Angels, to YOU. Fifty. That's quite an accomplishment (yes, we have new standards and measuring sticks in the Time of COVID). Seven full weeks. Five sets of my favorite number. Ten sets of half my favorite number. The big 5-0. People are cracking, but we are counting! Counting another day at our home bases; counting ourselves lucky that we and our family and friends are healthy; counting calories; counting raindrops; counting crows; counting down. Counting down to the day when we are ready to stick our masked faces outside and see what it's like to cross paths with our fellow corona avoiders, corona survivors, corona carriers. It's going to be Different out there, but so are we now. And let's do our best to believe that at least some of that Different is going to lean towards Better. We can at least make sure that's the case with ourselves. So, get ready. Over the next 50 days, it's time to keep getting Better. But, for now, since it's raining, my mask's in the wash, and people are scary, I'm just going to stay inside a little longer and maybe even offer up another haiku for you: Looking outside I / test the waters and think, "To- / morrow sounds better." Dream peacefully, Angels, because tomorrow will provide us with another chance.

As the sun sets on Day 51, I am reveling in a quiet Sunday evening folding laundry while watching *Call the Midwife* and enjoying Walter snoozing beside me. Ever have moments when you can't believe all this is happening? This is one of those moments…until I mistakenly – but necessarily – switch over to the news. Molly and I often comment on this phenomenon when we head out for a dog walk on a sunny spring afternoon. Weird. Like a lot of this. Well, I'll take it. Any moment of relative peace is something to celebrate. I wish all of you many moments of peace this week. Sleep peacefully and / rise tomorrow ready to / give it your best try. Good night, Campers!

As the sun sets on Day 52, I tip my hat to people helping other people (feel free to sing that in your best Streisand voice, if you wish). WAIT!! Hold the presses!! I just went out to visit my raised bed. While the starts have been starting along (red cabbage, parsley, and rosemary very happy; spinach and kale looking better; lettuce and arugula surely getting nibbled on below the surface), all has been quiet on the seed side...until Now!! I now have visual proof-of-life of snap peas, carrots, and bush beans!! I am terribly excited, and I know all you fellow veggie farmers share my excitement. I shall hold out hope that the cukes, peppers, oregano, and basil will also make a dramatic appearance eventually. Wow. I grew my first veggie babies. And I have our lockdown to thank. Seriously. I've talked for years about putting in a raised bed, and right when I should've been hammering and shoveling and planting and watering, Summit crunch time would arrive, as would my myriad excuses. Well, not this time, veggie fans! This time, the big box store delivered, and so did my starts and seeds! This summer, we feast! Well, maybe this month; it's a small bed. No matter! I'll take it! I hope you, too, have had a victory today, however small or large or delicious. Let's take it and build on it. Tomorrow is coming! I slowly creep out / the door and up to the edge / looking over. Hi!! Sleep well, my fellow veggie lovers, and we'll see what pops up tomorrow!

As the sun sets on Day 53, I tip my hat to nonprofits, the good work they do, and the good people who support them. Today was GivingTuesdayNow, a global generosity movement launched in response to the need caused by the global pandemic. Typically, GivingTuesday in the U.S. is held the Tuesday after Thanksgiving, but times that are not Typical (like these) precipitated a second giving day. See? Good people are out there, and they are paying attention. I have heard more than one mental health expert share that one of the best ways to counteract the mental funk that comes with lockdown (well, they might've used a phrase other than "mental funk") is to focus on Gratitude and doing something nice for others. Well, we were the recipient of some of that gratitude and nice doings around here today, and so, we tried to pass it on. When you are feeling down, turn your focus to picking others up. It sounds simple, but there is a certain sneaky wisdom in it. I sit here on Giv- / ing Day hoping that some good / has been shared all 'round. Dream of better days, Campers, and wake to play your part in them!

As the sun sets on Day 54, I tip my hat to *Xena: Warrior Princess*. For some reason, this show has been brought to my attention from time to time since it was on in the '90s (remember those?), but I had never seen it…until the Time of Staying at Home All the Time. Fortuitously, my corona companion had never seen it either. Cue a well-timed Syfy marathon, and a binge-fest was born! I wish for each of you a pandemic binge-fest of your own, whatever show it entails. It's like a good book that sucks you in…there's nothing quite so enjoyable, entertainment-wise. And we all need some good entertainment these days. Grab your dinner and / head for the couch. It's time to / see what happens next! Binge happily, Angels, and see what's on tomorrow's watchlist.

As the sun sets on Day 55, I sense some general exhaustion with the current situation. Folks are tired of being stuck at home; tired of all the uncertainty, whether around timelines or guidelines; tired of avoiding others when they really want to sit in the sun together sharing a happy hour, some of which I observed this afternoon on our dog walk. Who can blame them, really? We are herd animals. And we are herd animals who want to do what we want, when we want. I'm refocusing on being satisfied with what I have at home, which is so very much compared to so many others. The weather this weekend is supposed to be glorious, so I think I'll pull some weeds, water my veggie babies, and sit in my lawn chair. Who says I don't make plans anymore? This evening, however, went like this: Fell asleep on the / couch in the glow of the set. / Guess it's time for bed. Sleep soundly, Campers, for tomorrow is a day when you will be at home!

As the sun sets on Day 56, I realize this is our 8-week quarantiniversary. I think the traditional gift is a gallon of moonshine; the contemporary gift is Indica. I will be sure to check the front porch tomorrow (where the mail and delivery folks leave our packages). Tonight, I'm tipping my hat to our dairy delivery guys. I always wished the era of the milkman would return; I just didn't expect it would be under these circumstances. Monday will be our third such delivery. I'm diggin' it, and it sure saves some trips to the store. I realized today that I haven't been to the regular grocery store since March 12, and let me tell you, that has NEVER happened before. I used to go many times during the week (or, even three times in one day…but that was not a good day). Where am I going with this? Not sure. Looking forward to some great weather and veggie farming this weekend. I wish some similar simple pleasures for each of you, too. I hear there will be / some good weather this weekend. / Where'd I put my shorts? Dream vividly, Angels, and do something(s) fun tomorrow!

WEEK #9

Saturday, May 9, 2020 – Friday, May 15, 2020

"If West Wing Still Isn't Safe, Is Any Office?" (Peter Baker and Michael Crowley, *The New York Times*, May 9, 2020)

"(Governor) Inslee Orders Some Restrictions Lifted: Implementing a Plan Announced Last Week, State Allows Curbside Retail Activity, As Well As Landscaping and Pet-Walking Work" (Joseph O'Sullivan and Ryan Blethen, *The Seattle Times*, May 9, 2020)

"Housing Market Adjusting After Slow Spring Start" (Jacqueline Allison, *Skagit Valley Herald*, May 9, 2020)

As the sun sets on Day 57, I tip my hat to sunshine, veggie babies, and my spouse. Sunshine made me happy while tending to my veggie babies, while my spouse mowed the lawn (cut the grass? is this regional?? help!) Sunshine made my veggie babies grow which my spouse (and I) sampled tonight for the first time with our pizza while watching Wonder Woman. I didn't even have to make a hard sell. My spouse is a patient woman. I hope you all had some happy adventures outside, too, and maybe even inside! We watched Wonder Wom- / an tonight. My spouse is a / superhero, too! Sleep restfully, Campers, and give a nod to all the Mothers tomorrow!

As the sun sets on Day 58, I tip my hat to all the Mothers in our lives. The ones we have or had, the ones we want to be, the ones we admire. I hope they all got what they wanted today! When I was small and / the thunder rolled, I would go / down the hall to Mom. Sleep unimpeded, Angels, for you deserve a good rest!

As the sun sets on Day 59, I tip my hat to weed control. I spent a few hours the past couple of days doing some between the raised bed and the fence. It was a great diversion, and it was good to feel the sunshine and sweat a little. Was my level of attention absolutely necessary? No. Was it a fun project for the veggie babies? Yes. I hope you, too, have some similar projects or diversions to keep you chugging along. I also managed to save a sparrow a couple days ago from a most unfortunate demise. Said sparrow had caught its head in a weird gap under the eaves, and I just happened to see it while taking down the storm windows. I had to work at it a while, and I was afraid the little thing was going to break its neck; however, on the last try, it came free and flew off in a flurry to much fanfare in the rhododendron. I really hope it's doing OK. I can't believe it made it. I'm taking it as a very good sign! Little sparrow, stuck / up high. Little sparrow can- / not fly. Off you go! Sleep soundly, Campers, and spread your wings tomorrow!

As the sun sets on Day 60, I tip my hat to you, Angels. 60 days. The big 6-0. Six of my favorite number. Two months. Oh, wow...I haven't been to my beloved local grocery store in exactly two months. I'm getting very spoiled by grocery delivery in the meantime, another one arriving tomorrow, in fact. I'm thinking of each of you as things drag on and a potential spike looms. Stay safe and stay hopeful! That last one's not always easy, but General Leia and Xena have reminded me about Hope lately; so, I'm choosing to listen to them. Staying up late is / getting harder. Will I soon / sleep twenty-four hours? Dream hopefully, Angels, and keep doing your thing!

As the sun sets on Day 61, I tip my hat to the TV show *Call the Midwife* (yes, I'm tippin' my hat to a TV show...sign o' the times, I guess). This show deserves a tip, though, because it never fails to remind me how very kind and decent humans can be to one another, and it also provides some lofty words of comfort in the narrated segments at the beginning and end (narrated by the grand Vanessa Redgrave, no less). I've been watching the last few evenings, and it honestly reminds me that I am part of the broader community of the entire human species. Long stretches of my days can feel kind of numb right now; the compassion in this show makes me feel something again, and it's something very good. Find something every / day to remind yourself that / you are not alone. Sleep peacefully, Campers, for we are all in this together.

As the sun sets on Day 62, I find myself frustrated. Frustrated that my pandemic routine has kept me from my reading chair. I realized that I have yet to escape to my sand chair on the deck for a nice, long reading session. This is one of my favorite things to do for some stress relief. Why have I not done this? I have a sneaking suspicion that it is related to the same reason I stay up so late, my mind races, and I have trouble falling asleep. Not cool, corona; not cool! It's time to make a change. I stand on the precipice of an outstanding weekend, and it's time to start hitting that chair on the deck. I will do it for me! I will do it for Molly! I will do it for Olive and Walter! I will do it for you, Angels!! For one cannot be there for others if they are not there for themselves [geez, I just got lost in all those pronouns]. Take time to do what / you enjoy so that others / can then enjoy you. Sleep, Angels, because we all need it, even when we think we don't.

As the sun sets on Day 63, I find myself excited! Excited for the weekend that is just beginning. Excited for the blank canvas ready for attack! I feel it is going to be a Fun one! Dog walk fun; reading in my deck chair fun (or on the couch since showers and rain are predicted); veggie baby fun; movie fun; cake and ice cream fun. Less pandemic, more fun. Less anxiety, more fun. Join me!! The weekend stretches / before me with a promise / of Fun. Join me, please! Sleep well, Campers, for tomorrow is our Netflix Party!!

WEEK #10

Saturday, May 16, 2020 – Friday, May 22, 2020

"Collapse in Sales is the Worst Ever For U.S. Retailers: Gradual Rebound May Follow Reopening but Shoppers Are Shifting Habits" (Ben Casselman and Sapna Maheshwari, *The New York Times*, May 16, 2020)

"(Governor) Inslee: Contact Info No Longer Required to Be Collected By Restaurants" (Tan Vinh, *The Seattle Times*, May 16, 2020)

"County Gets Update on State Finances" (Brandon Stone, *Skagit Valley Herald*, May 16, 2020)

As the sun sets on Day 64: Virtual movie / night with friends. So many drinks. / I go to bed now. Sleep well; tomorrow will be great; yadda yadda yaddaaaazzzzzzzzzz.

As the sun sets on Day 65, I realize this is Day 65. That sounds like a lot tonight. Not in a bad way, really; just a lot. I'm happy to report that our Fun weekend delivered, and I hope yours did, too! I was reminded how important it is to step away from news, step away from tech, and step into things you enjoy. It is OK and necessary to have some fun; feel a bit lighter. I've always believed in the "Work Hard, Play Hard" approach, and it's really true. We do have to work. Some things are hard. But that's the way things go, and we will not escape it. So, dig in and do your best work and then do your best playing. Or, maybe sometimes do all that in the reverse! And tonight, a Haiku inspired by the home front: Advice from my folks: / One day at a time. Keep it / between the ditches. Sleep deeply, Campers, so we can tackle the week ahead!

As the sun sets on Day 66, I tip my hat to dreams of Camp. We all need things to look forward to, and Camp is one of the good ones! Shirts, badges, fellow Campers, food, drinks, games, camp-fires, sleeping under the stars, Camp breakfast the next morning. Bring it on! And remember, dear Angels…Camp Whatchamakeit is a spirit and not a place; therefore, pandemics have nothing on Camp! In fact, Camp spirit is more important now than ever. Stoke it; nurture it; spread it far and wide. Huzzah!! Virtual confer- / ence the next two days. I may / never be the same. Dream of Camp, Angels, and we shall keep planning our exploits tomorrow!

As the sun sets on Day 67, I find myself feeling that very specif-ic kind of exhaustion that comes from spending 8 hours attending a virtual conference (and knowing you are going to do it all over again tomorrow). Tech truly exhausts me. I really feel for all you frequent Zoomers out there. Please remember to take frequent breaks, eat well, and get your sleep. I spent eight hours on / the computer today. How / do people do this?? And I'm not proud, but this one, too: People annoyed me / today. How can that be when / I am on lockdown?? I'll get better. Sleep restoratively, Campers, and make sure to spend time away from your tech tomorrow.

As the sun sets on Day 68, I find myself feeling like a survivor. I survived a two-day virtual conference! What a weird time in which we are living. And to think that many of you do this all day, every day. Yikes. No wonder stress and depression are receiving some of the attention they are due. It's about time. Maybe we will get our acts together and work on mental health, along with our health care and educational systems and our food supply chains. One can hope. A two-day confer- / ence; a Zoom restorative / Yoga class. Good night. Sleep deeply, Angels, for tomorrow is another weird day!

As the sun sets on Day 69…hey, stop giggling! This is a very, very serious nightly missive. Nope! I can't even. That's just a big, fat lie. Giggle away, if you must! Today's main feeling was relief. Relief that I could be on tech or off at my own choosing; relief to get back to my routine; relief that we are still here and healthy. I also felt gratitude for shopping by mail, as some food and office supplies and even some surprises arrived over the last few days. Back to relief…relief that I didn't have to drive around and go into stores. Ick. That still doesn't sound good, even with my bandana mask, although I was never much of a shopper before the virus arrived. Back to gratitude…for my friends who commiserated with me about how this was supposed to be Summit week and who made me giggle (back to giggling). One of these friends inspired tonight's haiku, in fact. She offered up the awesome phrase "twiddle idle thumbs" which made me giggle, so here goes: 'Tis true what they say: / to twiddle idle thumbs is / to foster numb buns. I sincerely hope we're back to giggling now. Dream magnificently, Campers, and we shall put our thumbs (and our buns) to good use tomorrow!

As the sun sets on Day 70, I tip my hat to being Alive. No, not in the dramatic COVID sense, just in the I'm-a-human-being-who-gets-to-be-alive-right-now-and-has-so-much-to-be-grateful-for sense. Also, Happy 10-Week Anniversary, and 10 is my favorite number, as you may recall. And it's a three-day weekend! So, I'm pretty much crushing this Friday night (nope, Saturday morning). Seriously, though, think of all we have to be grateful for right now. I won't list it all out (nor could I if I tried), but I would wager our Pros far outweigh our Cons. I'm going to focus on that as I tackle another weekend. More time for chores and fun of my own choosing; less time on tech. The worries are there, Angels, but don't let them drag you down. My Yoga teacher mentioned a TED talk about the idea that the people best able to handle adversity are those who can focus on the Present. The Past is done, and we can't go back; the Future is unknowable. The only things we can influence are those that are right in front of us in the Present. Let's seize the Weekend Present, have some fun, and recharge our batteries for next week…which we won't worry about because it's in the unknowable Future. So, you're off the hook. Don't blow it. We stand on the prec- / ipice of three magical / days. Let's seize this chance! Sleep soundly, Angels, and wake with wonder at the Present you will create!

WEEK #11
Saturday, May 23, 2020 – Friday, May 29, 2020

"Employers Get Little Direction Over Staff Tests: Patchwork of Plans for Reopening Safely" (Steve Eder, Ellen Gabler, Sarah Kliff, and Heather Murphy, *The New York Times*, May 23, 2020)

"In Yakima, Flood of Coronavirus Cases Drives Apple Packers to the Picket Line" (Hal Bernton, *The Seattle Times*, May 23, 2020)

"Skagit County Asks to be Allowed Into Phase 2" (Jacqueline Allison, *Skagit Valley Herald*, May 23, 2020)

As the sun sets on Day 71, I am outraged and wistful. Outraged at the birdie buzzsaws who demolished my pea plants; wistful about the week anniversary of our Netflix Party. I miss my Campers, but I'm trying to carry on and do my chores and my relaxing this weekend. But Netflix. And parties! And birthday fun!! I challenge you Campers to dream up another reason for us to celebrate. Go!! Every day is some- / one's birthday; so, every day, / we should all eat cake. Dream of cake, Campers, for tomorrow, we shall have some!

[Day 71 = First Guest Missive by…Cameron!]
As the sun sets on Day 71, I tip my hat to the mystery of time. It seems impossible that we have been in this state of uncertainty for that length of time. And at the same time it has almost settled into a new normal that some parts feel 'normal' and it has all been but the blink of an eye. I am grateful to each of you for helping mark the time and the experience, for helping define daily expectations and thus comfort. Angels, you have all been exactly that, angels of grace and light and love and care and laughter. Tomorrow will come and we are better for being in it together. So here's to tattoos/ that keep us real and steady/and to tomorrow. So…I've got a long way to go in the haiku realm, but I did slide in under the wire for a guest missive. Love and appreciate you all!

[Response:]
Words can't express how / wonderful it is to hear / Cam's angelic voice. Thank you for accepting the Nightly Missive Invite! Very well done!! Time is, indeed, such a mystery, and you Angels make it pass sweetly. Catherine, if you are interested, you're up next! Any night this week that you feel inspired, and remember, it's also OK if you aren't. No pressure! Hooray for varied voices!!

As the sun sets on Day 72, I find myself Happy. Happy that this is a three-day weekend; happy that this gives me time for chores on my own time. I've learned that I desire and thrive in Unstructured Time. I'm rather slow and deliberate, so that unstructured time lets me set my own pace. Which is slow. And deliberate. I've also learned that I'm not a great multi-tasker and that it's hard to re-focus after being interrupted. So, unstructured time and I get along. Back to happy about a three-day weekend. One extra day to get stuff done without being interrupted by pesky things like work. I guess I really am built to quarantine! Lucky me. Slow and deliber- / ate wins the race, unless there / is a fire. Then, run. Dream happily, Campers, for tomorrow you have permission to be unstructured, if you wish!

As the sun sets on Day 73, I tip my hat to J. K. Rowling because you know why. I'm up too late watching Deathly Hallows, Part 2 on Syfy. Life is good. (You-Know-Who is decidedly not.) I hope each of you got to indulge in something you enjoy this holiday weekend. Maybe even several somethings. It's good to take a breather, recharge, and gird our loins for the (partial!) week ahead. We are ready, Angels! We can do this! A boy, a scar, a / wand, two friends, a victory. / Go forth like Potter! Dream of Hogwarts, Angels, and wake to do the right thing!

As the sun sets on Day 74, I am reminded why Tuesdays are the most nondescript day of the week. It is as far away as you can get from either weekend, and it has no clever nickname (like Hump Day) or special status (like Friday or those two weekend days). It's not even Monday, although I suppose that could be seen as a plus. The only thing you might be able to give it is Taco Tuesday, which actually isn't that bad, but still. Tuesday. How nondescript you are. Before the time-when-we-shan't-move-freely-about, I would purposefully schedule something fun on Tuesdays, like coffee with a friend, so that I had something to which I could look forward. Well, you can imagine how that's been going. So, I had to buckle down, do some lame chores, and spend too much time in the kitchen as has become my norm. However, the clock continued to roll as it tends to do, dog were walked, dinners were chewed, *Xena* was watched, and here I am...finishing the work tasks somehow not completed during normal working hours, watching my late-night sitcom re-runs and news, and standing on the precipice of another Hump Day and Zoom Yoga. Hey, look at that...I made it! And if you are reading this, so did you!! Well done! Check the box. Brush the / teeth. Hit the hay. Flip the cal- / endar. It's Wednesday. Sleep well, Campers, and I'll try to write a better haiku on Hump Day!

As the sun sets on Day 75, I tip my hat to the camel and the Hump Day it now represents. I hope a fun Hump Day was had by all. After realizing that it was allergies that have had my wagon draggin' the past few days, I dug deep and rallied and had a pleasant Hump Day afternoon complete with some Zoom Yoga. Now, I'm reconciling myself to the fact that my county may not be able to move to Phase 2 of the "Safe Start Washington" Plan. Can't say I'm shocked, but it's still a bit of a Hump Day bummer. Hump Day, Hump Day, Hump Day. I feel better again! Plus, tomorrow is Thursday...my favorite day of the week. Why, you may ask? (Well, you might.) I like things that are a little offbeat, and I like antici-pation; therefore...Thursday! Everyone loves Friday, so I couldn't pick that one, and Thursday means the anticipation of Friday. No matter what happens on Thursday, you can just say, "Oh, well... tomorrow's Friday!" I realized, too, that I was born on a Thursday; so, we're really made for one another. Hmmmm...methinks I may need to get some sleep. Sitting in the dark / watching *Friends*. So this is how / my grand Hump Day ends. Sleep well, Angels, and wake to my favorite day!

As the sun sets on Day 76, the close of my favorite day of the week, I find myself pondering the coming Summer. I'm a bit wor-ried about our country tonight...pandemic, race relations, unem-ployment, Presidential election. I could go on. However, rather than wringing hands or becoming paralyzed or bitter or angry, I am leaning towards attempting some calm compassion. We defi-nitely don't have to agree with the numbnuts [I had to look up that spelling], but we do all have to row in this same boat; so, instead of trying to yell the loudest, I may just smile and nod and speak out calmly when I feel that is needed. Now, that sounds well and good at the moment; I invite you to check me when I slip up. Because I will. Because I'm human. And we all are. We all are. Yep, that numbnut is me, and I am them. We are more alike than we are different, it just doesn't always feel that way. So, good luck out there this summer, and let's do what friends do and keep each other accountable. We are going to need one another. The day after Hump / Day is the best day. And you / can hump if you want. Stop giggling; that can be anything you want. Dream of the Summer, Campers, and wake to Friday...the one everyone loves.

As the sun sets on Day 77, I tip my hat to bagels. Yes, bagels. Tomorrow morning, our local bagel shop (unimaginatively named The Bagelry) will be delivering an assorted baker's dozen and some cream cheese. I will then be delivering some of that baker's dozen to two neighborhood households, including one headed up by one of our local nursing heroes. I am as excited about the deliveries as I am about stuffing my face with the best bagels in town... for the first time in more than 77 days (11 weeks!) I don't even eat bagels all that often, but when I do, I go to the Bagelry. They are an institution in downtown Bellingham, and I am so glad they are still kickin' (mixin'?) A lot happened today (that day everyone loves), but what makes it into the Nightly Missive? Yep, the promise of fresh bagels. I told you, I'm into anticipation. But I can hardly wait. Maybe I'll just stay up and wait for them on the front porch. I should have given / Friday more credit. It was- / n't bad after all. Sleep soundly, Angels, and wake to a weekend of gluten, if you are into that stuff. If not, a joke: How do you protect your bagels? You put lox on them! Bonus joke: What kind of bagel can fly? A plain bagel! Bonus joke #2: What did the ghost put on their bagel? Scream cheese! And we should end on a cringe-worthy joke, of course: Did you hear about the new OB/GYN bagel shop? It's called Pap Schmear. Good Night!!

WEEK #12

Saturday, May 30, 2020 – Friday, June 5, 2020

"President Warns Looting Will Lead to Shooting: A Phrase Hark-ing Back to Police Violence" (Maggie Haberman and Alexander Burns, *The New York Times*, May 30, 2020)

"(Governor) Inslee's New Plan Eases Reopening: Washington's Largest Counties Could Soon See Many Businesses Back in Operation, But Nearly All Workers Have to Wear Masks" (Joseph O'Sullivan and Ryan Blethen, *The Seattle Times*, May 30, 2020)

"Skagit County Seeks Approval for Phase 2 in Safe Start Plan" (Brandon Stone, *Skagit Valley Herald*, May 30, 2020)

As the sun sets on Day 78, I refer you back to Day 9: As the sun sets on Day 9, I reflect on a suggestion by the Archbishop of Canterbury to light a candle tonight for Hope. From the fire of the SpaceX Falcon 9 rocket that launched the Crew Dragon capsule into orbit at 12:22pm Pacific to the fires that burn across our country 12 hours later, let's all light a candle and Hope we can rise from the ashes. Get some sleep tonight, Campers, and let's buckle down (and up) tomorrow.

As the sun sets on Day 79, I find myself disappointed that it's not another three-day weekend. But perhaps I'm being greedy. But no, because I've decided that every weekend should be three days long. Saturday often ends up being about chores and catching up on things that don't get done during the work week; Sunday frequently leads to the late afternoon "Sunday Blues" as we call them around here. Sunday anticipation of Monday is the one kind of anticipation I guess I don't really dig. Ah, well, so it goes. Time to buckle down. Sunday slips into / Monday, this one even her- / alding a new month. Sleep well, Angels, and wake to a fresh, new month!

As the sun sets on Day 80, I report on my day's high point, low point, and gratitude (this is something a friend used to do with her family every night at dinner, and I like the sentiment, even if my own practice is spotty). High point: Brandi Carlile streaming concert, including several valuable calls to action related to racial justice and Pride month and a surprise encore with her kids of one of my current favorite songs. High point #2 (because I feel doubling up on High Points should be permitted): packaging up Camp shirts for my college friends and continuing to spread that Camp spirit, which we really need right now. Low point: The sitting U.S. President threatening to call in the military on U.S. citizens. I just read an article recounting 12 times the President has activated the National Guard since the 1952 Armed Forces Reserve Act. All but two were related to racially-based issues. The most recent was in

1992 in L.A. following the Rodney King verdict. Our country is addicted to racism. We need to admit we have a problem, make amends, and start the healing. Now. Gratitude: I have ears and eyes and a mind and a voice, and I intend to use them. We created this mess, and we can fix it if we have the will. Get some sleep, Campers, because it's time to step up. And I know you will.

As the sun sets on Day 81, I find myself tired, but in a good way. It has been a long, intense eight days. I think I've let down just a bit because I saw some signs of Hope today. From friends having thoughtful discussions and getting involved to images of diverse peaceful protests, law enforcement joining in, and politicians opening channels of communication for the work still to come. Might we be starting down the road to real change? Only time will tell, but I am more hopeful tonight. Also, Election Day is exactly five months from today (now that the clock has crept past midnight). Sleep well, Angels, for you have made it through another Nondescript Tuesday, and you know what that makes tomorrow!

As the sun sets on Day 82, I celebrate a great Hump Day and another imminent favorite-day-of-the-week just over the horizon. So much going on. So many thoughts, feelings. So much to do. We are built for this. We can do it. We need to help each other along the way. I see that look in many people's eyes. It's a good sign, Campers; a good sign indeed. A rainbow of peo- / ple marching in the streets. Change / is afoot today. Dream of the world you want to see, and wake ready to work towards your vision!

As the sun sets on Day 83, I feel the need for a moment of quiet. I heard the phrase "holy hush" today in reference to moments of silence, and I'm wishing for a moment of quiet peace for everyone tonight. Today was another packed one, and I'm very grateful for all I've learned; I also need a fair amount of quiet time in normal times, so I'm ready for some…even though I keep typing. Want to join me? Close your eyes; take a / slow breath in and out. Give your- / self a bit of peace. Sleep peacefully, Angels. Yep, just that… sleep peacefully. That's your only job until tomorrow.

As the sun sets on Day 84, I note that our time together has now stretched out to 12 weeks. For those who play with numbers, 8 plus 4 equals 12 (well, I suppose that goes for those who don't play with numbers, too). I'm also thinking about the fact that tomorrow is the 76th Anniversary of D-Day and of the relationship between that unimaginable act and tomorrow's "Peaceful Solidarity Rally For Justice." I like it. It makes me feel like we are all part of something much bigger than ourselves. We don't know all the answers or how things will turn out, but we are all part of these struggles. And they are worth it. So, do your best. Also, be sure to relax and try to have some fun! It's another weekend, our 13th together, in fact. Regroup, relax, revel. Take care of yourselves. The world needs all of you. Bouncing between hard / work and rejuvenation. / This is what we do. Sleep well, Campers, and wake to a weekend of possibilities!

WEEK #13
Saturday, June 6, 2020 – Friday, June 12, 2020

"Virus Closures Leave Students Falling Behind: Gaps of Race and Class Are Likely to Widen" (Dana Goldstein, *The New York Times*, June 6, 2020)

"A More Somber D-Day Remembrance as Pandemic Keeps Many Away" (Raf Casert, *The Seattle Times*, June 6, 2020)

"DOH to Enumclaw: We Are "Committed' to a County-By-County Approach" (Ray Miller-Still, *The Enumclaw Courier-Herald*, June 3, 2020)

As the sun sets on Day 85, I tip my hat to everyone out there trying to make their community better. Those efforts can be big gestures (e.g. bringing our country closer to its highest ideals) or smaller ones (e.g. holding a movie night with friends and supporting each other wherever they are). It all matters! It really does. What kinds of things do you need? Someone else does, too. One day, you give. The next day, you receive. See the symmetry? When we see it and act on it, we all thrive. When we don't, well, we don't. Simple. But complicated. If we could only get out of our own way, as several of my teachers have said. Let's get out of our own way and get into a better place. We can do it. Work and play and both / together. Reach out and give / someone a hand now. Dream broadly, Angels, and let's see what we can do for each other!

As the sun sets on Day 86, I tip my hat to everyone who's surviving 2020. What a year. We are all being asked to deal with so much. It's tiring. And worrisome. But that's the hand we've been dealt. This is our test right now. No one said life was going to be easy… which is good because if they had, they'd be a big, fat liar. Every person and every generation is tested. Does this test feel a teensy bit extreme? Yes. But that's probably how other generations felt, too. The point is how we respond. I hope everyone had a chance to regroup, relax, and revel this weekend. Here we go! Staring down ano- / ther week in the crucible. / Get fired up, Campers! Sleep soundly, and we'll give it a go tomorrow.

As the sun sets on Day 87, I am reminded what it's like to Get Some Sh*t Done. This had to have been my most productive Monday in eons (so, you know, like one week Quarantine Time). My mind has been racing for so long, I forgot what it was like for it to move at a more normal pace. Was I still a super-freak? Yes, decidedly. But I was able to check some things off that infernal To-Do List. It felt good. What'd you get done today? Something? Congrats! Nothing? Don't worry; tomorrow's another opportunity. And remember, it's all relative. Some days you get sh*t done; other days, you aspire to get sh*t done. And it's 2020, so if you manage to get out of bed, you're allowed to count that as something. When your mind is rac- / ing, everything is swimmy / and jumpy. Calm down! Dream serenely, Angels, because another Tuesday is just around the bend.

As the sun sets on Day 88, I tip my hat to the medical profession-als. Again. Still. I ventured forth today for my first medical ap-pointment since lockdown. I was very impressed with the proce-dures the facility had implemented to keep their staff and patients safe, and I was reminded how much better I feel about being out and about when those around me are taking recommended pre-cautions. Looking at the numbers, we are not out of the woods yet by far, and some areas seem to be headed back into the woods while we continue to wait for a vaccine or cure. After 88 days, it's easy to become fatigued on the virus front, and there certainly are other vital issues vying for our attention now. It's challenging, but keep your eyes on the balls. Yep, the eyes and the balls are plu-ral now, perhaps more than ever. Find those coping mechanisms, and activate them ASAP. Stay informed, and stay home if you can. Standing in the whirl- / wind that is 2020, / keep your eyes open. Sleep well, Campers, and steady on.

As the sun sets on Day 89, I tip my hat to the lessons of the gar-den. I actually thought I'd be writing about the lessons of Yoga, as I achieved my most successful Yoga action to date: I realized I didn't need the dynamic class I was signed up to attend this afternoon; instead, I opted for the evening restorative class. Yeah, that's the ticket! A lot of lying around on props and working on pranayama (Yoga breathing). It was absolutely the right choice. I was going to share one of the lessons of the night: Breathe in Peace; Breathe out Love. Pretty great, right? And so very appropriate to the times. But no, that's not what I want to share. Oh, wait, I just did. So, you're going to get a two-fer tonight. After Yoga, I tidied up the Yoga studio/Molly's office/new addition and went out to water the

Veggie Babies. Remember them? We're still hanging out together. And you should have seen what I found out there! I want you
to see, so here are two pictures of the same row of veggie babies,
taken a mere 2.5 weeks apart, that relay the Lesson of the Garden
[photo of what had been considered Total Devastation and subsequent photo of same-but-apparently-not-so-devastated peas roaring back]. Dream of the great mystery of the pea shoot, Angels,
and believe that we can come back, too.

As the sun sets on Day 90, I'm feeling like today has been a bit of
a mixed bag. [This is a 2020 recording.] From the highs of a good
webinar (work) and an actual in-person but appropriately-masked
and socially-distanced visit from a fellow Camper (play) to the
lows of tonight's COVID news (B.S.), I feel tired. I'm afraid this is
our new normal now. Best to stay informed and figure out how we
want it to go. But I'm tired, so I'm going to start figuring that out
tomorrow. Minutes feel like days; / days like months. This year can
be / a bit annoying. Get some sleep, Campers, and know that your
weekend loometh!

As the sun sets on Day 91, I reflect that this is our 13th week together. Lucky 13! Right. Well, last night, I was feeling a bit down
about the virus news. Tonight, our neighborhood blog included a
link to an article that provides some reasonable-sounding advice
re: to how to keep safe as numbers rise and this grinds on, as it is
going to do: https://www.nytimes.com/2020/06/09/well/live/
coronavirus-rules-pandemic-infection-prevention.html A smidge
of reasonable advice always makes me feel better, as do examples
of people rising above. Talk about a lesson tonight: Washington
State's oldest COVID survivor is 106 years old. She was inter-
viewed on the news tonight (by her granddaughter who is a Seattle
reporter), and the reporter observed that she sounded good. Her
response was, "Well, I have a lot to smile about tonight." Lesson
received. I was fretting last night while the 106-year-old survivor is
smiling on. Lesson definitely received. Let's all make an effort to

smile a lot this weekend. I mean, I want to see some real Cheshire Cats out there! Keep your wits about / you, and keep smiling. Inside / and outside as one. Dream deliciously, Angels, and keep on smilin' on.

WEEK #14

Saturday, June 13, 2020 – Friday, June 19, 2020

"From the Boss: Sign a Waiver to Go to Work – Firms Seek Protection; Employees Worry" (Ana Swanson and Alan Rappeport, *The New York Times*, June 13, 2020)

"Starbucks Ends Ban on BLM Symbols: Staff Can Wear the Items Until the Company's Tamer T-shirts Arrive" (Paul Roberts, *The Seattle Times*, June 13, 2020)

"Plateau Protestors: Black Lives Matter" (Ray Miller-Still, *The Enumclaw Courier-Herald*, June 10, 2020)

As the sun sets on Day 92, I tip my hat to Saturday. Yes, I know…I said everyone likes Saturday, so that can't possibly be my favorite day. This particular Saturday, however, was particularly lovely because it involved being outside, working out, eating good food, seeing a good friend and her dog (masked and distanced…well, not the dog), watching our favorite show, harvesting in the garden, and not being on tech for hours and hours (and still more hours). I like an organic day; they feel longer and less rushed to me. Scheduling every minute of every day is the pits. I hope you, too, had an organic, pleasantly-paced day. If not, good news…tomorrow is another great weekend day that is just waiting for you to wake and enjoy it. Sometimes, less is more. / Taking it slow can be ex- / actly what you need. Sleep peacefully, Campers, and know tomorrow holds many unexpected pleasures, if you just look around.

As the sun sets on Day 93, I tip my hat to all you survivors out there. We are far apart right now, but I see you and hear you and enjoy your adventures and yes, even your struggles. Our conversations are such a microcosm of Life. Well, they are Life, really. It is rich and deep and messy and joyous and frustrating and exhilarating. So many things right now seem sucky, but so many actually aren't. We're still here, we're still together, we're still learning. It just looks and feels a little different, but it might actually be burning a little brighter and hotter. What's the meaning of all this? I'm not sure exactly, but there are sure a lot of feels to feel and thoughts to think. It's like the Grinch's puzzler. Actually, that's a pretty great quote to puzzle tonight: "It came without ribbons. It came without tags. It came without packages, boxes, or bags. And he puzzled and puzzled 'till his puzzler was sore. Then the Grinch thought of something he hadn't before. What if Christmas, he thought, doesn't come from a store. What if Christmas [quarantine?], perhaps, means a little bit more." It's all in how we look at things, I suppose. The weekend draws to / a close. Our weekend adven- / tures live on inside. Dream of the week ahead, Angels, and make it a good one!

As the sun sets on Day 94, I tip my hat to all the musicians we love. In fact…Music always says / it the best. I'm gonna keep / quiet and listen. Oh, except for one more thing…the *Friends* episode with my favorite quote about chickpeas was just on, which I always take as a good sign. Guest star George Clooney says, "God bless the chickpea." I always think of that when I have hummus. Just thought you'd want to know. Sleep well, my little Chickpeas, and dream of a riveting Tuesday (it could happen).

As the sun sets on Day 95, I tip my hat to all you fine friends who helped me through another Tedious Tuesday. With your stories and jokes and pics and good humor, it was not at all tedious. Thank you for entertaining me! Tonight, I offer up a quote from Henry David Thoreau sent by one of my fine friends (you know who you are): "If a man does not keep pace with his companions, perhaps it is because he hears a different drummer. Let him step to the music which he hears, however measured or far away." I love it! Thoreau himself has given us permission to march to our own drum. Let's all do it. Harmony is more interesting than a solo anyway. We need each other and those drums. If you're feeling really crazy, throw in a kazoo or some maracas. All instruments welcome! Dream of the great symphony of our lives, Angels, and wake to write your next bars.

As the sun sets on Day 96, I reflect back on a truly packed Hump Day. Work: Major breakthrough/brainstorm on two fronts during a particularly inspiring webinar. Trust me, I'm not boasting. I haven't experienced either phenomenon on any front in a very long while. I guess I was due, if only per the law of averages. Home: CSA and bread pickup in the 'hood; dog walk; Yoga Zoom; Book Club Zoom. That's a lot, even back in the Before Times. Personal: lots more thoughts and feels. Little bit of a spinny, swimmy mind again, but at least a little bit of it might end up being spun and swum into something productive. Standing in the pock- / et office in the wee hours. / Hump Day, you got me. Sleep well, Campers, and pass me the coffee!

As the sun sets on Day 97, the word that stands out this evening (nope…this morning) is Together. This word came up numerous times today, during work and in text strings, during a Yoga benefit and in various conversations. We are herd animals, folks, and we need each other, perhaps in different doses, but we need each other all the same. I was doing some noodling on how to Summit and how to see friends in the Time of COVID, and I am convinced that Togetherness is going to be different for the foreseeable future. However, we have to try because we need each other. So, time to stay informed and get creative. Our mental health depends on it! Spending time at home / has many positives, but / I'm tired of my face. Dream of sharing space safely, Angels, and wake to new possibilities!

As the sun sets on Day 98 (155th Anniversary of Juneteenth), we celebrate our 14th week together (and 14 is Molly's favorite number). We are getting perilously close to the century mark, Campers! How the heck did that happen?? Today was a good day: more learning, more sharing, Happy Hour with friends, Molly's summer began at around 4pm, and we enjoyed what has become our traditional Quarantine Friday Dinner of "Fancied-Up Frozen Pizza" and Xena, plus some really, really good Cabernet. A little online shopping, some *Frasier* while penning this missive, and then, it's off to reading in bed. Silver linings, folks. I tip my hat to all you Campers who are also finding the silver linings every single day. You know, maybe we make some attempts to make the lining the main event. Instead of a bunch of Blah being the main thing and the Silver stuff being just the liner, we flip that story around. We are just embarking on our latest weekend adventures, so it's the perfect time to try! Look for those silver / linings and make them the main / part of your sweet day. Sleep deeply, Campers, for you have some shiny memories to make tomorrow! And I can't wait to hear all about them.

WEEK #15
Saturday, June 20, 2020 – Friday, June 26, 2020

"On Juneteenth, Tulsa Pairs Joy With Defiance: A Message Sent Ahead of a Trump Rally" (Astead W. Herndon, *The New York Times*, June 20, 2020)

"City Schools Set Reopening Plan; Families Can Opt to Stay Online" (Hannah Furfaro, *The Seattle Times*, June 20, 2020)

"Expo Center Offering Drive-In Movies" (Ray Miller-Still, *The Enumclaw Courier-Herald*, June 17, 2020)

As the sun sets on Day 99, I tip my hat to you brave weekend warrior women out there celebrating the Summer Solstice. I see baby chicks; I see canoe-based imbibing; I see brave party planning. And it is good. It is all very good. I must refer back to earlier Saturday comments about how nice it is to spend some organic time away from the computer on the weekend. Let's do it again tomorrow! Clucking, rowing, plot- / ting all the weekend long. Wish / it would last longer! Dream of new adventures, Campers, and wake to a summer of possibilities!

[Day 99 = Guest Missive by Cameron]
As the sun sets on Day 99 (we're gonna party like it's 1999!) I tip my hat to the lesson of the llamas. I understand they are somewhat trendy in the U.S., but here in Ecuador they are staple farm animals. In fact we have 4 of them here at El Refugio where we are staying. They are typically staked to a spot in the ground by about 30 feet of rope. This gives them a fairly wide berth as they munch the grass in their vicinity and add to the picturesque view of the hillside where they are keeping grass and weeds at an appropriate level. As I walked by the same llama over the course of two days, I noticed that its rope was getting shorter and shorter as it wound itself around the stake in the ground. The llama seems to be a little on the dull side as this phenomenon takes place day in and day out. Wherever said llama is staked, it runs itself in circle, getting all tied in knots and making its own situation worse, until the rope is so tight/taut that all the sweet animal can do is sit next to the stake. It seems to me that there is a lesson to be learned from the llama. If we can be at peace where we are staked, we can enjoy it; if not, we wind ourselves up in knots. Let's not be llamas/let's enjoy and love where we/are and learn to thrive. Sleep well my angels and don't be a [llama emoji].

[Response:]
A truly Magnificent guest missive!! I loved it! What a valuable message: "If we can be a peace where we are staked we can enjoy it;

if not we wind ourselves up in knots. Let's not be llamas/let's enjoy and love where we/are and learn to thrive." I will work on applying this today. Thank you, Margarita!!!

As the sun sets on Day 100, I stare slack-jawed at those triple digits. Someone pinch me. Is this really happening? Yes. Yes, it is. My, we have shared some shares, haven't we? And by that, I mean I have shared and you have had to read (or delete…I'll never know). Well, don't forget the offer for Guest Missives. The Nightly Missive belongs to all of us, even though I'm usually hogging it. The more the merrier! I've been thinking more than usual this year about the Summer Solstice, and it always reminds me of an episode of *Northern Exposure*. Anyone remember that TV show? Super quirky and awesome. Well, it's set in Alaska (although they filmed in Roslyn, Washington, which is awesome and home to the oldest continuously-operating saloon in The State and a great pizza place and a really unique cemetery, so we should all go there sometime!), and one episode is set around the Solstice. So, it being AK and all, it's light almost 24 hours a day and no one is sleeping and they are all alternately creative and crazy (more so than usual) and much hilarity ensues. It's 1:30am here again, so I'm feeling a little bit like a citizen of Cicely, AK. We visited Molly's cousin in Anchorage in June a few years ago, and I think the writers of the show were on to something. It was pretty crazy, and you did get a weird surge of energy after a while. And everyone else was wandering around with this slightly crazy look in their eyes, too. So, those two zeroes in Day 100 are starting to look like crazy eyes to me. So, I think it's time to go to bed. Triple digit days / together. Who would have thought / it would come to this? Sleep well if you are able, Campers, and flash that creativity around tomorrow!

As the sun sets on Day 101, I tip my hat to Highway 101 out on the Coast. I did not expect to tip my hat to Highway 101 out on the Coast, but seeing that number in Bold, how can I not?? What a ride! Hey, remember road trips? Anywho…. I actually have a serious, or at least heartfelt, message for you tonight. I've noticed over the past 101 days that, not infrequently, some among you – perhaps even all of us at one point or another – have expressed some significant Self-Doubt. While this is a completely normal human condition, it always makes me sad to hear people I admire and care about struggling with this. When those doubts creep in, I think back to when I was very little, and I learned the song "Yes, Jesus loves me." Now, whether or not you believe, I remember being very little and thinking, "Whoa, no matter what happens there is always someone who loves me." Now, sometimes things get pretty rough (pandemic, anyone?), and it can be a little hard to believe that Jesus or anyone is out there just hanging around loving you; so, without getting too schmaltzy, I want to offer that I love you, too. And so do all the other Angels on this text. So, you are covered, Angel. When that self-doubt creeps in, and we know it will at times, just know that you are covered. So there. Also, when that self-doubt creeps in, and we know it will at times, I also have you covered where Silly Jokes are concerned! What did the buffa- / lo say when his little boy / left for school? Bison! Holy Cow, that silly joke was also a haiku!! What are the odds?? That's it. I'm done. That joke rules, you are loved, good night. Sleep well, Angels, and rest assured that I am marveling over the joke haiku.

As the sun sets on Day 102, I am a bit bummed. I just read that our County will not be able to move to our State's "Phase 3" on Friday due to a rise in confirmed cases that have been traced back to large social gatherings. Our State is also moving to a face mask requirement starting Friday. Come on, Personal Responsibility... I need you to make that comeback! Such easy, recognized measures, and people refuse to be "inconvenienced." Barf. These things fall squarely under the Golden Rule. Let's look out for our neighbor! In other news, I participated in my first Zoom Commission meeting tonight, and it wasn't bad at all. It might even have been more enjoyable than some of our traditional meetings. Silver lining, I see you! I hope you all had a good day and a better evening. I'm muttering in the dark. Not a good sign. Good thing tomorrow's a busy day, and you know what else…it's Hump Day again!! Channel your inner / camel and think of the fun / on the other side. Dream of hidden stores of energy, Campers, and tap into them tomorrow!

As the sun sets on Day 103, I smile fondly at thoughts of each of you. Good grief, I think I might be turning permanently schmaltzy or something! Well, I guess I could turn into worse things. Hump Day was a very busy day up here…lots of learning and some errands (food and drink-related, of course) and a whole bunch of other life-on-lockdown stuff. I (still) need to make more of an effort to get out onto the deck and into my chair. I am lacking fresh air. More sun, more breeze, more birdie buddies. Even if I'm working in my chair, those things make me feel better and brighter. I hope you, too, can get more of those things! The out of doors feels / more real than the in of doors. / Get you some, Campers! Dream of birdie buddies, Campers, and wake to greet them (as they might greet you with their incessant chirping even when you're trying to sleep in because you were up half the night).

[Day 103 = Guest Missive by Catherine]
As the sun sets on day 103, I think about the fun fact that before this pandemic, this thread was active maybe once a week? Sometimes only a few times a month? We reached out when major things were going on, good or bad, but sporadically at best. Now, it's part of my daily routine to sit down and catch up with all of you and what's been going on in your lives. I imagine sitting together in someone's dorm room, at the local hangout, in the Quad, at the viewpoint, and chatting with you all, and I'm so thankful for our connections that have survived and, I hope, grown even stronger over the past 25 years. Thanks for knowing I'm here even when I'm quiet. I hear you all and I'm taking it all in. I do have so much self-doubt and uncertainty in my life…and I appreciate so much the fact that you're all here and love me no matter what. https://www. goodreads.com/quotes/412210-and-what-is-a-friend-more-than-

a-father-more My favorite mug (thank you Mel) that I drink out of whenever I can reminds me of you all. I looked up the rest of the quote, and I hope you won't mind my taking Elie Wiesel's words and turning them into a haiku: Good friends let me "hold/ [my] tongue without shame and talk/ freely without risk." Thank you all for sharing your lives, love, and brilliance with me.

[Response:]
Wow!! Thank you, Catherine!! That is a beautiful missive. Silver lining, indeed! And creating an Elie haiku?? Masterful.

As the sun sets on Day 104, I find myself embroiled in work machinations. Trying to salvage something meaningful in the midst of a pandemic is no small feat. It is, however, worth the effort. I've been thinking, mulling, plotting, training, worrying, kvetching, and agonizing. I think I've come up with some good options, but I only shared them with my main helper today. To my great relief, they were very well received. So, perhaps I am not crazy, regardless of what my head has sounded like! Relief. That's a really good feeling I haven't felt in a very long time. This whole exercise has made me think about how helpful it can be to take the time to pause and sit with something, especially something like a hard decision. We live in such in instant gratification society that we expect everything, even things like hard decisions, to come immediately. I had to stew on this one, and I don't think I could have worked my way through it quickly. So, let's all give ourselves permission to pause and sit with something when the way isn't clear. The insta-grat approach doesn't always serve us well. It's OK to take a beat. Things often have a way of clearing up when we do. Taking the time you / need to think things through can be / a form of self-care. Sleep peacefully, Campers, because rest can bring you some of your best ideas.

As the sun sets on Day 105, we mark our 15th week together. Wooooh, baby, that's a while! I'll get right to it: the lesson of the slug. As you know, I have been marveling over the Resurrection of the Pea Plants. To recap: pea plants were planted; pea plants sprouted; pea plants grew some beautiful bi-colored leaves and promising tendrils; pea plants were rudely decimated in a matter of hours (birds were suspected and slugs were later confirmed); pea plants were thought to be lost; pea plants were allowed to take time to heal and consider coming back; pea plants came back; pea plant farmer marveled. Well, we have another garden miracle, Angels! I wandered out a few nights ago to do the watering by the glow of headlamp. I hadn't mentioned it yet, but the leaves of the bean plants must also be delectable to the resident birds and slugs because they have been sporting lots of nibble marks and looking pretty rough. Same for the cucumbers. Well, I leaned over with my headlamp, and the glow revealed at least two bean plants that are now sporting flowers! Those blessed beans are surviving and maybe even thriving now! And those crazy cukes survived the nibbling and have grown in size and foliage. Are you kidding me?? I marveled some more and then laughed out loud at the lesson of the slug which goes thusly: slugs are plentiful and voracious, but if you (I mean, "if a plant") takes a little time to heal, it can come back better than before, no matter the damage. Sleep well, Angels; ponder the lesson of the slug and channel your inner bean.

[Day 105 = Guest Missive by Phoenix]

Hallo, there —it is I, your guest Poet. Thought I had fallen asleep on duty, didja? Well, not true, Campers, I was binge watching *Travelers*, a promising show for someone who doesn't do much TV. It has time travel, quirky characters embodying other bodies, and that guy from Will and Grace who doesn't seem to age any more than Paul Rudd for some strange reason. All positives! I'm going to call this the close of Day 105 for posterity's sake, but to be honest, I'm not tracking time the same way in my corner. This was week one of summer break, week eight of our tribal furlough, and also the start of the last fortnight of my husband's forties which has set an ever-so-slight tone of impending doom over the house of late. All

I can think to get him is that extra jug of hand sanitizer I saw under the sink at work...and a Whole Lot of quality time with his family this summer! So, anyhoo, about that uplifting poem! I cheated and looked up some haikus from the Japanese masters, thinking I would get cute with it. And behold! I find that the act of translation from the Japanese combined with the restricted style adds an air of erudite mystery to the whole affair, which quite charmed me. So, I will pick two Japanese haiku praising summer to share with you, and we will see if the morning brings depth or resonance to the lines, or if ,instead, we will merely enjoy them for the random images they joyfully convey: Don't hit it/The fly rub the hands/ Or the legs. The cool breeze/With all of his strength/The cricket. Sleep soundly, Campers, and take the new day in as we take in a new language, with the ears of travelers!

[Response:]
Thank you, Phoenix!! A beautiful & thought-provoking missive, indeed. Re: the haiku, is the 3-5-3 scheme a function of translation, or a different form of haiku? I've been using 5-7-5 the whole time! I love that you speak Japanese now. Impressive!! #QuarantineSkills

WEEK #16
Saturday, June 27, 2020 – Friday, July 3, 2020

"States Backtrack on Relaxed Limits As Cases Explode: New Restrictions in Florida and Texas – West and South See New Highs" (Patricia Mazzei, Sarah Mervosh, and Shawn Hubler, *The New York Times*, June 27, 2020)

"How Well Did People Heed New Mask Rule? Residents Have Mixed Reactions to Governor's Order Making Coverings Mandatory" (Elise Takahama, *The Seattle Times*, June 27, 2020)

"Local Women Call On Councils to Tackle Systemic Racism" (Ray Miller-Still, *The Enumclaw Courier-Herald*, June 24, 2020)

As the sun sets on Day 106, I tip my hat to Saturdays. No wonder people like these! Unstructured time, I salute you!! While we chose to forego a friend's small retirement gathering, we did get to visit safely on the front porch with a close friend. And it was Good. Watching another benefit concert show now. I tip my hat again…this time, to Talent! Man, are there some talented folks out there! I've always wondered where Talent comes from. I mean, we all have gifts, but some people just stand out. Amazing. Off to read my book and go to sleep at a decent hour! Meandering through / my Saturday. It sure feels / good to take my time. Dream serenely, Angels, and enjoy another day at your own pace!

As the sun sets on Day 107, I tip my hat to Sunshine. I finally made it to my chair in the backyard this evening! I read for about 30 minutes, put my book down, and closed my eyes to feel the warm setting sun and the breeze and to listen to the birds. Then…I woke up. I actually fell sound asleep for a few minutes! I don't think I've been that relaxed since before my trip to Huntsville in late February, right before the Current Unpleasantness. Thank you, giant ball of gas and plasma in the sky! You are beautiful. And you have not been around enough yet. Let's get this Summer thing going! Light in the sky, warmth / on the skin, makin' those veg- / gie babies grow, y'all! Sleep well, sweet Campers, and don't forget your sunscreen.

As the sun sets on Day 108, a tip o' the hat to Simplicity. Quickly, to bed now! / You have an early training / tomorrow morning. Sleep deeply, Campers, and enjoy the simple pleasures of a good night's rest.

As the sun sets on Day 109 [Dad's 84th birthday], I tip my hat to Adventure! Tonight, I adventure virtually via the National Geographic channel and a couple documentaries about Mount Everest. I am a complete sucker for extreme climbing stories. While I have no desire to attempt such feats, I love reading about them and watching the astounding videography of the documentaries. It really is basically another planet up in the Dead Zone. Meanwhile, across the country, a certain Angel adventures in the real world (or, we could say "IRL" which I learned today means "In Real Life"). Said Angel and her family embarked this morning on an Epic Road Trip in the Time of COVID. They are taking their precautions and giving it a go. I salute them and will eagerly follow their Adventures IRL virtually from my couch. God Speed, Road Warriors! Hit the road this sum- / mer, whether literally / or in your own mind! Dream of the open road, Angels, and wake to adventure in the planet down here.

As the sun sets on Day 110, I have so many things running through my head, I'm not sure what to write about tonight. Transitioning the Summit to an all-virtual event (please keep that on the down-low until we announce); my Dad's 84th birthday yesterday and now a pending hospital visit tomorrow to clear a blocked kidney tube; town hall on policing; ever-rising COVID numbers; Presidential election; spouse and her own challenges and adventures; dogs on antibiotics (nothing serious); prepping for the neighborhood 4th of July Chalk Festival. It's kind of a lot. And I'm feeling kind of exhausted. So, without further ado: Find what interests / you and get in the game. It's / what we're here to do. Dream of making your mark, Campers, and wake to get started!

As the sun sets on Day 111, I tip my hat to creativity in the COVID Times. People are getting creative out there in so many cool ways! Businesses and communities are finding new ways to connect, and musicians are finding new ways to play for their fans. Tonight, those two things collided in a great local streaming concert. We probably wouldn't have gone in person in the Before Times, and it was fun to think of all the neighbors listening in, as well as folks across the country. Might this be another Silver Lining? I think it is. It gives me hope for a virtual Summit in October, too. Here's a two-fer tonight: Be open to new / ways of connecting with each / other in these times. If we keep an o- / pen mind, there's no telling the / new fun we can have! Dream of new ways to connect, Angels, and wake to lean into our New Normal.

As the sun sets on Day 112, I tip my hat to our computer guy. How I love someone who is willing to completely update my computer in a matter of a few hours and not judge me for not wanting to do it myself. This has been such a long time coming. What. A. Relief!! Tonight, I propose embarking on another book reading together. What do you say? This one is an updated (in 1979) edition of the 1962 classic *Happiness Is…A Warm Puppy* by Charles M. Schulz. So, we go from a monkey to a dog for our words of wisdom. Personally, I think we're smart to stick with (other members of) the Animal Kingdom for our wisdom! Here are our first three lessons: 1) Happiness is knowing who you are. 2) Happiness is watching an old movie. 3) Happiness is getting together with your friends. Wow, I kid you not…those are the first three lessons! Gather 'round, y'all, and / soak up the words of wisdom / from Snoopy and friends. Dream of holiday weekends, Campers, and wake to the happiness of adventure!

WEEK #17
Saturday, July 4, 2020 – Friday, July 10, 2020

"Celebrations Set on Mute This Fourth" (Julie Creswel, *The New York Times*, July 4, 2020)

"Boys of Summer Are Back - Team Grateful for Return; Games Without Fans Set to Begin in Three Weeks" (Ryan Divish, *The Seattle Times*, July 4, 2020)

"UW Outbreak Gives Peek at Containment Challenges" (Katherine Long and Asia Fields, *The Seattle Times*, July 4, 2020)

As the sun sets on Day 113, I wish you all a Very Happy 4th of July!! I hope you enjoyed lots of sun and fun and food and friends and fun and laughter and lots more of all those things I just mentioned. Cuz that's the stuff, Angels!! I hope this won't be too disappointing, but I am going to push tonight's "Happiness" lesson to tomorrow because really the only thing you need to do tonight is take the Hero's Journey that I will send momentarily [Molly created the Hero's Journey for our neighborhood Chalk Art Festival; it is a Wonder Woman-inspired "activity course" that encourages people to be active and inspires them to find their inner superhero]. It was so amazing to see our neighbors – ones we know and ones we don't! – take their journey and strike their pose at the end. Molly's abilities in this area are boundless. Enjoy, and we will visit with Snoopy again tomorrow! We watched the kids and / adults jump, climb, lasso, breathe. Then, their pose appeared! Dream sweetly, Angels, and try your pose in the morrow!

As the sun sets on Day 114, I realize that yesterday was a prime number day (113); I missed that at the time, but hooray!! Thank you for allowing me to stray last night from our new "Happiness" adventure. I was worried it would seem like a bait and switch. Well, back to it! Here are our next three lessons: 1) Happiness is a new jogging suit. 2) Happiness is finding someone you like at the front door. 3) Happiness is lots of candles. Hmmmm…well, you can find lessons anywhere, but that's a bit of a mixed bag for me. I will ponder on it. The one I can definitely latch on to is #2…assuming they are masked and 6 feet away, of course. Revel in your week- / ends, Campers, and think back on / all the fun you had! Dream of a solid Monday, Campers, and wake to a week of happy possibilities!

As the sun sets on Day 115, I'm a bit jumpy tonight. Tomorrow, we officially announce the move to a virtual Summit. Yikes. It's the right thing to do, but tell that to my nerves. I need a distraction. Peanuts to the rescue! 1) Happiness is a pile of leaves. 2) Happiness is a waterbed. 3) Happiness is disco dancing. That sneaky Snoopy…tempting me with the disco ball. Well, it worked! That makes me smile and think of '70s Parties in college. Do your homework, make / your plan, and stick to it. Things / will fall into place. Now, I just have to believe that! Sleep well, Angels, and disco dance through your Nondescript Tuesday.

As the sun sets on Day 116, I'm just glad the sun is setting. Today was a long, trying day, and I'm ready to move on to another HUMP DAY. Yes, I said it. Moving on to our Happiness lesson now because I need it: 1) Happiness is taking three airline stewardesses to lunch. 2) Happiness is a night light. 3) Happiness is one dollar for the movie, 35 cents for popcorn, and 15 cents for a candy bar. Oh, boy…even Peanuts is making me grumpy. Help! Perhaps a haiku instead: Not every day can / be the best day. Some days are / just days. Try again. Sleep restfully, Campers, and welcome the camel in the morning.

As the sun sets on Day 117, I'm thinking that sounds like a large number! And large numbers now make me think of my age…especially since we were laughing today about being more interested in watching the birds. They were quite cute and entertaining, I must admit. Good grief. Which reminds me of Peanuts: 1) Happiness is finding out you're not so dumb after all. [Geez, maybe I should stop there!] 2) Happiness is finding the little piece with the pink edge and part of the sky and the top of the sail boat. [Well, that's very pandemic-puzzle-appropriate!] 3) Happiness is knowing how to tie your own shoes. [Unless you're like me and you wear flip-flops every day now.] Keep your spirits up, Angels, as the pandemic grinds on and the New Normal swirls around us. Find a little patch of solid ground, stretch out on it for a bit, and check out those birds. They might just give you a little perspective. Birds, sun, breeze, seeds, feath- / ers, all together. Gaze at / wisdom on the wing. Dream of happy things, Angels, and watch them wing your way tomorrow!

As the sun sets on Day 118, I find myself coming down off a good ol' afternoon freakout. It wasn't so much a freakout, perhaps, as it was a conscious raging at the shit show that has been this week, this month, this year. The kind of moment where you just throw in the towel (or your laptop out the window) and run screaming out the door and around the block with your hair standing on end (which there is more of since you still don't want to go to the salon). Anyone out there feel me? Yeah, I know you do. I shall turn to Peanuts, but things are still dicey; so, Charlie Brown better watch his back: 1) Happiness is a piece of fudge caught on the first bounce. (OK, weird…but I can get behind that one.) 2) Happiness is a good old-fashioned game of hide and seek. (Here's an idea: I'll hide and nobody seek, and I'll see you in 6 months.) 3) Happiness is knowing all the answers. (I won't even touch that one.) May you all entertain your own personal freakout should you need one, which you might and that's OK, all the while remembering that tomorrow is Friday; so, who really gives a [poop emoji]. Freakout, poop emo- / ji, freakout, poop emoji, / freakout and poop, y'all. Sleep and dream, Campers, and wake to the day of Happy Hours.

As the sun sets on Day 119, we celebrate our 17th week together. My birthday falls on the number 17, so I am going to take that as a good sign. Well, what a difference 24 hours can make, not to mention one's friends. Thanks to my friends, I am feeling a bit better today; still totes crazy, but better. Kind of a good reminder to just keep pushing through; a little time can give you a new perspective. Perhaps Peanuts has something to say along these lines: 1) Happiness is show and lie. (Huh?? That is not a typo. Discuss.) 2) Happiness is a smooth sidewalk. (True, just ask Molly. We learned that on the 4th!) 3) Happiness is climbing a tree. (I can personally confirm that this is true.) So, what do you say we leave this shit show of a week behind and slide into a nice weekend? Time to regroup, rest, renew. A little breathing; a little bird watching. When the poop emo- / ji hits the fan, it's time to / lean on your friends some. Sleep peacefully, Angels, and know that your friends are wishing you the best.

WEEK #18

Saturday, July 11, 2020 – Friday, July 17, 2020

"Pace of Deaths Is Accelerating In Large States" (Farah Stockman, Mitch Smith, and Giulia McDonnell Nieto del Rio, *The New York Times*, July 11, 2020)

"Proposal Targeting International Students' Ire Draws Universities' Ire" (Katherine Long, *The Seattle Times*, July 11, 2020)

"Sounders Make a Statement at Opener" (Jayda Evans, *The Seattle Times*, July 11, 2020)

As the sun sets on Day 120, I shall lean on your kind offer of a simple Nightly Missive comprised mainly of a nod to Sauvignon Blanc. Yum. Also, Peanuts: 1) Happiness is walking in the grass in your bare feet. 2) Happiness is a camping trip. 3) Happiness is sleeping in your own bed. Um, yes…I can get behind those. Saturday can be / a day of great healing. Friends / and a movie. Yes! Dream sweetly, Campers, and know that you have done a great service.

As the sun sets on Day 121, I revel in a sunny Sunday. A little work, a few chores, a long dog walk, an annoying tech update, but I am going to rise above…all in all, a nice day. And watching the weather tonight, I realize I should celebrate our temperatures more than I already was. Whew, summer is here! Anyone for some Peanuts? 1) Happiness is scarfing junk food. 2) Happiness is three friends in a sandbox…with no fighting. 3) Happiness is an umbrella and a new raincoat. Ponder the wisdom of The Gang, Angels, and get your snoozing in…it's time for a new week!

As the sun sets on Day 122, I find it is late, and I just finished a tech consult with my IT guru. Also, this week is already feeling suspiciously ridiculous. Not a good sign on a Monday. Let's just get straight to the Peanuts lessons: 1) Happiness is standing around waiting for the chicks. (#Time'sUp, Schulz!) 2) Happiness is having someone to solve your problems. (Oh, it sure would be, wouldn't it??) 3) Happiness is the hiccups… after they've gone away. (Yes, hiccups. That's our biggest problem this year.) Let us regroup, Campers, for life calls us to action these days, or at least to perseverance. Reach out in front of you, as if you were creeping through the house in the dark, and feel your way towards Tuesday. Muddling through is still getting through. And that's good enough right now. Things are coming hard / and fast, sometimes too hard and / fast, but still, you fight. Sleep deeply, Campers, and we'll muddle through Tuesday together.

As the sun sets on Day 123, I peeked at the next piece of Happiness wisdom, and I propose that it is the only thing needed this evening. I cannot expound upon, improve, or even ruin it. Here goes (one and done): *Happiness is a warm puppy.* Dream of sloppy puppy kisses, Angels, and wake to fight again tomorrow…on Hump Day!

As the sun sets on Day 124, I would like to report that I have received an important message. It came to me this evening as I fretted about, and you know what it was? The message itself was simple, but it was profound, especially these days. Here it is: Everything is going to be OK. That's it. It just popped into my head. Strangely, I do feel better this evening, and my fret level is way down. I hope this simple but powerful message hits you the right way, too. Let's exhale and check out tonight's Happiness lessons: 1) Happiness is a blow-dry hairdo. (Unless there's a pandemic on and you are avoiding the salon.) 2) Happiness is remote control T.V. (Yes and YES!!) 3) Happiness is knowing you have a pretty face. (At this point, I will settle for having a face.) OK, Hump Day survivors…on to Thursday! Sleep happily, Campers, and embrace the magical, powerful message that it's going to be OK.

As the sun sets on Day 125, I'm having a little bout of "WearA-MaskAHole"-itis. Mask up, Washington! (I just saw a PSA to that effect with lots of cute little masked smiley faces going about their daily lives.) I won't go on and on (even though you are a captive audience…assuming you are still reading this), but I swear…if I go through all this in the attempt to stay healthy for an eventual flight home and some non-mask-wearing a-hole infects me, I am going to be one unhappy (and uncomfortable) Camper. OK, I know you are all living in the same world with many of the same concerns, so I will just thank you for listening during one of my moments of struggle and move on. I know each of you are having your own moments. I feel you. I'm here for you, too. With that, let us turn to tonight's Happiness lesson: 1) Happiness is a thumb and a blanket.

(I could actually go for some of that right now.) 2) Happiness is forty-nine flavors. (Of adult beverages, obviously.) 3) Happiness is finding a caddy who doesn't fall into the hole. (Golf is dumb. Just kidding! Golf is very challenging, and the drinking is typically way more fun.) Hmmm…two mentions of drinking. Tomorrow must be Friday! Dream of Friday, Campers, and wake knowing that your dreams have finally come true!

As the sun sets on Day 126, we mark our 18th week together. As Dave Niehaus, legendary voice of the Seattle Mariners from 1977-2010, used to say, "My, oh my!" Makes me tired tonight, honestly, as does the end of another work week during a global pandemic that shows no sign of slowing in our country. Oh, did I go on right there? Seems to happen these days. Let's get to those Happiness lessons! 1) Happiness is flying south for the winter. 2) Happiness is expecting someone special. 3) Happiness is eating out. Anyone else think some of these take on a much different meaning than what was probably intended? OK, it's a wrap, Campers, just like this week. Sleep well so you're ready to dive into your much-deserved weekend!

WEEK #19

Saturday, July 18, 2020 – Friday, July 24, 2020

"To City's Alarm, Federal Officers Police Portland - 'It Feels Like Fascism' - Accusations of Exceeding Their Authority and Violating Rights" (Sergio Olmos, Mike Baker, and Zolan Kanno-Youngs, *The New York Times*, July 18, 2020)

"Friendly Fire Killed Bothell Officer; Accused Instigator Charged in Case" (Paige Cornwell and Sara Jean Green, *The Seattle Times*, July 18, 2020)

"Obituary: John Lewis, Icon of Civil Rights, A Stalwart in Congress" (Calvin Woodward, *The Seattle Times*, July 18, 2020)

As the sun sets on Day 127, I tip my hat again to Prime Numbers. We haven't had one for 2 weeks (Day 113). This is very exciting (to me)! Hi, Prime! In other news, today was Saturday…a beautiful, sunny, warm, leisurely Saturday. Pancakes, veggie babies, tall drinks, dog walks, warrior woman shows. No complaints. Nothing like a nice / Saturday to bring a smile / and lift your spirits. Plus, some Happiness! 1) Happiness is sharing. 2) Happiness is a cat nap. 3) Happiness is a new bicycle. Now, that's a fitting list for a Saturday! Dream of stars and comets, Angels, and light up the sky tomorrow!

As the sun sets on Day 128, I have a slight case of the Sunday Blues, as we call them around here. While I look forward to taking some time off here and there this coming week [Campers, any chance you could each take a Nightly Missive Wed-Fri?], I have to plow through some things Monday and Tuesday. I'm kind of gritting my teeth over my chores lately. Everything seems irritating. I hear that can be a sign of depression; so, it's time to take a step back…right into my lawn chair. Life could be challenging enough in the Before Times; now, there's a pandemic bubbling in the background all the time. Are you feeling some of this, too? I think it just means we're humans in the year 2020. Hang in there. I'm with you. We can muddle through together. Probably time to re-visit that Gratitude exercise, too. Every day, note at least one thing for which you are grateful. Even though the [poop emoji] is swirling, being grateful is not hard to do, and it's proven to help. Plus, it puts those goods vibes out into the world, and there's not one human who couldn't use a few of those. So, hang in there and check out these Happiness lessons, too: 1) Happiness is an invitation to a party. 2) Happiness is sunlight, air, plants, water, soil, birds, microorganisms… 3) Happiness is finding someone to type your term paper. I'll take a #2, please. Sleep soundly, Campers, because tomorrow is a chance to express gratitude.

As the sun sets on Day 129, I tip my hat to all you Angels. I am so impressed by and Grateful (there's the Gratitude) for your responses to last night's Irritation missive. You have done no less than respond by listening to one another, encouraging one another, commiserating with one another, and supporting each other's plans for upping the exercise. COVID Fatigue is real and is super [poop emoji]-y. The dark cloud is always looming on the horizon...or positioned directly overhead while pelting you with hail and lightning. It makes it hard to relax, hard to feel like you are parenting well (to small humans or to canines or felines), and hard to let go of a freezer of ruined food...because the freezer is COVID stocked. You know, I have to agree with the assessment... all of that Super Sucks. Maybe we have to turn the ship again. I had a breakthrough on my covidteenth webinar last week: I'm going to try to start shifting from "New Normal" to "Next Normal." In other words, stop fighting it, accept it is here to stay indefinitely, and start thinking of it as Normal. Then, maybe we can throw ourselves into things like planning Virtual Summits instead of the very special in-person event that everyone says is so important because of the face-to-face interactions. Sigh. But you get my drift. Let's try to face what's here to stay while we are exercising. Will it into being! And if that doesn't work, lean on your Angels here. Some Happiness is in order: 1) Happiness is reaching the top. 2) Happiness is mellow. 3) Happiness is overcoming your fears. Now, that's what I'm talkin' about! Say those things while exercising, and we'll be halfway there! Dream about your vision for tomorrow, Angels, and work hard to fulfill that dream!

[Day 129 = Guest Missive by Spicoli]
As the comet appears on day 129, I have a few inspirational words. They came to me today but they were isolated and random. Not actually connected. Strength and endurance comes with intimacy. Intimacy is like the fuel for all other things. Including sparkling which is the next thing that I recommend. And the last think is to create - create anything - make your own kind of anything.

Creating lets you sparkle, sparkling can help with intimacy. And these are the words!! Live well and safely!!!

[Response:]
A masterful and inspirational start to the week, Spicoli! I am inspired to try to Create and Sparkle when I take my time off. Well done, and thank you very much!

As the sun sets on Day 130, I tip my hat to Taco and Tuesday (that's the cat and the day, folks). We did it! Another Nondescript Tuesday under our belts. It has been beautiful weather here, and my, how that improves one's mood. I have been working steadily for two days towards my slower days, and I am giddy with excitement about Less Tech. I like tech as a Tool, and I even admire its creativity, elegance, and usefulness in many cases; however, too much tech time really saps my soul. I have to disengage and go play outside frequently, or I feel drained. I hope you, too, are able to take time for the things that recharge you. Maybe it's that new exercise routine; maybe it's a rousing game of hide-and-seek; maybe it's simply PBR and chips for dinner. Whatever helps you exhale and smile. Let's see what the Peanuts gang suggests: 1) Happiness is an "A" on your spelling test. 2) Happiness is living in a high-rise. 3) Happiness is a bread and butter sandwich folded over. Sure! Why not? Thank you, in advance, Guest Missivers for covering Wed-Fri and sharing your thoughts. Be sure to have fun with it; no stress. Talk to ya again on Saturday! Sleep soundly, Angels, and wake to know that you deserve some Happiness today!

[Day 130 = Guest Missive by Spicoli]
Night 130. OK, 4 thoughts rose to the surface at various times today. If opportunity doesn't knock, build a door...the essence of bravery is being without self-deception...increase your bandwidth - you can...patience when times are stressful, the antidote to anger is compassion. That's what I got - thanks for being out there, Campers!!!

[Response:]
Thank you for the missive, Spicoli! Much food for thought there. I especially like the ones about bravery and compassion. I did a rare morning Yoga class w/ my main teacher, and her theme was being a Warrior for Peace. More Warrior Woman stuff! No easy task today, I'm afraid. Hope you all are having better luck.

[Day 131 = Guest Missive by Margaret]
As the sun sets on Day 131, I keep thinking about the phrase "Next Normal." My son's school confirmed today they are definitely going virtual until early November when they can reevaluate. So, there's that. It's a relief to just have a solid answer. So, now we prep for that Next Normal, and roll with it. We've spent a lot of my son's life talking about "transitions," because he's always been resistant to them. Even when it was just "stop what you're doing and put on your shoes." And I get that. He's finally settled into the Now of what he's doing when we tell him to change.

My Snoopy Happiness is ... is back at my mom's house. But she did send me home with a Pooh book when I left Saturday. So here's an excerpt from that:

"He recited his Morning Rhyme:
Just two things to do,
To truly be Pooh.
The first thing was to be in the here and now as much as he possibly could without a whole lot of thinking about it. (This was easy enough for a Bear of very little brain.)
The second thing was to be as kind as he possibly could toward everyone, including himself. (This was easy for a Bear of very big heart.)
'It's not hard to be me,' thought Pooh. 'Just be Here and Now, and be Kind.'"

Farewell Hump Day, my loves. Tomorrow is Thursday - my favorite day of the week. You can still be productive, but the weekend is right around the corner. (Why is there no bear emoji?)

[Response:]

That is some Beautiful Missiving, Murt! Thank you! That Pooh is one smart bear. I re-read some Winnie a few months ago, not too long before the Current Unpleasantness. I had forgotten how wise he and his woodsy friends are. Thank you for the reminder and the excellent advice. I am going to try to practice it during my Tech Timeout. Have a great Thursday-Best-Day-Of-The-Week, all!

[Day 131 = Guest Missive by Spicoli]

Night 131...also a prime number. I have been sent the message "build on your similarities," but I will share three images from my day of monitoring in a sports field where I got to use the bathroom in the change room and then travelled on a ferry and down a country road. Love you guys - three images to follow [Happy Camper sign; Thank You for Social Distancing bumper sticker; Win With Class chalk talk].

[Day 132 = Guest Missive by Cameron]

The sun set on day 131 and has in fact risen on day 132 (but who is counting), and I tip my hat to grace.... grace for the forgetful... grace for when we are late...grace for the not getting the important things done. And yet it is in its own right an incredibly powerful and important concept. Grace can change the world/oh thank God for Grace because/ I need it badly!

Have a grace filled days angels. Love you all and whoopsie.

[Response:]

A masterful and experiential reminder of the fact that we ALL need some Grace from time to time (or, more often than that, as the case may be). A beautiful sentiment and a memorable haiku. Also, terrific use of the word "whoopsie." What more can we really ask from a missive, Angels? Enjoy your Friday, all!

[Day 132 = Guest Missive by Spicoli]
Night 132.
Authenticity and compassion
Work towards authenticity
Or life becomes a feast of pity
Ask difficult questions
Sing off key
The antidote to anger is compassion
When the rage starts to flare
Open your palms, your hands and your heart to compassion.
That's all

[Response:]
Well done on the missives, Spicoli! I am sorry I forgot to respond to last night's. Want you to know that I am enjoying your thoughts and your style. Words to work on. Compassion. A good reminder. I need more, including for myself...but mostly for others. Hope you Campers are doing OK! TGIF, y'all!!

[Day 133 = Guest Missive by Mel]
The fog rolls in and the evening settles in on day 132 [133]. That is a very many days for the world to collectively hold our breath. Irony not intended. Shit, on many levels with that one. Remember when we were all, if you can hold your breath for 15 seconds you are OK? And have you seen the Tiger King? The good ole days. We've had 132 of them now. Say that out loud. One hundred and thirty-two days. In this time of a dark barren landscape, we've had time to mine for gems we'd never have stopped to dig for until we had time. Now we seem frozen in it. Our gems? We've found a way to get back in touch with each other in a real (albeit virtual you effing virus) way. To see inside our daily lives and marvel at the women we've become and the families and lives that we've carved out over decades of triumph and sadness. Of living. Which the virus threatens to steal from us, and will if we allow it to from either the wee beast's pathogen itself or our fear of dying. My Dad

said tonight, oh we expected this from Mike. I said what, dying? Dad: we all expect to die. We just hope it isn't right now. My Angels, don't let the fear of dying keep you from living today. Find a moment in each day to say yes-this is why I'm here and how very grateful I am to be experiencing this. See the micro happiness as the macro burdens of this time are dark and heavy. Snag Cam's grace and dodge the dark shit as much as we can. Celebrate her entire family's triumph over that which has innately terrified us for 132 days and nights. And remember-no matter how dark and how heavy this time is or may become-we have this time. We are together. And there is nothing more sacred than trusting God and leaning upon one another to see the light begin anew on a new dawn tomorrow. God has us, and we will beat all of this through love and with friendship. The words of this song mean a great deal to me, thanks to the love and support of each of you through this dark season. Arise in the morning to a new light and find a moment of hope within it to sustain us through tomorrow. I love you Angels. https://youtu.be/q_5t2sTaYlw

*I googled haiku. I'm still confused. F the hi-k-u.

[Response:]

A most excellent missive (with a hidden haiku, too)! Micro happiness; grace; together; love; friendship. Honestly, there isn't anything we can't do with those things. Look how lucky we are! We have the tools. When you don't feel like you can pick yours up and use them, another Angel will do it for you. Thank you for the encouragement! Now, on to the weekend!

[Day 133 = Guest Missive by Spicoli]

As we say good-bye to the Comet, we can get ready for our old friends the Perceids, and it made me realize that although we are mostly water, we are all made of star dust one way or another. How funny that people get wrapped up in anything else. What their view of cosmology says, or their leaders say, or their family lore says. The molecules that make us up were all primarily space dust.

Also, without dreams our lives would be dull and pointless, so give time every day to dreams!

[Response:]

Spicoli, we are on the same wave length...I have mentioned to Molly twice recently that we are all made of Stardust. I've been thinking about that frequently, especially as I was visited a second time in my head by The Statement, "Everything's going to be OK." Something out there - that we are all a part of - wants us to know that. Now, will it be what we think of as Pretty? Not necessarily. But it will be OK. So...have a truly "OK" Saturday, Campers, because I think that means it will be Great!

WEEK #20

Saturday, July 25, 2020 – Friday, July 31, 2020

"Charities Now In Need of Aid To Stay Afloat, Services Are Imperiled as Pandemic Builds" (Nicholas Kulish, *The New York Times*, July 25, 2020)

"Political Posturing Over Violence at Protests Decried as Distraction" (Jim Brunner and David Gutman, *The Seattle Times*, July 25, 2020)

"State Orders Changes After COVID Death at Orchard Labor Camp" (Hal Bernton, *The Seattle Times*, July 25, 2020)

[Day 134 = Guest Missive by Cathy]

As the sun sets on day 133 [134], I found out that 133 is an Angel Number not a prime number as I originally thought. Trusted Psychic Mediums assured me that we must pay attention to this number when we see it. Here is what they are saying about this number: "it indicates that you are happy where you are and satisfied the way life is going; you have a strong sense of security and stability because you worked very hard to achieve this life that you are enjoying now; you have stayed true to your purpose and focus on your goals." So, we got that going for us! It is so easy to focus on the [poop emoji] show that is happening around us with the Rona, politics, horses with extremely long appendages, but we do have much to celebrate and be thankful for, which has molded us into the wonderful warrior women that we are today. I am constantly in awe of your dedication and passion to your life's work, compassion and empathy you each exhibit on a daily basis, your thoughts and intelligence that keeps me on my toes, your humor and ability to make me laugh until my belly hurts, a shoulder to cry on without judgement and much more. If there is one thing that I am thankful for during this time it has been reconnecting with you in a way that we had not been since college. I had extreme problems with FOMO in college, and I love that all I have to do to hear from my favorite people is open an app. I will close with a quote from my favorite president, President Bartlet, "What's Next?" (The phrase is used in his dialogue to signal to his staff when he's ready for what lies ahead. Disclaimer: I am re-watching *The West Wing* and pretending that it is real). So, Warrior Women: What's Next?

[Response:]

Angel numbers, West Wing, and Warrior Women; celebrating one's friends. Ring Leader, drop the mic and take a bow. You have done Angel Number 133 a great service! Thank you for sharing your voice!!

[Day 134 = Guess Missive by Laura]

Wow, are you all in for a treat—I fell asleep whilst reading with my son and now have been awakened by a strange toilet flushing. OK, give me a sec and I'll be profound....Sorry, I didn't mean to do assigned reading [pages 211-216 from *Letters from the Earth: Uncensored Writings* by Mark Twain], it just struck me that this essay has oysters and extinctions and the self-centered Man, and all explained so well by one of my heroes. I hope that all of you can find a way to basilisk in the sunshine today!

[Response:]

Thank you for the missive!! I look forward to my assigned reading. "...basilisk in the sunshine...." I love this so much b/c you either 1) meant to type that, or 2) auto-correct inserted it because you use it frequently. Either way, it is a Win!! Have an OK Sunday, Campers!!

[Day 135 = Guest Missive by Elizabeth]

As the sun sets on day 134 [135], I've been pondering a recovery day vs. a day off. In previous workout seasons, everyone would talk about your "days on" vs. your "days off" as if "off" was a negative. With the new focus on fitness, strength, and whole health, I appreciate that we give as much respect to a "recovery day" as we do a "training day." We need a mix of both to be at our best. Angels, we have all renewed our accountability to fitness, to moving, to recognizing the importance of getting those natural and healthy chemicals triggered in our bodies as a way to fight COVID fatigue, the [poop emoji], and the mental space that becomes available during fitness. Recognize that a recovery day is a positive activity, and I would also say that we need to apply this to other aspects of our lives. We "train" as parents, professionals, family members, and many other hats. I challenge you to plan your "recovery" times in those areas just as you do in your fitness plan. It is Sunday night, and I have planned my fitness training and recovery for the week. I am challenging myself and each of you, angels, how are you planning the week? Do you have your fitness training and recovery planned? How about the recovery in your households: is it an evening that you don't have to prepare dinner but ask someone else or order in? What about professionally, what does recovery in the midst of a week look like? Is it doing fitness in the middle of the day to step away, or is it blocking off a bit of time to be creative and not worry about all the items on the to-do list? In all aspects of life, are you balancing your "training" and your "recovery"? Just as our physical muscles need it, I would say, it is as important for our mental, emotional, and spiritual muscles, as well. Rest well, Angels! Remove the guilt of not training 100% of the time in all areas, and I'd challenge each of us to find Joy in the recovery.

[Response:]
What a wonderful missive. Such an important reminder that recovery and rest and just Being are absolutely as important as our training and activity and to-do lists. We are taught in Iyengar Yoga that "restoratives" (fully-supported resting poses) are as important as our "asanas" (active poses). Restoratives turn on the relaxation response and fight the cortisol and adrenaline that always seem to be running through us, especially now. Aunt Button is absolutely right…make sure to include some recovery on that to-do list of yours. It's just as (and often more) important than all the other items on it. One way I've been practicing that this week is asking for help. Thank you, all, for helping me recover! I'm getting stronger; look out!

[Day 135 = Guest Missive by Laura]
Well, Fellow Campers, I am looking up the day because I'm not counting them….OK, yes, Day 135. Ahem, I'm sitting out front and feeling a twinge of Lesson Learned. Back when Spicoli said to go out and find the comet, I did so and was duly impressed. I was alone on that short drive down the farm roads and quite happy to be on a solo adventure for once. But when I sat there with the binocs and was Wowing to myself, I only stayed for maybe ten

minutes, if that. I was so busy thinking how great it would be to show my people in a few days, and I put together a trip to my mom's house with the fam for that weekend. Well, that weekend we saw it but much higher and fainter than my solo trip, and I regretted talking it up to everyone for four days. It's never as much fun to be told how great something is and then not be able to recreate it. And now, I have returned from a third trip with just my husband to try to find my same farm road experience, and we couldn't see it at all, probably already below the horizon. Good ol' hubby is a trooper, but what I'm left with is Carpe that Diem, dammit! Grab dem carps with yo' bare han's, as my granddaddy Coker might say, because you really aren't going to be in that same place twice. Live it, right now, because now is the time we have. I 've been waiting, waiting for people to get on board with masks, waiting for this to end, waiting for the rains to end, and then waiting for the sun to pass the house to make good shade to sit in, waiting for that perfect time, waiting for stars to align. I think, just maybe, the trick isn't so much to seize the day with lists and great accomplishment, but rather to See the Day, See the Night, See the Moment. I do look forward to our time together, but I also See you now anyways, and I'm going into tomorrow with a See Today mind. Love you all so very much, The Glorious Phoenix (really need a Phoenix emoji).

[Response:]
Excellent advice per your missive, Phoenix! See the Day. Less waiting; more seeing. Such a valuable lesson. Also, see your Mom, Symbol. I hope you all have a good time doing nothing together! Stay cool out there, Campers!

[Day 136 = Guest Missive by Leslie]
As the sun sets on day 135 [136], I'm pondering a simple practice that fits in nicely with the mindfulness, presence, and break-taking wisdom of my fellow angels: pacing. Realizing today that my agreement to allow 2 undergrads to take my 600-level class for 300-level credit would mean I had to create a 3rd online course (when I'm

supposed to only do 2 because the other half of my job is putting my fellowships office online) revved up my anxiety to a pitch commensurate with the length of this sentence. You've all been there: the treadmill gets turned up and the [poop emoji] starts flying faster that you can bat it away. Heck, we're all living there perpetually these days. Strangely, 2 things from work collided to alleviate the [poop emoji] storm: 1. The difference between the grad & undergrad experience of the course would be one of depth and pacing, and 2. Spending time with a favorite writer on writing to grab an essay for the fellowships site (Anne Lamott; please read "Shitty First Drafts" if you never have & ever plan to write anything ever again), I remembered the story behind her book entitled *Bird by Bird*. Her brother had 3 months to write a long report on something like 30 species of birds and waited until the last day to get started. Overwhelmed and in hysterics, he asked their dad how he could possibly write his report, to which his dad replied, "Bird by bird, bud. Just go bird by bird." For those of us who live for the checkmark on a to-do list, it's a good reminder to deal with the one task in front of us and not be overwhelmed by the others waiting in line.

I'll leave you tonight with a word from my favorite childhood character, Frances. It seems appropriate to inject a little estrogen into our group of favorites, plus y'all need to meet her if you've never heard of her and she has a great name. This is from "Lorna Doone Last Cookie Song (I Shared It With Gloria)" which is about the last cookie in a sampler: "Lorna Doone, Lorna Doone, / You were last but you weren't wasted. / Lorna Doone, Lorna Doone, / We'll remember how you tasted." Sleep tight, Angels, and don't forget to take your work, chores, problems, and even cookies bird by bird.

[Response:]
Another brilliant missive from another brightly shining Angel. Thank you! So good to hear your voice in the missive slot! Same with all our other Guest Angels these past days. I have enjoyed it tremendously. Your excellent points about Pacing and your men-

tion of *Bird by Bird*, as well as the question of how to eat an elephant, remind me of a story from when I worked for a local Tribe on a truly overwhelming archaeological recovery effort (this was my first job out of grad school and set the stage for everything since). We were in Year Three of sifting 10,000 cubic yards of material (650 double dump trucks) by hand. Every day was considered a funeral. We started each day with what we called "morning lineup" with various cultural practices and words from our elders and crew boss. Over time, the crew boss would periodically call on each crew member to say something to the group. I was always very nervous about being called on because I really wanted to say the "right" thing. I was called on one morning during a period when we were all feeling quite overwhelmed by our monumental task. I acknowledged our herculean task and said we would just have to do it "one bucket at a time." It must have made an impression on the crew boss because that saying came up many times in the years following. So, grab a Lorna Doone, Angels, and pace yourselves with some compassion. We've got miles to go before we sleep (tip o' the hat to Mr. Frost). See you for another Taco Tuesday!

[Day 136 = Guest Missive by Laura]
Well, tonight I think that my son said it best—as he fell asleep, he asked if you say something happened five months ago, when did it happen because is there a zero month that you have to count. Then, when I said let's figure that out tomorrow, he mumbled Make Kindness Your Superpower, and rolled over and gave it up. Day 136 in the bag, my dears.

[Response:]
Out of the mouths of babes, Campers. How can you improve upon that inquisitiveness and those words of wisdom? You can't, that's how. So we sleep, we dream, and we wake to another Taco Tuesday when we will practice Kindness. Not a bad goal at all.

As the sun sets on Day 137, I return to the keyboard with a simple, heartfelt Thank You. Thank you for making it possible for me take a much-needed step back over the last week. Thank you for the fantastic Guest Missives. Thank you for continuing to entertain and educate me. I have noticed, and I have appreciated. You all are my Gratitude for the day. And now, we return to your regularly-scheduled Happiness lesson: 1) Happiness is eighteen different colors. 2) Happiness is storing up solar energy. 3) Happiness is winning a trophy. There it is. That's all for Taco Tuesday. I am very pleased to join you again, refreshed and reinvigorated. Sleep well, Angels, and Thank You.

As the sun sets on Day 138, I share with you The Latest Lesson of the Garden. Remember when the pea plants were savagely attacked and literally nibbled down to their tiny stems; then, when extended some time and patience, darned if they didn't bounce back and sprout a new set of beautiful leaves and small tendrils? See first pic for a reminder. Well, another miracle has occurred. When given a bit more time and patience (and sun and water and encouraging words by headlamp, of course), look what happened!! See second pic for a Big surprise. I really cannot believe it...those darned persevering pea plants done produced some pea pods. Seriously unbelievable (unPEAlievable-??) Current count is 4 pea pods picked; a fifth has been spotted, just growing away. The first 2 sampled were delicious. Sunshine and high hopes in a crunchy pod. Now, that is some nourishment! Makes me very Happy. On that note: 1) Happiness is an "A" on your spelling test. 2) Happiness is living in a high-rise. 3) Happiness is a bread and butter sandwich folded over. Sure! Why not? I hope you all had a good Hump Day. Dream of persevering peas, Campers, and even if you feel worn down to just your stem, wake to stretch out some new tendrils.

As the sun sets on Day 139, I begin with a request for some good thoughts. My Dad has lost some more ground this week, and Olive's weakening hind end is expanding to more coordination and balance issues. It is very hard to see bodies breaking down, whether it's your own graying hair and creaky knees and back or your loved ones, human or canine. And yet, it's unavoidable. So much these days feels uncertain and unpredictable, but you can count on getting older. I'm actually not trying to be negative, just matter-of-fact. This is part of life, but your attitude and exercise and gratitude and all those other good things we talk about here can stave off the stiffness and creakiness. Speaking of attitude, perhaps some Happiness lessons are in order! Yes; always. 1) Happiness is your first kiss in the rain. 2) Happiness is finally getting the sliver out. 3) Happiness is being able to reach the doorknob. Sleep well, Angels, and channel your inner pea pod as you make the most of your Friday!

As the sun sets on Day 140, we mark the end of our 20th week together. I start with a big ol' Gratitude for all your kind thoughts for my Dad and my Dog. I sincerely appreciate it. Their bodies are betraying them, but their spirits are strong. I am paying attention to the lessons they are teaching us. Today was very busy with a trip to the vet (much relief followed) and big Summit work (much relief followed). Then, this evening, a good friend came over for a distanced visit in the backyard. Olive loves this particular friend, even though she did the unthinkable and got her own dog, and it was fun to see her get excited, weave her way outside, and wag her tail while getting some pats. More lessons: keep at it, even if your pace slows; always show gratitude. Happiness, too, is a good pursuit: 1) Happiness is being glad you're you. 2) Happiness is getting to the semi-finals. 3) Happiness is having an audience. A busy day, a / nice night, and lots of feels. Week / twenty's in the books. Sleep soundly, Campers, and wake to wag your tails generously!

WEEK #21
Saturday, August 1, 2020 – Friday, August 7, 2020

"A School Reopens, and the Coronavirus Creeps In" (Eliza Shapiro, Giulia McDonnell Nieto Del Rio, and Shawn Hubler, *The New York Times*, August 1, 2020)

"The Holiday Weekend Will Last Saturday, Sunday, and Monday for Ecuador Independence Day" [Staff Writers, La Hora (Ecuador), August 1, 2020)

"Coronavirus in Ecuador: 1432 New Cases in 24 Hours; 740 of Those in Quito" (Staff Writers, Metro (Ecuador), August 7, 2020)

As the sun sets on Day 141, I find myself pondering the passage of Time. I have learned recently that Time really does pass at different rates depending on your situation (well, that is a gross understatement of some Stephen Hawking/Neil deGrasse Tyson stuff, but I'm going to assume you, too, have experienced this phenomenon). How did today feel so much longer than a weekday?? I felt like I had so much more Time to do the things I wanted to do. Is it because I wasn't watching the clock so closely? Is it because I was doing things that I chose to do? Is it because I focused on the thing I chose to do and not all the things I thought I should be doing instead? I just love an "organic day" where I can move from one thing to another when I choose, and this was one of those days. A little work, a little exercise, a little play, a little cooking, a little reading, a little TV, a little dog walk (well, one dog walked while I pushed the other one in her cart which she enjoyed very much indeed). It truly felt like a long, hot(ish) summer day. It also happened to be the 1st of August, which I can hardly believe. Time may have stretched out today, but it keeps on marching. Dream widely, Angels, and we'll see how Time flows tomorrow.

As the sun sets on Day 142, I tip my hat to the lessons of the canine. As you might imagine, I have been observing Olive closely all weekend. To our great relief, she has been improving daily. While doing so, she has reminded me of some very important lessons, primarily Patience and Living in the Moment. Olive is very smart and independent and self-aware and capable, and she definitely knows she is not some of those things right now. Despite that, she has stayed calm and keeps plugging away…when she's tired, she takes a nap; when she wants to find us, she lurches outside; when she's hungry, she begs for human food because she doesn't want her kibble right now. Yesterday, I watched her stagger up to the deck steps, stop, gather herself, and walk slowly and deliberately up those two steps that, to us, are hardly anything but that to her are mighty challenging right now (and probably look like they are moving and pitching and rolling). While worried and confused in the beginning, she let us take charge and believed we would help her as we promised her every few seconds. Once we all understood what was happening, she accepted it, took her Dramamine willingly (that chicken flavored pill pocket didn't hurt!), and is patiently moving through the recovery time. It's a teensy bit humbling to realize that I wouldn't handle a similar challenge with a smidge of the grace my canine is showing. But what I can do is notice those lessons of Patience and Living in the Moment and just try. Life is a journey / and sometimes you get knocked down. / Get back up and Go. Happiness, too, is a good pursuit, and we have reached our final lesson! Ready? Happiness is one thing to one person and another thing to another person. You got that right, Peanuts gang! Thank you for all the wisdom. Happiness imbues many different things; just look around. Dream of living your lessons, Campers, and tomorrow, we'll give it a shot!

As the sun sets on Day 143, I find myself a bit weary after Day 1 of a seven-day virtual conference. Seven days? Come on! Silver lining: I had plenty of time to practice multi-tasking, which is not my forte. I also had plenty of time to observe my Office Assistant, Olive, who continues to improve. She feels good enough to work on her training skills, i.e. she is training us again, this time to put chicken broth on her kibble and to push her in her cart for an evening stroller-about. She is a very good trainer. My mushy brain is drifting towards lights-out, so perhaps a haiku is in order: Rise and shine and cof- / fee up. It's time to start your / day at the keyboard. That Morning haiku could be balanced by this Afternoon one: File your notes and crack / one open. You have survived / another long day. Well, no one said the Nightly Missive would always promote deep thoughts. Sometimes, a Monday is a Monday. Good Lord, it's time for Taco Tuesday again. There goes Time a-flowin' again. Sleep and dream, Angels, because multi-tasking happens at all hours.

As the sun sets on Day 144, I find myself a bit bewildered, as well as tipping my hat to my Dutch oven and gas range. Strange combo? Yes. The bewilderment describes my day up until about 5pm; the Dutch oven and gas range kicked in after that during some much-needed regrouping. Bewilderment plagued me most of the day because I tried to do too much multi-tasking during Day 2 of the seven-day virtual conference (whoever thought a seven-day virtual conference was a good idea should give their big idea some more thought). As I may have shared here before, I am not a great multi-tasker. I am so "not great" that I forgot I mentioned it as recently as…last night. Nice. Well, I double-doozied myself today between too much tech time and trying to multi-task during it. By 5pm, I was frazzled, worn out, and bewildered. Why bewildered? My brain was so scrambled, I couldn't pick up on the most important things, like Lessons of the Garden and the Canine and Searching for Sparrows. Not good, Campers; not good! I finally put all that to the side, played some frisbee with Molly, and went inside to cook dinner, which I actually enjoy. Turned on the news (always dicey, but I also want to stay informed), and tried my hand at frying cod in the Dutch oven. And it worked!! Messy? Oh, yeah. Crispy, brown, and delicious? Also, a resounding Yes. Perfect vehicle for tartar sauce? Happily, yes, again. Put the veggie box to work, too, and had fresh slaw and fresh green beans with some awesome mushrooms (I love the fungi). Cooking got my brain back in order and my tummy happy (a much better double-doozie than the prior one). So, now that it is cool and dark and the kitchen has been purged of its multitude of grease splatters, I think the lesson is take a breather when you know you are red-lining. If you can disengage from the noise and do something you like, especially something physical, you can bounce back and, dare I say it, feel ready for Hump Day at a virtual conference. And you also might be smart enough to tackle your next day differently. Because you know who you are (and who you aren't), and it's time to live that way. When you feel like a / deer in headlights, step back and / find another way. Sleep soundly, Campers, and shape tomorrow to suit your style.

As the sun sets on Day 145, I tip my hat to elevenses. I'm contemplating a campaign to have them officially recognized. I know who I am (and who I'm not) – at least most of the time – and it's time I start overtly embracing and advocating for elevenses. I first learned about them from Paddington Bear, and I was recently reminded that Winnie the Pooh also enjoyed them. So, how can they possibly be wrong, I ask you? As I tried to be smart enough to tackle my Hump Day differently, I noticed I was burning through the calories at my standing desk and wandering to the kitchen for a smackerel of something between sessions (another nod to Pooh on "smackerel"). Prime time for such a smackerel? Around 11am. It makes so much sense (as does tea time around 4pm, but that's another campaign). It doesn't have to be a lot, but a little something might just get you through your 11am session on preservation ordinances. I invite you all to join me tomorrow in some elevenses (I will probably just be waking up as you enjoy yours). It may just be the bridge between morning and afternoon that you (and your tummy) are looking for [I shouldn't end this sentence on "for," should I?] We are herd animals, Angels, so we need one another, we like to graze, and we often move in groups (except now, of course). Honor your inner herd tendencies, and while you are having your elevenses, know that your herd-mates are thinking of you. Dream of tea and toast and honey pots and marmalade sandwiches, Angels, and wake…feeling hungry, I imagine.

As the sun sets on Day 146, I return to the idea that sometimes a day (here, a Thursday) is a day (i.e. Thursday). Between the virtual conference (Day 4 of 7 is in the bag!) and all manner of Summit tasks, this was just a plain ol' hard-core work day. This is actually OK with me. A day like today would have been impossible back in March. My March pandemic brain was waaaay too jumpy to concentrate, let alone know what it should concentrate on. It's actually a relief to be able to concentrate again and to have a decent work-related to-do list to tackle. My, what a low bar I have. You know what else is a relief? Friday! I see you, Friday, just over the sleep horizon. I'm comin' for ya! Sometimes, a day is / just a day. Check that work off / and pour a stiff one. Dream sweetly, Campers, and earn that weekend tomorrow!

As the sun sets on Day 147, I tip my hat to International Beer Day. Has there ever been a better-timed Day of Something? I think not. As I reflect on the past week, two words come to mind: Survival and Celebration. We all survived another week of work, family, pandemic, chores, news, cooking, Zooming, relaxing, learning, worrying, playing. So, let's all Celebrate now! We celebrate the big things, the little things, the victories, the missteps, the highs, the lows, the memorable, the fleeting. It's all part of you; it's all part of the journey. We are all the sum of our many parts. You are not one-dimensional. You are a prism reflecting all the life around you. You know what else acts as a prism sometimes? Beer. Beer can reflect the life around you. Beer can also be related to survival and celebration. So, well done, Prismatic Beer Drinkers! You made it through our 21st week together. Sleep well, Angels, knowing that you are not one-dimensional and that tomorrow you will reflect all the things that make up a great Saturday.

WEEK #22
Saturday, August 8, 2020 – Friday, August 14, 2020

"Russia is Trying to Assist Trump in Race, U.S. Says" (Julian E. Barnes, *The New York Times*, August 8, 2020)

"How Many People Are Allowed to Ride in a Car Over the Holiday Weekend: Only 4, Strict COVID Restrictions" (Staff Writers, La Hora (Ecuador), August 8, 2020)

"Quito: What Is Happening With Expired Documents, Bus Stations, and Vehicle Registrations?" (Staff Writers, Metro (Ecuador), August 8, 2020)

As the sun sets on Day 148, I feel a little bit like I'm in the eye of a hurricane. That might be a bit dramatic, but I heard from three good friends who are having health issues, either themselves or a parent (not the COVID, thankfully). Add to that my own family health issues, a global pandemic, an existential work situation, and all the stuff that has come with all of that, and it is feeling a bit stormy around here. At the same time, it has reminded me that life is in constant flux for everyone all the time. That's a lotta flux swirling around. So, maybe it's "normal" in terms of the Universe, but it sure feels more so today. Deep breath; stay calm; lean on the people and things that keep you grounded. Maybe even write a haiku! When the shit storm swirls / around you, take cover and / believe it will pass. Flux happens, Campers; let's see where it takes us. Dream serenely, Campers, and let the shit storm pass over you.

As the sun sets on Day 149, we return to the garden, and let me tell you...it was a jungle out there tonight. What started out as an innocent enough visit with the watering can turned into a full-on slug and snail campaign. Rather than kill the invaders, I choose to relocate them to a small compost pile I created for them on the other side of the yard. Each time I thought I'd taken the last one over there, another one revealed itself in the glow of my headlamp. By the time I took snail number four to the old country buffet, the first two were, shall we say, getting to know one another. When I brought slug number three over, slug number one was getting to know snail number two. Come on, Gastropods...I garden to relax, not to see all that! Ick and ewwww. I did have to laugh when I made my last trip over to the buffet because the two very friendly snails were now headed off in exact opposite directions. That lesson of the garden was quite obvious. Besides spending some time as a gastropod interloper, I also spent several delightful hours in the backyard visiting with a good friend (at a safe distance with masks, when necessary). The weather was ridiculously nice, and it felt so good to chat about all manner of things. A rather nice way to spend a Sunday afternoon...the same Sunday afternoon that the seven-day virtual conference concluded. Hallelujah!! I'm free. Sit and chat in the / sun and breeze. Remember when / you did as you please. Snoozle on, Angels, and we'll slug it out in the new week!

As the sun sets on Day 150, I tip my hat a second time to the sitcom *Parks and Recreation* (previous tip was waaaay back on Day 49). We are working our way through what is perhaps my favorite sitcom of all time, and it is so much fun. I really enjoy laughing every night, and I highly recommend it to you. A friend asked recently if I have a favorite episode. It's only my second time through the series, so I don't claim to be an expert; however, tonight's episode will most definitely be in the running. Fire up a streaming service that has *Parks and Rec* and navigate to Season 4, Episode 4 (Pawnee Rangers) as soon as possible. You will see why, Campers. Today was another straight-up Monday: work, work, work, spin, cook, TV, sunset dog stroll, work, missive, read. I thought some thoughts, but now my thinker is thought out. We wend our way through / another Monday and find / the end is quite sweet. Sleep gently, Campers, and give that thinker the rest it needs to tackle Taco Tuesday (and don't forget to laugh easily and often).

As the sun sets on Day 151, I tip my hat to a simple game of catch. Molly and I have a new pandemic pastime that is quickly becoming a habit: every evening at quitting time, we go outside and play catch (softball), toss the football, or (try to) toss the frisbee. We enjoy the sunshine, the breeze, the grass, and we debrief about our day. I cannot believe how good it makes me feel and how much I've started to look forward to it. Playing catch is SO familiar to me, and I've always loved it. It makes me feel like a kid. It's also proving to be a fantastically effective way to transition from work to play. I highly recommend that you find your game of catch. Maybe it's a walk or a bike ride or a dance party or any manner of things. It doesn't have to be hard or take up a lot of time. Just enough to break you out of your brain and back into your environment. Then, you'll be ready to head in for dinner and Xena. Oh, wait…that's just me. Dinner and your evening entertainment. Catch the ball, throw the / ball and feel your inner kid / smile. Time to pivot. Dream of making the big catch, Angels, and spend tomorrow with your inner kid.

As the sun sets on Day 152, I tip my hat to Turkey Tuesday. Yes, I know it's pseudo-officially Taco Tuesday, but we had turkey burgers yesterday (well, 2 days ago by the clock now) and they are worth a mention. We have a recipe where you mix in spinach and cumin and garlic and then top them with a garlic aioli. Brioche buns don't hurt either, nor does the cooking method of pan sear and then steam. Yes, please!! So good. We had leftovers tonight (last night now). Yes, please, again. Why am I writing about turkey burgers? I'm not exactly sure. Simple pleasures? Pleasant surprises? Delectable dishes? Helpful hints? Fantastic fowl? Convenient cooking? Beautiful buns? Well, I guess there were a few reasons. Take your pick. Working too late in / the glow of the TV. What / am I doing up? Dream sweetly, Campers, and treat yourself to something yummy tomorrow.

As the sun sets on Day 153, I relish another Lesson of the Canine, courtesy of Olive again. To our great relief, Olive made great strides over the first week following the onset of vestibular disease, aka Old Dog Syndrome. However, over the past 2-3 days, she has taken a step or two backwards. Her hind end, in particular, is giving her problems in terms of stiffness, coordination, and weakness, and it will even give out on her suddenly. Her head tilt is back at times, too, but I have decided it is charming and makes her look quite inquisitive (as if she needed help with that). Despite her body giving her problems, she still wants to GO, as in GO on a WALK. So, tonight, Walter and I first went on a fast-paced, long loop; then, Olive got a one-block turn. I thought it might help her to move around a bit. She was excited and barking as I "saddled her up," even as she lurched around a bit. I used her harness that has a handle so I could help her up/down the front steps, as well as support her during bigger lurches. Well, off we went! She still wanted to patrol and sniff and take stock, even while doing her drunken sailor imitation. I've watched her closely the past 2 weeks, and I know she's still in there and as smart as ever; she isn't embarrassed when she stumbles or falls; she is still ready to GO whenever the opportunity arises. She is going to do what she can do as long as she can do it. And I'm going to help her…when she'll let me. Now, if that isn't a valuable lesson, I don't know what is. I really, really want to be like my dog. Be ready for ad- / venture at all times. Grab the / chances when they come. Sleep fiercely, Angels, and tackle the day with the tools you have; they are enough.

As the sun sets on Day 154 (the close of our 22nd week together), two thoughts come to mind: 1) I'm really looking forward to taking time out and playing this weekend, and 2) I'm really disappointed that *Wonder Woman 1984* didn't open today (and even October 2 is highly suspect). Come to think of it, though, COVID is responsible for both thoughts. On the bummer side, no movie; on the silver lining side, virtual Camp with college friends! It's all in how you look at things. One coin, two sides. That's just like one of my mottoes, too: Work Hard, Play Hard. We've all done the first part; now, let's tackle that second part! How will you spend National Relaxation Day?? The Zooming and the / chores are done. Time to embrace / the fun and the sun. Sleep sweetly, Campers, and reward yourselves tomorrow!

WEEK #23

Saturday, August 15, 2020 – Friday, August 21, 2020

"Postal Service Warns States It May Not Meet Mail-In Ballot Deadlines" (Luke Broadwater, Hailey Fuchs, and Nick Corasaniti, *The New York Times*, August 15, 2020)

"Francisco Carrion to be the New Ambassador From Ecuador to the United States" [Staff Writers, La Hora (Ecuador), August 15, 2020)

"New Public Transportation Schedule After Announcement From the Committee on National Emergency Operations" (Staff Writers, Metro (Ecuador), August 15, 2020)

As the sun sets on Day 155, I write to you from the Campfire, along with Walter, the birthday boy. He's 8 today, and while I'd like to think he likes Camping, I think he really just likes popcorn. New Campers have joined the fold today, and it is Good! It is very Good. I hope everyone had Fun, supported one another, and said "YES" loudly and often. Campers, know that you can take this Camp spirit with you wherever you go and whatever's happening. Your Campers have got you. Fun times, sad times, good times, bad times. They're all a-comin' for all of us, so we will be there for each other when they do. We're all on this journey Together. Jump in with both feet! We'll catch you. (And, hopefully, you'll do the same...otherwise, that's gonna hurt.) Camp Whatchamakeit / is camp. In your backyard. Jump / on in and say Yes!! Dream of fun and merit badges, Angels, and wake to a whole lifetime of Camp!

As the sun sets on Day 156, I tip my hat (and my heart) to all Camp Whatchamakeit Campers everywhere. You are an inspiration! Thank you for being game and for playing. Play is often in short supply in the adult and the pandemic worlds, and we really need it! It's good for the spirit and for the cheeks (the ones on your face...from all the laughter). I hope all Campers had a good weekend and are now feeling supported as they head into another work week. We can do hard things, Campers. Keep it up! Camp is the people / and the spirit. Take it wher- / ever you go now. Sleep serenely, Campers, and take your Camp spirit right on into the week.

As the sun sets on Day 157 (prime number!), I am reflecting on the final episode of *Xena* which we watched last night. What a pandemic adventure it has been! I am legitimately sad that we reached the end; however, it was inevitable (and we own the whole series on DVD now, so we're going to watch it again). You all have very graciously entertained my love of the Lessons of the Warrior Women, and I am grateful. I would like to share a Lesson from Xena and Gabrielle (for those unfamiliar with the series, Gabrielle is Xena's best friend/loyal companion/soulmate). As in real life, Xena tends to get most of the credit. She is the Warrior; she is strong, smart, beautiful, brave. However, as her full story is revealed, you learn she is also deeply Flawed. Fortunately for us mere mortals (because she was a really bad actor for a while, even earning the moniker Destroyer of Nations), she has a change of heart and dedicates the rest of her life to fighting for the Greater Good, as well as seeking Redemption for her past. Enter Gabrielle. She is the Bard and Poet. As in real life, she typically plays second fiddle to the Warrior, often needing rescuing from the Gods and Warlords and never receiving much credit…except from the Warrior herself. They are Yin and Yang to one another, and we actually get to see them realize and acknowledge this fact. The Warrior acknowledges she can't save others or redeem herself without having learned the Bard's lessons of love and forgiveness; the Bard can't continue to love and forgive others with the having learned the strength of the Warrior. What seems in opposition is actually in harmony. Neither can be as great individually without the other. Am I waxing on (and on) once again about a Warrior Woman story? Yes. Is this one particularly inspiring because it illustrates how we need one another, learn from one another, and draw strength and love from one another? Also, Yes. I think these are lessons worth learning and contemplating. I think it's also worth realizing that each of us has the Yin and the Yang inside our individual selves, too. The good, the bad; the dark, the light; dare I say, the Warrior and the Bard. And we need both sides of ourselves. We sometimes spend time too much precious time trying to squash one or elevate the other, but we'll always have both. They make us who we are, and we'll only be our best selves when those things are in harmony. OK, admittedly, that was a lot. Inside you are both / the Warrior and the Bard. / Welcome them both in. Dream of epic poems, Angels, and wake to write your own!

As the sun sets on Day 158, I tip my hat to Nature Therapy. A good friend went up to Mt. Baker yesterday and referred to it as his Nature Therapy. Not to be outdone, we went to the flats at low tide today and walked forever. Wind, clouds, sun, birds, fishies, shell-fishies, small planes, water, islands, crabs, eelgrass, rocks, boats, kiteboards, boogie boards, mud, sand. It felt good. And real. And healing. Get outside, Campers! Hug a tree; make a grass angel; smell a flower; admire a bird. We are of Nature, and modern life tends to cut us off from her. Get back out there and say, "Hi!" She won't let you down. Sleep deeply, Campers, and answer the call of Nature.

As the sun sets on Day 159, I look back on a difficult day. This is the kind of day that you just want to leave behind. I surprised myself at one point by feeling an emotion I rarely feel: rage. It did not feel good, and rather than move fairly quickly through it like I normally would, I just sat in it for a while. It didn't even really fit the situation, so I know it was a bunch of things coming to a head over a smaller thing. Ick. I'm just kinda sick of everything right now. One thing did break through the dark cloud over my head, though, and that was this string. I thought of all the good advice shared, the encouragement, the commiseration, the determination. And I thought, "You know, all of that has been really good, and when I'm not being such a poop emoji, I will draw on some of that good advice and try to apply it." It's 10:30 at night, and I'm still waiting on not being a poop emoji, but when I do (probably tomorrow at this point), I'm totally going to take some of your advice and try it out. Because it's good advice, and tomorrow is a new day, thankfully. Sometimes, your feelings / surprise you. And sometimes, you / just let them. So, there. Sleep well, Angels, and as far as I know, the sun will rise again tomorrow.

As the sun sets on Day 160, I bask in the glow of more Nature Therapy down at the flats. Another beautiful day. More clouds this time, but a perfect temperature and breeze. Lots of marine and bird life around. Very few *Homo sapiens sapiens*. Trains along the shoreline and small planes taking off over the bluff. Delightful. Then, back to work, but with a better attitude, even with Summit tech tests this evening. Thank goodness for my fun tech team! We Zoom here, we Zoom / there, we Zoom everywhere. Why / all the Zoomin', y'all? Dream of cool sea breezes, Campers, as we drift on towards the weekend.

As the sun sets on Day 161, I tip my hat to my Friends (hint: that's YOU!) My Fab Friday included both a virtual coffee with my women friends on the block and the weekly happy hour with you Angels. So, after a week of everyone listening to my nightly rantings and supporting me in my brush with rage, I also got to see many of my chums today [I've never used the word "chums" before, and it was weird]. It is an embarrassment of riches around here, Friends! The weekend looks promising, as well, with two separate Camp events on Sunday. I'm not sure what I did to deserve this (hint: I did nothing to deserve this), but I sure appreciate it. Friends, fun, friends, fun. Fun, / friends, fun, friends. Lucky me, luck- / y you, lucky us. Sleep well tonight, Angels, and know that you are greatly appreciated!

WEEK #24
Saturday, August 22, 2020 – Friday, August 28, 2020

"Some Schools Keeping Quiet on COVID Cases: Lack of Data Muddles Efforts to Reopen" (Dan Levin, *The New York Times*, August 22, 2020)

"Police Catch Band of Four Who Rob at Gunpoint" (Staff Writers, *La Hora* (Ecuador), August 22, 2020)

"Quito: Bus Travels Packed As Passengers Race Home Before Daily Martial Law Begins at 7pm" (Staff Writers, *Metro* (Ecuador), August 22, 2020)

As the sun sets on Day 162, I tip my hat to DC Comics and the *Wonder Woman 1984* team of Patty Jenkins (Director), Gal Gadot (Diana Prince/Wonder Woman), Chris Pine (Steve Trevor), Kristen Wiig (Barbara Minerva/Cheetah), and Pedro Pascal (Maxwell Lord). DC is hosting a 24-hour global virtual fan event since none of the Comic-Cons can be held during the COVID times. The entire event began with the WW panel, and they did a great job with it (this counted as Summit research, right?) As most of you know at this point, I don't cry…unless I see a Horse running or an Outsider triumphing (that second one might be a new reveal). Well, it could be because I was tired, but I teared up twice during the 20-minute session. The first time, Gal (because we are on a first-name basis, of course) was commenting on a piece of fan art. The artwork was a take on the Norman Rockwell style, and it showed a little girl of around 6 years old standing in some way-too-big-for-her red high heels looking up into a full-length mirror where Gal's *Wonder Woman* smiled back at her. It was adorable, but what got me was Gal's commentary which included the observation that WW is so important because "when little girls see it, they believe it." I know what she means. Representation is important. How many male superheroes did we see growing up with no female superhero to be found? Don't get me wrong, I like Superman and Batman, but until I saw WW a few years ago (June 4, 2017, to be exact), I didn't know what it was like to see a female triumph (and struggle) the way we always saw the male superheroes do it. It really was different, at least for me. I wonder sometimes what it would have been like if a WW like this existed when I was 10 years old (all due respect to Lynda Carter and the WW TV series, but we all know that's awesome in a late-1970s way). The second time I teared up during the panel was prompted by a general trend in fan art. I'm new to all this comic culture, but I've learned that fan art today often involves taking a superhero like WW and representing her according to the ethnicity or culture of the artist. One piece depicted WW as an Indian woman; another showed Gal's WW hugging a black WW, both strong and triumphant and happy. These are the elements of WW and Xena and other Warrior Women that I love...the elements that transcend a superhero story and teach us things that are worth striving for in our actual lives. I guess the comic book nerds have known this for a long time. It's easy to write off their fandom, but I'm pretty sure this is the level that moves them. It's basically a modern-day mythology (and many comics are deeply grounded in ancient mythology, but that's another missive for another day... by a different author). Finally, the session ended with the second official WW trailer...and I will just say that It Was Good; watch it soon! Look inside for your / superhero; look outside / for many others. Dream of the good parts of humanity, Campers, and wake to be a Hero, too!

As the sun sets on Day 163, I tip my hat to Fun...just a bit wistfully. First, I was extremely fortunate to have had a very fun weekend with a Camp Whatchamakeit Archaeology Edition movie watch party and an abbreviated Camp W. Wine Group edition gathering. Both events truly were fun, and I am so lucky to have had the opportunity to spend time with friends. The abbreviated Camp gathering, however, left me feeling a bit wistful. It was wonderful to see everyone, but the masks and distancing and no hugs made me feel kinda down afterwards. I am sure you all have had similar experiences. I haven't had as many of those since we are playing things so conservatively, so it was a bit of a surprising bummer. Was it better than not seeing them? Absolutely. Was it an annoying reminder of where we still are? Also, yes. Sigh. Well, we just do what we can right now, don't we? I hope you all had a great weekend and that you're ready to give the new week a shot. Was it fun? Yes. Was / it kinda sad? Also, Yes. / Thanks, 2020. In case that one was a bit of a downer, how about we end on this one instead? Another Sunday / draws to a close. Know that you / have cheered this Camper. Sleep peacefully, Angels, for Monday is also a good day for wine.

As the sun sets on Day 164, the garden instructs us yet again. Over the weekend, it reminded me how sharing your bounty helps both you and others (even if it's just a cuke and a handful of beans). Tonight, it showed me the value of patience and tenacity. I wandered out to water by headlamp, and what did I find but another pea! A really nice, healthy, pluckable pea. There were even a couple others that probably won't mature into much, but there they were. Unbelievable!! As we move through these times that test us on all fronts, remember the garden and how it just keeps growing, regardless of sun, wind, rain, slugs, snails, roly-polies (pill bugs), and all other manner of challenges and stressors. Growing is its job, and it just keeps doing it. Patience. Tenaci- / ty. Persistence. These are the / things we need to thrive. Dream of rich soil, sun, and water, Campers, and wake to send out your shoots and runners.

As the sun sets on Day 165, I am reflecting on the importance of our pets in our lives. There is nothing like our relationships with our pets, as you all well know. My college friend and her family had to say good-bye to their dog, Dora, today. I think Dora was 16 or 17 years old. I feel for them, as I know you can appreciate. I can't even really communicate my feelings on this matter because it is way too close to the softest parts of my gooey center. So, let's just tip our hats to Dora! As another friend of mine said recently, I believe she is in that place where all good dogs go. I also write tonight with a request for assistance tomorrow night. I am going camping for a night and may not have cell service; so, I'm wondering if anyone would like to do a Guest Missive. Jump on in, if you are so moved. It would be wonderful to hear your voice! We care for them and / what do they do but give un- / conditional love. Dream of pets past, present, and future, Campers, and wake to care for all living things.

[Day 166 = Mary's gone campin'. No Guest Missiver emerged.]

As the sun sets on Day 167 (prime number!), I tip my hat to the Great Outdoors. Much of the COVID times has been about the Grate (On Your Nerves) Indoors, so my overnight camping trip at Deception Pass State Park on Whidbey Island was a deep-ly-appreciated change of scenery. Plenty of campers were enjoying the large campground, but the layout of our campsite made it feel private. Happily, the vast majority of campers were respecting the rules, official and commonsense. Deception Pass is right on the saltwater, which was another very welcome element. We also had a fantastic firepit that I played with for nearly 5 hours, and I slept extremely comfortably in the back of my Subaru (it was nice not to have to deal with a tent for a change). Sunshine, trees, saltwater, birds, and oceans of coffee from the camp stove. Very refreshing and rejuvenating. I don't really have many profound thoughts to share because my mind was quieter out there (and now, I'm so tired, it's basically blank). Rather, I just want to paint a little picture for you to enjoy in your own mind and maybe even inspire you to dip your toes into the Great Outdoors. It can cure what ails ya, or at least give you a break from and a new perspective on it. Go outside, hug a / tree, smell the air, skip a stone / in your second home. Dream of firepits and s'mores, Angels, and wake to lay your plans.

As the sun sets on Day 168 (24 weeks together!), I tip my hat to Imperfection. Like several other missives, tonight's begins with a trip to the garden by headlamp. I guess I shouldn't be surprised anymore, but what did I find but 3 more peas on that most per-sistent of pea plants. Another beautiful cucumber and a few more beans were also waiting amongst the leaves (and the slugs and snails). Now, why Imperfection, you may ask, if you are still read-ing this? Well, let me tell you, those leaves and plants are looking a little rough at this point. Any serious gardener would have given up and pulled these veggie babies weeks ago (months ago where the peas are concerned). At this point, I'm looking at them like my 2001 Subaru...I just want to see how long they'll last! They are highly Imperfect, yet they keep producing. Sun, rain, grow, grow, grow. So many of us put so much pressure on ourselves. Perfec-tionism abounds. It doesn't have to be that way, though. We can each produce beautiful fruits despite our many, many Imperfections. Good grief, those veggies are smart! Do your best, warts and / all. Everyone has flaws. It's / what you do with them. Dream peacefully, Campers, and wake to give yourself a break as you bask in the weekend.

WEEK #25

Saturday, August 29, 2020 – Friday, September 4, 2020

"Biden Gears Up to Hit the Trail in Swing States" (Katie Glueck, Annie Karni, and Alexander Burns, *The New York Times*, August 29, 2020)

"Columbia Protestors Hit the Streets After Blake Shooting" (Andrew Caplan and John Monk, *The State*, August 29, 2020)

"Clemson Ticket Plan Has Feel of Postseason Game" (Todd Shanesy, *The Spartanburg Herald-Journal*, August 29, 2020)

As the sun sets on Day 169, I tip my hat to Not Working. About 169 days ago, as the Before Times drew to a close, many people scurried home from their office buildings and established the now all-too-familiar Home Office. Many funny (and some not-so-funny because they are so true) memes ensued. As people learned the intricacies of the Home Office, I realized I have worked from home for over 15 years. While I generally appreciate and am suited for working from home, there has been one big challenge over the years: truly separating from work in the evenings and on weekends. As many of you have learned over the last few months, it can be a real challenge not to work all the time, especially if you like what you do. During the rare times when you have a few idle minutes and on slower days like the weekend, it can be hard not to wander in, grab the laptop, and knock out a few tasks on the To-Do List. Well, today, Angels, I abandoned that laptop and focused on a proper Saturday. No work; just livin'. It is so easy to get the work tunnel vision, but you've gotta look up once in a while. Real life is out there, waiting for you to notice. Head down, working all / the livelong day. Raise your wear- / y head to live life. Sleep soundly, Angels, because there's some real livin' to do tomorrow!

As the sun sets on Day 170, I'm relishing the smell of rain. Why, you may ask, is a resident of the Pacific Northwest relishing the smell of rain? Well, we haven't had much of it around here since July, and this evening, we are having some gentle showers. Just enough to water those veggie babies, lower the temperature a few degrees, and release that summer rain smell that can stir you and make you exhale just a bit. Not a bad feeling at all and so appreciated. Watching the weather happenings across the country, I am feeling especially grateful for our mild summer weather. I know others would not be welcoming more rain. But here at this house tonight, the rain is gentle and welcome and rejuvenating, and it carries the promise of better days ahead. Summer raindrops and / temperatures fall. Steam and / spirits rise tonight. Dream of fresh starts, Campers, because blue skies are coming!

As the sun sets on Day 171, I'm thinking about Hard Work. Everyone on this string has been working hard lately. Even I have been working hard lately, both on the upcoming Virtual Summit and on my pizza-making skills (haha…but tonight's was elevated). I'm reflecting on hard work because I had another big Monday of work and because my Dad's headed to the hospital again tomorrow for a periodic procedure. I don't think I know two people who have worked harder than my Mom and Dad. They are true worker bees. One of their pieces of advice has always been, "Work hard and do your best." I see a lot of that around me these days. We might not feel like we are working in our most efficient manner these days, but we are working hard… teaching, interviewing, designing, nursing, learning, parenting, ranching, surviving. Keep it up, Angels! One foot in front of the other. Nothing worth doing is easy, but you have everything you need. Set your sights, roll up / your sleeves, and get to work. You / can make it happen. Sleep deeply, Angels, because tomorrow is another chance to work towards your goals.

As the sun sets on Day 172, I look back at last night's Missive on Hard Work, and I feel…tired. Today was another day of Hard Work, and I am feeling it at this point. However, tonight's Tiredness feels different than earlier bouts of what I see now was Pandemic Exhaustion. Those were largely due to things like desperation, hopelessness, worry, uncertainty, even fear in the early days. Tonight is more about, "Gee, I spent all day on a computer. I learned some new stuff and got a bunch of other stuff done. I'm ready for some sleep." There isn't a pall of anxiety hanging over it all. It's funny I'm even pausing to note the difference, but it does feel different. Wow…I feel different because I feel "normal tired" and not pandemic exhausted. If this isn't a sure sign it's 2020, I don't know what is. I'll take it, though! Up with Normal Tired; / down with Pandemic Exhaus- / tion! Please and thank you. (The last four words of the Near-Nightly Haiku must be credited to Ron Swanson from *Parks and Recreation*.) Sleep restoratively, Campers, and feel some normal feels in the morning; they are still there.

As the sun sets on Day 173 (prime number!), many things are happening around here: it's a full moon, *Wonder Woman 1984* is supposed to open in one month (hmmmm), Election Day is two months from tomorrow, the Virtual Summit wraps in seven weeks, Molly's school started handing out schedules and supplies to 600 students today. That's a lotta numbers and happenings. New month, new outlook. The last two Missives have been about Hard Work and Normal Tired; tonight's Missive completes the triptych with Looking Ahead. It feels more normal to be looking ahead and working towards some goals (school, movie, Summit, election). Those irritating new guardrails are still there, but maybe we're learning to function inside them in new ways. I am still going to heed the 2020 roller coaster, but I'm going to try to keep inching forward. Even spinning wheels / often end up grabbing hold, / moving you forward. Dream of forward momentum, Angels, and get on your way.

As the sun sets on Day 174, I'm thinking about how glad I am that tomorrow is Friday, and it's no ordinary Friday either…it's Friday of a three-day weekend! Bring it!! I had all kinds of thoughts today, but once again, the garden makes a late-breaking impression. Two more cukes, a nice bundle of good-sized green beans, and… can you guess??...two tiny pea pods on that most persistent of pea plants. I mean, that plant deserves to be in the Planet's Premiere Persistent Pea Plant Passageway of Popularity [aka Hall of Fame]! We're a match made in veggie heaven…it just needed a little extra time, and I don't know what I'm doing. Perfect! An accidental victory. Those are pleasantly surprising when they sneak up on you. Keep your eyes open / tomorrow, Campers, you are / due for something nice. Sleep with great anticipation, Campers, and be ready to be Victorious!

As the sun sets on Day 175, we celebrate our 25th week together. One week shy of half a year. Let the record show that today, 175 days in, two different groups of friends, including this one, discussed how to travel safely by airplane. While this isn't the first time this topic has come up, it is the first time people were talking about how they plan to do it safely. I noticed the shift from, "No, way" to "Here's my plan." I'm still leery of how far I have to travel, but even I have my plan. Small, gradual shifts. Learning over time. Things feel a little different. Let the record also show that today is the 25th Anniversary of the *Xena* premiere. Channel your inner / Warrior Woman as you board / that plane in your mask. Ha! That one snuck up on me. I think it accurately bookends the last 25 years. Dream of electrostatic disinfectant sprayers and HEPA filters, Angels, and jet off into the holiday weekend!

WEEK #26
Saturday, September 5, 2020 – Friday, September 11, 2020

"Job Gains Shrink, Showing Frailty of U.S. Recovery" (Ben Casselman, *The New York Times*, September 5, 2020)

"USC Could Run Out of Space to Quarantine Virus Cases" (Bristow Marchant, *The State*, September 5, 2020)

"New T.K. Gregg Center Hosts Swim Meet as First Event" (Jed Blackwell, *The Spartanburg Herald-Journal*, September 5, 2020)

As the sun sets on Day 176, I submit a Junior Warrior Woman for consideration: *Moana.* I watched the end again on TV tonight. I really wish I had seen this one in the theater. It is so beautiful visually and musically, and it has a wonderful message, not to mention another strong female lead. I am so glad we are living in this new era of female protagonists! I aspire to be a strong female lead, so much so that this is the Nearly-Nightly Haiku: Sometimes, you fall a- / sleep on the couch after watch- / ing *Xena* again. Sleep soundly, Campers, and sail sweetly into your Sunday!

As the sun sets on Day 177, I find myself watching another animated kids' movie on TV (yes, this is my life now). Tonight, it's *Wreck-It Ralph.* I like this one, and I really like the sequel, *Ralph Breaks the Internet.* I was just about to observe that this one is not really on the Warrior Woman spectrum; however, it does have a glitchy little heroine (Vanellope von Schweetz), and there is an amazing Wonder Woman connection with the sequel...Gal Gadot voices one of the female leads (a race car driver named Shank from a video game called Slaughter Race...I know that's a lot of detail, but I wanted to type "Slaughter Race"). So, right there is basically the air-tight proof that all roads lead to Wonder Woman or Xena. Hope you all are enjoying the holiday weekend and deepening your life experience as I am clearly doing. Holiday weekend; / watching some movies; figur- / ing everything out. Dream in animation, Angels, and we'll figure things out tomorrow.

As the sun sets on Day 178, I give a huge Tip O' the Hat to teachers and students everywhere. While this is a Tardy Tip for those of you have already started back, it is a more Timely Tip here in the 'Ham. School (100% virtual) starts tomorrow in the Bellingham School District. God love and help you all. I cannot imagine being either a teacher or a student right now. You are all Warrior People, and I really do wish you the very best. Hang in there, and try to look for ways to make the best of things. I also tip my hat to the woman who runs our neighborhood blog. She is a musician and wrote these words back in 2015 when she "went to Maine to help my sister Kitty die. Bits of writing float back up from that time. Here's one: I am training wheels for death: / A slightly wobbly glide into new territory / Trying to avoid crashing on the way down this hill / An unfamiliar balancing act / But so far the slope is gentle." She shared that in tonight's blog, and I just liked it. We wobble and try to balance while seeking to avoid a crash, and sometimes we are surprised that it isn't as hard as we expected. I wish that for you this week. Sleep peacefully, Campers, because the way stretches out before us.

As the sun sets on Day 179 (prime number!), I feel Taco Tuesday turned on us a bit. First days of school in masks, coyotes, COVID, wildfires. Actually, it feels just like a Taco Tuesday in 2020. Good grief! We are asked to deal with more and more. It's kind of mind-boggling. Our tools remain the same, though. Deep breath, lean on your friends, one bite at a time. Maybe it's time for some silly jokes again. Tonight's theme will be Coffee because coffee is the nectar of the gods (and you thought that was ambrosia) and because I was just researching Starbucks corporate gift cards. Here goes, courtesy of scarymommy.com (you have been warned).... How does Moses make coffee? Hebrews it! Why did the coffee file a police report? Because he was mugged! What do you call it when you walk into a café and you feel sure you've been there before? Déjà brew! What kind of coffee was served on the Titanic? Sanka! Why did the espresso keep checking his watch? Because he was pressed for time! What currency is used in space? Starbucks! Feel better? Or, maybe you're thinking about coffee now instead of the other stuff? You're welcome (*Moana* reference). Dream of hot coffee, Angels, and wake to have some.

As the sun sets on Day 180, I'm sitting in the dark feeling kind of stunned. (I almost said I'm a little speechless, but you know that can't be true.) Between all the things happening at this house, at my friends' houses, and in the news, I can hardly believe this is our reality. And that's saying a lot in Year 2020! My head is spinning. I think that's why I'm throwing myself into Summit work. It's something to focus on, and it feels more "real" than all this other stuff, even though the virtual transition is still pretty unbelievable. What is the turning point going to be?? Because there has to be one... right? I think I need a few more silly jokes from scarymommy.com, this time about Animals. Ready? (Are we ever really ready for these?) What did the farmer call the cow that had no milk? An udder failure. Why do fish live in salt water? Because pepper makes them sneeze. Why don't ducks grow up? Because they only grown down. Why did the lion always lose at poker? He was playing with a bunch of cheetahs. What do ducks put in their soup? Quackers. What happens when you cross a wolf with a sheep? You have to get new sheep. I'll be here all week, y'all!! Life happens, news drops, / smoke billows across the West. / I see you '20. Dream of serenity and a normal day, Campers, because wouldn't that be nice?

As the sun sets on Day 181, I tip my hat to Thursday the 10th... my favorite day of the week and my favorite number! That's cool. I am easily amused. Tonight I share something from Yoga that I really like. There are many, many (many!) Yoga traditions; this teaching is from Kriya Yoga specifically, the "Yoga of Action." The sage Patanjali wrote that Kriya Yoga involves three things [and I am most definitely summarizing here...each one of these can be interpreted many, many(!) different ways]: 1) DO something (there's the Action); 2) REFLECT on it; 3) DEVOTE yourself to it. I have always liked this. Apply it to anything you please. Take action; consider it; dedicate yourself to it. Do something; think about it; stick to it. Perhaps some food for thought. It is always nice / to discover different / ways to see the world. Sleep soundly, Angels, and try a new outlook tomorrow!

As the sun sets on Day 182, I tip my hat to 26 weeks together. Twenty-six weeks, folks! Six months. Half a year. And what a year it is. I also tip my hat to all the people and feels of a September 11 anniversary. Nineteen years since my college friend in the Central Time Zone called me while I got ready to go work and asked if I knew what was going on. I turned on the TV, and we watched in total silence for quite a while until we said just a few words and hung up. I don't think I've ever been that shocked. I don't know about you, but I can honestly say my outlook on life has never been the same since. That is not hyperbole; that is the truth. When I think about how carefree the '70s, '80s, and '90s were in comparison to the last two decades, the aughts and the teens, I can hardly believe it. It does make me feel a little sad and wistful, but this is the way it is. It's our challenge to meet. Just like the Year 2020. What else is there to do but to give it your best shot? There's no telling what / will happen next. Just make sure / you give it your best. Give a nod to those we lost, Campers, and work to make tomorrow better (or just lay your plans…it's the weekend, after all).

WEEK #27

Saturday, September 12, 2020 – Friday, September 18, 2020

"Blazes Untamed, Officials Prepare for 'Mass' Deaths" (Jack Healy, Jack Nicas, and Mike Baker, *The New York Times*, September 12, 2020)

"Columbia Area Army Soldier Receives Medal of Honor" (Sarah Ellis, *The State*, September 12, 2020)

"His Carving Skills Landed Him on Food Network" (Lillia Callum-Penso, *The Spartanburg Herald-Journal*, September 12, 2020)

As the sun sets on Day 183, I'm winding down after a strange, yellow-gray, twilight kind of day. Usually, around here, days that look the same the entire day are of the gray variety. Clouds and rain. Can't tell if it's 11am or 3pm. Today, it was that feeling, but the color was all wrong. And it was smelly. Thinking tonight of all those living with the flames that have created all this smoke. Add the Air Quali- / ty Index to the list of / new things I now track. Dream of wind and rain, Angels, and hope they arrive soon.

As the sun sets on Day 184, I tip my hat to the Italian Plum (*Prunus cocomilia*, although this is the Old World variety, I think). Today was another twilight day, so jam took center stage. A somewhat time-consuming yet easy activity for those trapped indoors. While I was reminded that regular jam calls for a truly insane amount of sugar (next time, I'll try a low-sugar recipe), I can't wait to try the finished product. I really love the smell of the cooked plums, and the color is gorgeous. Let's hope it sets up overnight. It will be fun to give some away and nestle the rest in the freezer. In other news, the Seahawks played (really well) today. It was strange to see live professional sports, even though they've slowly been returning. I wish I could concentrate long enough to care. Perhaps I should try harder. Nothing like a really long sports season to pass the time, which it sounds like we'll be doing for a while longer. At the end of this, I will ironically have gained some cooking skills, but since restaurants won't exist anymore, it won't do me any good. In the meantime, though, I will enjoy that jam. Dice them, boil them, su- / gar them, pectin them, jar them, / store them yummy plums. Dream of smoke-free adventures, Campers, and wake to see what you can see.

As the sun sets on Day 185, I tip my hat to everyone on these text strings doing their best to survive 2020. From teachers to parents to business owners and employees to emergency responders to nurses and on to their kids, pets, families, and friends. You all are brave, and you are survivors. Keep going. Do things that you like and keep going. Last night, we had one of Molly's favorite things for dinner; tonight we had one of mine. Serious discussions are being held about starting to eat dessert first. Evening games of catch continue despite the wildfire smoke and work pressures. Nightly episodes of *Parks and Rec, Xena,* and/or our new Prime binges are eagerly anticipated. With wide, incredulous eyes and shrugging shoulders, we carry on. Fires, hurricanes, floods, / smoke. It sounds like the Postal / Service, but it's not. Sleep soundly, Angels, because WTH.

As the sun sets on Day 186, our very latest Taco Tuesday, I reflect again on brave humans who just keep going. My friend and "I.T. guy" and I had a Zoom test session with a presenter who is speaking at a virtual event on Thursday, and I feel encouraged by those who are as flummoxed as I am about what is happening to us but who are still trying to make the best of it. No one I know loves Zoom, but we realize we have to do it for now; so, let's do it well and have some fun with it. I've seen similar attitudes in Summit speakers and registrants. Like last night's missive, the message to me is: Keep Going. I also tip my hat to Tiny Kittens because someone I know just got one, and its cuteness is off-the-charts delightful. Like last night's missive, do things you like…and look at pet pics as often as possible. I'm in the mood for another silly joke tonight: What did one toilet say to the other toilet? You look flushed. Please don't filter these / missives. I don't claim to be / a comedian. Dream of your favorite joke, Campers, because you deserve to hear things you like.

As the sun sets on Day 187, I bask in the glow of our latest Prime binge. We loved Season 1 of *Hanna,* and we were very pleasantly surprised to see a second season released this summer. Yay, pandemic entertainment! We finished Season 2 tonight, and we were not disappointed. Not a show for the younger kids, but if you like thrillers with a couple great female leads (and a great male lead in Season 1), check it out. So good! I've said it since early March…

the real revolution will begin when there are no more new shows to release. TV is now the opiate of the masses, and you know how much we need our opiates right now. Perhaps when there are no more new shows to release, we all start acting out our favorite pandemic binges. In great detail. Work, work, work; yoga; / cook; Prime binge; *Friends* reruns. It's / time for bed again. Hmmmm… maybe I should be concerned. I'm not sure how much value I'm adding to the world. I shall try again tomorrow. Dream of your favorite shows, Angels, because you know you have them. And they are good.

As the sun sets on Day 188, those two 8's are making me feel cross-eyed. Or, maybe it was all the Zooming today. [I just hit the wrong key when typing "Zooming" and it made me think of a joke of my own: What is Xena's favorite video conferencing platform? Xoom! I crack myself up.] I actually had a positive Zoom experience tonight, and it gave me a boost to see and hear from friends, watch them enjoy the evening's activities, and listen to them brainstorm for the future. Imagine that…thinking about the future. A good sign, indeed! I also wore my School House Rocks "Vote" T-shirt and plugged voter registration. 47 days until Election Day! Hey, that's how old I am. And it's my fave day of the week. I am on such a roll! I was also in a time warp this week because I got off the Zoom and was honestly (and very pleasantly) surprised to realize that tomorrow is Friday. Pizza night and a new Prime binge (Season 2 of *Homecoming*). What more could I ask for? Well, quite a bit, really, but what more could I need at this particular point in time? Nothing. Pass the popcorn. Work hard and do your / best. Eventually, Fri- / day will come again. Sleep with great anticipation, Campers, and wake to skip towards the weekend (carefully, because it is still 2020, after all).

As the sun sets on Day 189 (27 weeks together…more than half a year), I tip my hat to Supreme Court Justice Ruth Bader Ginsburg. The Notorious R.B.G. 87 years old (March 15, 1933-September 18, 2020. Appointed to the Supreme Court by President Clinton and served August 10, 1993-September 18, 2020. "Some of my favorite opinions are dissenting opinions. I will not live to see what becomes of them, but I remain hopeful." Opera. Fiery dissents. Work ethic. Brilliant mind. Planks. Survivor. Dream of who you'd like to emulate, Angels, and wake to honor them with your efforts.

WEEK #28

Saturday, September 19, 2020 – Friday, September 25, 2020

"Justice Ruth Bader Ginsberg is Dead at 87" (Linda Greenhouse, *The New York Times*, September 19, 2020)

"SC Virus Death Toll Tops 3,000 as 766 New Cases Confirmed" (Greg Hadley, *The State*, September 19, 2020)

"Teachers, Staff on Start of New Virtual Schools" (Samantha Swann and Chris Lavender, *The Spartanburg Herald-Journal*, September 19, 2020)

As the sun sets on Day 190, I'm not sure which way to go tonight. On the one hand, there are memorials, fires, tropical storms (named using the Greek alphabet now because we've run through the English one), a pandemic, homeschooling…OK, I'll stop. On the other hand, though, there are memorials, first responders, relief efforts, and people, including friends and neighbors, who are re-dedicating themselves to causes they care about. I guess it's time to revisit those lessons of Hope from General Leia and Xena that we've pondered here. We are never guaranteed a certain outcome or an easy road or a happy ending. What else can you do but keep swimming? Hope is still out there, waiting for us to notice. Things change. Nothing is / static. You've gotta roll with / it and keep moving. Dream of apple pie, Campers, because it's almost fall, and pie makes everything better.

As the sun sets on Day 191, I am grateful for a couple simple things: weekends and clean air. It's funny how simple things can mean so much. We walked down to the waterfront with the dogs this afternoon, and we stood looking out over the water and breathing in the now-clean air. And it was Good. It also reminded me that last night's nod to Hope is for realsies…the prior smoky week was rough, and at times, in combination with everything else going on, it felt like it would never end. But you sighed and supposed it would eventually. And guess what? It did. And today was gorgeous. And Fall is falling on Tuesday, and the rains are coming. Keep swimming, Angels. The smoke rolled in. The / smoke settled down. The smoke went / on its way at last. Sleep well, Angels, and we'll continue the journey tomorrow.

As the sun sets on Day 192, I am, unfortunately, pondering Facts and Keeping One's Word. For years, I've bemoaned the trend that well-reasoned debates are becoming like an endangered species. Now, we often cannot agree on basic Facts, so those debates become all but impossible. I'm deeply disappointed that we don't even seem to have a starting place for talking to one another.

Talking things out is where new, great ideas emerge, but it first requires some common ground. The War on Facts has been accelerated by the unrefereed universe of social media. If people cared about facts, that would be one thing, but many don't seem to care anymore. It's who can shout the loudest and who can deliver the greatest "gotcha" moment. BOOOOR-ING!!! That's way too easy. What's hard is a well-reasoned debate that results in some compromise and some positive movement benefitting the most people. Wondering whether or not we can rein some of this in really stresses me out because there's so much fear and anger, no one wants to give a little. And life just keeps pushing people into their corners. What's gonna happen?? I don't know. I only know that the only actions I can control are my own. I prefer Facts and keeping my Word. I know some would call that naïve, but I still believe How you do something is as important as What you do. Yes, also naïve, but that's the way I aspire to roll. Remember when the toughest thing you had to do was organize the class kickball game at recess? Or pick just one of 31 flavors? Or make sure you could make it to Choir on Sunday after the '70s Party? Well, heck. Adulting is lame. Tomorrow, I just have to make it to the flu shot clinic on time, so I'm just going to focus on that. Do I have to lis- / ten to someone if they're wrong? / Haha, but for real. Dream of something that brings you joy, Campers, and cling to your touchstones.

As the sun sets on Day 193, I tip my hat to Summer. Today was the first day of Fall/Autumn, and we enjoyed one more day of blue skies, puffy white clouds, perfect temperatures, and Fall sunlight. Tomorrow, the "atmospheric river" arrives (that is a real meteorological term). Lots of rain and gusty winds are forecast. So, basically, Fall is arriving overnight. Again. I am always amazed how quickly the weather turns around here. There's no middle ground. Grab the sides of the row boat and hang on, I guess. Time to dig out the raingear again. Perhaps it will wash us clean and give us a new perspective. Or, perhaps I will hide under the covers. No… perspective. No…covers. We'll see what happens in a few hours.

Bask in the glow; soak / up the rays. Summer is wind- / ing down once again. Dream of summer memories, Angels, and know that the sun is up there, even if there are rainclouds in between.

As the sun sets on Day 194, I report back that, while the rain and wind did arrive, it didn't seem nearly as bad because the temperature remained mild. More silver linings. It will be a different story in February. Until then, we play in puddles! This Hump Day was mostly work and news with a little Yoga thrown in. The roller coaster continues: work good; news bad; Yoga good. And around and around we go. Stay vigilant, Campers, for mischief is afoot, and not the good kind. Oh, my…it's time to read and go to bed… the infomercials are interesting. You hump through your Hump / Day and what do you have to / show for it? A yawn. Sleep peacefully, Campers, cuz we're gonna need it.

As the sun sets on Day 195, I tip my hat to random acts of kindness. I received a very nice note today, and it was such a pleasant surprise. We should all give and receive such surprises as often as possible. So, tonight, the missive is simply a suggestion: in the next 24 hours, starting from when you read this, send someone a note of gratitude or thanks or acknowledgment. We all need this kind of thing, now more than ever perhaps, and it's so easy to do. Reach out and put some Good out there. Sometimes, when you least / expect it, something happens / that makes you feel good. Dream of the good you will do, Angels, and wake to do it.

As the sun sets on Day 196 (28 weeks together, y'all), I'm exhaling at the end of another packed week. Packed with work, packed with news, packed with feels. I miss the Olden Days where one would just have a "normal" packed week without all the layers of extra stress underneath. This is what we have for now, though, so you just keep playing catch every afternoon, making pizza every Friday, and looking for the helpers (and being a helper). Keep plugging away. Lend a hand. Extend a gratitude. Hold on to that

Hope. When you reach the end / of the week, look for what will / launch you to the next. Sleep cozily, Campers, and be sure to exhale over the weekend.

WEEK #29
Saturday, September 26, 2020 – Friday, October 2, 2020

"President Plans to Name Barrett to His Court Pick" (Peter Baker and Maggie Haberman, *The New York Times*, September 26, 2020)

"Thousands in NC Evicted Between Virus Moratoriums" (Ben Sessoms, *The News and Observer*, September 26, 2020)

"Initial Unemployment Claims Drift Down Slightly in NC" (Ben Gibson, *Statesville Record and Landmark*, September 26, 2020)

As the sun sets on Day 197, I bask in the glow of another Yoga workshop. Just a couple hours, but a really nice Saturday addition. If I were smart (and I'm clearly not in this instance) I would do some Yoga every single day. Why, oh why, do we not do the things we know are good for us?? I have always wondered this. Why do we say "I don't have time" so often? Although, maybe that's not so strange when Time seems to move at different speeds on different days. It gets back to those Choices we make. And Responsibilities. Can I Choose not to have so many Responsibilities? I think I'm starting to chase my tail. Good thing I stretched today. I looked for a Yoga joke for you, and this one lines up nicely with the fact that our friend dropped off some fresh bagels yesterday: Why did the bagel struggle at Yoga class? It couldn't find its center. Dream of what's good for you, Angels, and wake to do some in the morning!

As the sun sets on Day 198, I am digesting the Stacey Abrams-produced documentary *All In: The Fight for Democracy* about voter suppression (free on Prime for those interested). I have always been interested in history, including American history, and took quite a bit in school. Man, can this be a messed-up place. I was just shaking my head with my mouth hanging open at times. I honestly believe the majority of citizens do not believe all this gerrymandering and purging of voter rolls is fair; we just don't educate ourselves, and if it's not in our face, we don't deal with it. I'm not sure if this attitude is willful or just how humans roll. Either way, our ignorance will catch up with us. Maybe this is another silver lining of the lockdown: we are less distracted by sports and reality shows and eating out and traveling and more tuned in to things like George Floyd's murder and the election. Maybe since we've been forced to extract our heads from our typical routines we will look up and see some things that really, really need our attention. Let's Hope. Vital things are like / a garden: you must tend to / them or they wither. Dream of the things that need tending in your world, Campers, and start tending in the morrow.

As the sun sets on Day 199, I am in the middle of my most stress-ful two-day Summit stretch, other than hosting the event itself. I'm not whining; it's just a fact, and I knew it was coming. My Summit Timeline don't lie. I just finished another big round of work with oodles of quality control. As a result, my brain is mush, and you get these two items: 1) If the inside of a fire hydrant has H2O, what's on the outside? K9P. 2) Tonight was a lot / of Summit work, so all you / get is this haiku. Sleep well, Angels, so you can take your Taco Tuesday by storm!

As the sun sets on DAY 200!!! Two hundred!! What?? I said, "200!!!" Wouldn't it be fun to celebrate together, as in, face-to-face?? It would, wouldn't it? Thanks, 2020. Tonight was the first of three (dear God, three???) Presidential Debates, or as I referred to it beforehand, "Debates." Turns out I was right but for waaaaaay weirder and even more disturbing reasons than I had anticipated. So, I tip all my hats to 200, but this is all I got at this point: I poured my wine and / sat down to do my duty. / WHAT did I just see?? Sleep if you are able, Campers, and wake to join me for the 200's.

As the sun sets on Day 201, well…I had some thoughts, but I think I'll just go with this: I'm watching the news, and I just want 2020 to know that it is Absolutely Absurd. Apparently, there have been more Murder Hornet sightings 15 miles north of here. Also, there were some pictures of a very red sunrise/sunset…because the wildfire smoke is back. It's nothing like it was a few weeks ago, but it does give the skies and sun that really nice Apocalyptic 2020 Glow. All this on top of the stress that there may actually be two more "debates." I don't have time for this shit. Ironically, I do have time for this shit because there's still a pandemic on, so I'm not going anywhere or doing anything; rather, I don't have time for this shit emotionally. Perhaps some jokes are in order: What did the baseball glove say to the ball? Catch ya later! What do you call the basketball play where you drink too much and then score? Slam Drunk! [that one's close to my hoop-loving heart] I kept wondering why the baseball was getting bigger. Then, it hit me. [if that ain't one for 2020, I don't know what is] Why did the football coach go to the bank? To get his quarter back. Hahaha! You know, I actually feel better. Hope you do, too. Dream of a world where people are nice, Angels, and vow to start creating that world starting tomorrow.

As the sun sets on Day 202, the news came in while I worked on more Summit planning that the President and First Lady tested Positive for COVID. 2020, you are a never-ending source of surprises and sucker-punches and suckiness. All I can say is wear your mask and keep your distance and hang on…there is literally no telling what might happen next. Maybe two (or more?) of the parallel universes are colliding or something. This "space pun" encapsulates how I feel at the moment: I'm so disappointed…I keep hitting the space bar on my computer, but I'm still here on Earth. Haha! Thank you, space and time jokes. (I'm addicted to space jokes, but someday I'll over-comet.) That's it. I'm out. Sleep well, Campers, because we have viruses to fight off tomorrow.

As the sun sets on Day 203, I tip my hat to Friends. Molly shared this article with me, and I want to share it with you, my Sunlight Friends: https://turnaroundusa.org/back-to-basics-why-staying-close-to-friends-who-feel-like-sunlight-is-as-important-as-food-and-water/ Life is busy and / challenging, but your Sunshine / Friends will see you through. Dream and stir up those great brain chemicals, Angels, and wake joyfully for the weekend!

WEEK #30
Saturday, October 3, 2020 – Friday, October 9, 2020

"President in the Hospital as He Battles Covid-Experimental Treatment Given-Stay to Last for a Few Days" (Peter Baker and Maggie Haberman, *The New York Times*, October 3, 2020)

"NC Senate's Decision Will Affect the Diversity of UNC System Board" (Kate Murphy, *The News and Observer*, October 3, 2020)

"Dale Jr. Foundation, Unilever donate $135,000 to N.B. Mills School" (Ben Gibson, *Statesville Record and Landmark*, October 3, 2020)

As the sun sets on Day 204, I tip my hat to accounting software. However, I'm up way too late using it, so a haiku and an adieu: Sometimes you have to / work on a Saturday night. / I'm glad it's over. Sleep soundly, Campers, and wake to enjoy the other 50% of your weekend.

As the sun sets on Day 205, I tip my hat to the various modes of communication available to us. I enjoyed catching up with friends and family this weekend via FaceTime, Zoom, and even the good ol' telephone. It is wonderful to be able to hear voices and see faces. Can you imagine if we were still limited to letter writing? I mean, that makes for some great Masterpiece Theater tension, but no thank you during year 2020. I do love a hand-written note or card now and then, and sometimes, I bemoan the fact that it seems like a bit of a lost art; however, in times like these, I like that tech. I hope you, too, had a chance to catch up with some of your loved ones. Consider writing someone a note this week. It could be short. It could contain a gratitude. It could even be a postcard. Surprise someone from the mailbox! Hopefully, you have a stamp somewhere at hand. Grab a pencil and / let someone know you're thinking / of them from afar. Dream of learning cursive as a kid, Angels, and wake to know your kids can't read it. (Hey, a secret language!)

As the sun sets on Day 206, I realize that maybe 206 isn't that big a number. What's that, you say? Not a big number? Are you nuts?? Well, yes, but here's why I say it. I just heard that this is Day 1355 of the current Administration.. So, 206 feels much, much smaller. They all feel quite weighty, though. I'm tired and ready for some shifts. I try to take care of the shifts I need to make personally, but I'm ready for some broader ones, too. In other news (that really isn't news per se), pets are a great diversion. Tonight, I shared some Pirate's Booty with Walter. Such a sweet face and such a deep appreciation for salty packing peanuts. When in doubt, go find your pet and snuggle them. Looking down, I no- / tice some drooling. Oh, hey, it's / just Walter begging. Sleep peacefully, Campers, and emulate your pets in the morning.

As the sun sets on Day 207, I reflect on some more lessons of the garden. Fall is falling, so a couple days ago, I pulled the veggies that are finished (beans and cucumbers). Would you believe that most persistent of pea plants is still going?? Not only did it have a few pea pods (a bit scraggly, but one of them was delicious!), it also sported a sweet little white bloom. The pea plant was left alone out of a deep respect. Two other pleasantly surprising finds: one of the cabbage stalks has sprouted some new leaves, and I found a mystery plant hiding under the rather extensive cucumber leaves and vines that I suspect may be one of my missing pepper plants. I was really looking forward to some hot peppers, but I think the cukes overtook them. They were the only things that never showed up. I shall try again next year. Keep at it, Angels. The things that Victory Garden did with little to no help from me continue to amaze. We can do so much, even when conditions are less than ideal. Just keep doing your thing and apply persistence. Eat and drink well; get your rest. And watch out for slugs and bugs. Dream of optimal growing conditions, Angels, and wake to flourish in them.

As the sun sets on Day 208, I tip my hat to coffee. We are now 12 days from the Summit, and I'm pretty sure I'm only alive because of coffee and hysterical laughter. Whatever gets me there. Between a packed day of Zooming and planning and the Vice-Presidential debate, my eyes are drying up and blowing away. Darn, they were pretty handy while they lasted. Remember this classic? What did the right eye say to the left eye? Between you and me, something smells! And a new one: Why do potatoes make great detectives? Because they always keep their eyes peeled. You're welcome. Sleep quickly, Campers, because I'm already asleep.

As the sun sets on Day 209, I'm wondering if any of you have seen the movie *How to Train Your Dragon*. I love this one. I remember going to see it in the theater with Molly's nephews. I wasn't expecting much, and I was very, very pleasantly surprised. I may have enjoyed it more than the nephews! (Plus, the popcorn was really good that afternoon.) It's a dragon tale about a dragon's tail. A classic story of Viking boy meets Night Fury dragon. Overcoming physical challenges, oddballs triumphing, parents and children, courage, loyalty, inter-species friendships, not to mention flying and fire-breathing. It truly has it all! It was fun to revisit as I trek up to the Summit. Sometimes, you need animated kids' stories. Great lessons, lots of chuckles, a little adventure, and a hopeful ending. I wish those things for you tomorrow as we close out our 30th week together. Dream of dragons, Angels, and fly through your Friday!

As the sun sets on Day 210, I wish you all a Happy 30th. Thirty weeks together. I, for one, am so glad we are together, at least in this weird way. Tonight, our first Fall storm has moved in. Steady rain and wind. Not as much of either as I expected but a nice reminder that Fall has fallen. So, that also means we've moved together from late Winter all the way through Spring and Summer and into early Fall. We have at least touched on all four seasons, with more to come, I assume. Fall and Winter typically make me turn a little inward, do a little introspection, maybe even a little hibernating. Once this Summit wraps, I am going to do just that for a bit. I hope you, too, have time to slow down and ponder, if you so desire. A little exhaling might be really nice. I just realized I / haven't haiku'd in a while. / Maybe tomorrow. Sleep snuggly, Campers, and wake to embrace your sloppy Saturday.

WEEK #31

Saturday, October 10, 2020 – Friday, October 16, 2020

"Low in Cash in '16, Trump Generated His Own Windfall" (Susanne Craig, Mike McIntire, and Russ Buettner, *The New York Times*, October 10, 2020)

"Teacher Who Died of Virus Put Students First" (Theoden Janes, *The News and Observer*, October 10, 2020)

"Police Officers Don Badges with Pink, Purple Highlights" (Donna Swicegood, *Statesville Record and Landmark*, October, 10, 2020)

As the sun sets on Day 211, I tip my hat to baking therapy. I was at it again today. Another batch of muffins. Thank goodness both of us love these particular goodies, or it could become a problem. Not sure why I enjoy it so much, but the end result sure doesn't hurt. A walk by the Bay with the pups revealed a very Fall mix of sun, clouds, wind, stormy-ish seas. That weather is coming – there was even light snow over one of the mountain passes – but it's OK. We know what to do: hibernate and when you can't, grab that fleece and Gore-Tex. On the food front, grab the Crock Pot. And maybe do some baking. Winter weather can / drive you inside but it's not / all bad…there's muffins! Dream of warm snuggles, Angels, and enjoy your Fall preparations!

As the sun sets on Day 212, it's possible I'm watching another Harry Potter movie on Syfy. Lasso of Truth: I'm watching another Harry Potter movie on Syfy. I wonder if fantasy and escapism have ever been more important than in year 2020. Well, I guess that's an exaggeration in general, but it feels pretty true for me, personally, right now. It's helpful to have escapes and diversions. I've gotta make sure not to escape to Diversion Land for another 8 days, though. My brain wants to trip off to Diversion Land…la, la, laaaaa. But no. Not yet. Sit. Stay. There will be time enough for watching movies in bed and eating junk food. Oh, dang…that sounds pretty good, too. But no. Not yet. Daydreaming is another good escape. Be sure to do a little tomorrow. Figure out what you want to do the next time you can take a trip to Diversion Land. The pandemic can't take those trips away from us, no siree! You can go anytime you like, although if you are on a work Zoom, you should probably cut your Video feed first. Uh-oh…time to go to bed. Zoom is infiltrating the Nightly Missive. Even though it's Mon- / day, you can still stroll on off / to Diversion Land. Dream of your favorite escapes, Campers, and visit them in the morrow.

As the sun sets on Day 213, I tip my hat to Fall Sunlight. I took a couple great walks this afternoon, one with each pup, and it was sunny and beautiful and clear. The sunlight and air had that notice-able crystal-clear, almost washed-clean quality that only Fall gives us. Nice! Exhale. Smile. Gather yourself. You can do it. Walk-ing with the pups, / admiring the Fall after- / noon. Look at that light! Dream of sunny afternoons and jumping in leaves, Angels, and wake to do a little of it (even if it's raining).

As the sun sets on Day 214, the story of the day was the Fall Wind. We were under a Wind Advisory today as another Fall storm rolled in off the Pacific. Once the rain tapered off this afternoon, we had sun, clouds, and that wind. So, what did we do? We drove down to the waterfront and walked the pups out to the point. Swells were rolling across the Bay, crashing into the breakwater, and smashing onto the pocket beach, along with some really large logs. The wind and swells stirred up the sediments in the Bay turning the water into a roiling brownish mass. Then, the sun broke through, making it a swirling golden-bluish mass. We stood at the point feeling the steady 15 mph wind and the 30 mph gusts. These aren't our biggest winds by any stretch, but they were enough to make it interesting and send the waves crashing and the spray spraying. Very exciting! Feel the wind, feel the / spray, hear the crashing. Watch those / two dogs get spunky! Dream of the motion of the ocean, Campers, but hopefully, you won't need any Dramamine.

As the sun sets on Day 215, my heart goes out to the weary. I sense a tiring week out there, so I send you wishes for some reju-venating sleep and soon! Perhaps a weather observation? Today, it was the Fall Clouds. To our east (opposite the Bay) lie the glori-ous Cascade Mountains, including "our" volcano, Mount Baker, or more accurately, Kulshan. Lots of clouds over the range today; no sign of Kulshan. This is not surprising from about October through May. Haha…some years it can be September through June. To-day, steely gray clouds were nestled against the mountain tops; then, they rose and rose and rose, up and up and up, into those big, white, towering clouds. They were the kind that grow right in front of your eyes. You can look at the top and actually watch it grow and expand and climb ever higher. It's kind of mesmerizing (although, Olive wasn't as mesmerized as I was). Olive and I then walked west towards the Bay; when we turned east again towards home, those clouds had bustled off over the horizon leaving just the gray clouds against the mountaintops. See ya, white puffies. That's it. That's what I've got tonight. The clouds grow and rise / right before your very eyes. / Time to feed the dogs. Dream of puffy white clouds, Angels, and check the skies in the morning.

As the sun sets on Day 216, I identify with those who were feeling weary a couple days ago. Working late into / the night. Can't wait for Friday. / Anyone with me? Sleep well, Campers, and soon, you will be able to reward yourself.

As the sun sets on Day 217, I tip my hat to the classic martini. And sleep. And friends. And the weekend. I have decided I am ready to put this event to bed. It has been 17 months, after all. I need some of that sweet, sweet Freeeee-dom!!! Steaming (crawling?) towards / that finish line. You do what / all you have to do. Sleep soundly, Angels, and party your pants off tomorrow…it's the weekend!!

WEEK #32
Saturday, October 17, 2020 – Friday, October 23, 2020

"White House Unleashes Blitz of Policy Changes As Election Day Nears" (Eric Lipton, *The New York Times*, October 17, 2020)

"North Carolina Breaks Day-Old Record For New Cases of Virus" (Lynn Bonner, *The News and Observer*, October 17, 2020)

"Iredell Sees Heavy Turnout at Polls" (Ben Gibson, *Statesville Record and Landmark*, October 17, 2020)

As the sun sets on Day 218, a haiku: Purchasing corpor- / ate e-gift cards is not as / hard as you might think. Sleep, Campers, because that sounds pretty awesome right about now.

As the sun sets on Day 219, I tip my hat to people willing to pull together for a common cause. I've spent the last few days contacting all the people who are contributing to the Summit this week (only one more work day to go!), and there are a lot of loyal, adventurous people out there. Hard to have an event without other people. Not sure what makes people do this, but I'm glad they do! Now, it is time to send out the Bat Signal to anyone willing to cover the Nightly Missive for the next few nights. I'm thinking Monday through Friday sounds pretty good (5 nights). Any adventurous authors out there? Step right up! Making sure all the / threads from seventeen months come / together this week. Dream of smooth sailing, Angels, and wake to the adventure; thanks for your help launching me!

[Day 220 = Guest Missive by Stephenie]
I don't know if I saw a volunteer for tonight…so, I will try. As the sun sets on Day 220 (yikes-not another number 20!) I tip my hat to people getting shit done! This may have already been a nightly missive Topic – most likely so – it's been 220 goddamn days. But I'm so impressed – we keep moving forward, checking items off the list, inventing new ways to accomplish big and little, old and new, albatross and monkey. Sleep well ye campers/ tomorrow we summit vir- / tually at last.

[Day 220 = Guest Missive by Cathy]
As the sun set (with a glorious sunset tonight) on Day 220, I tip my proverbial hat to all the interesting people you can meet in the Walmart parking lot while waiting for the police to show up. My daughter and I made the trek to the Walmart tonight to get some items for her Halloween costume. As I was pulling out to leave, I hear and feel the crunch of car on car-I had backed into another car

that was also pulling out at the same time. I pulled back in to assess the damage. (Only scratches to my badass bumper, but the other guy had a dent the size of my bumper in his backside.) Now, first up is the guy who saw it all-who was high as a kite. I could smell the booze through my mask. He tried to be super helpful, but I really just needed him to go and purchase his extra-large box of pop tarts and be on his way. Next came the Walmart Ambassador on one of the powered shopping carts. She introduced herself and pointed out her name tag proving her status and said she saw it all and that it wasn't my fault and she would be happy to talk to the police when they got there. A little while later, another employee came by and said that the outside camera was pointing directly down the aisle and would have caught everything on tape, if it came to that. Then, there was the series of nosy neighbors who had to give their 2 cents or just struck up random conversations about going back to school and the elections. Finally, after waiting for an hour, the nice policeman showed up to great fanfare. As I was waiting for him to process all our info, I watched as the sunset grew and changed into a wonderful mix of fall colors, deep red and radiant orange with a ting of yellow high lightening it all. It lightened my heart, and I felt the tension drain away. So, my wish for you is to find that hidden jewel of a sunset and kindness of strangers during the dark times. And always make sure you drive the bigger car! (No one was injured in the making of this missive.)

[Day 221 = Guest Missive by Spicoli]
So, last night, as the sun set on Day 221, I was forest walking with the hard feelings of saying goodbye. I was marveling at how sometimes in your life a friend really pulls off a major awesomeness, and when you celebrate that you aren't just being supportive, you are actually truly watching a superlative moment. Haiku: watching it happen / it isn't hyperbole / it is truly great. Sleep well, Campers, so when you bask in the next day, it is wonderful.

[Day 221 = Guest Missive by Elizabeth]

As I reflected on this 221st day, a day filled with performance management meetings, recruiting calibration, interviews, and one-on-one conversations to discuss growth and progression for the individuals, I remembered that today began with PASSWORD UPDATE. Why in all caps, you ask? It's just changing a password. Every 90 days we are notified of this required activity. Something so simple if not done right can take you out of commission. No offices to race into for IT support. The other side is...we have to enter our password many times a day. Instead of generating a random key, I started creating passwords to help reframe every time I entered it. I've had variations of wondering, wandering, choosing joy; so, today, I almost chose something generic or negative reflective of my headspace at the time. With a chance to control and influence my thoughts, I chose another mantra of "be present." So, instead of just typing random keys or names, I will be reminded to be present. So, what do you do that you can have as an aid and not just a task? How do we help ourselves reframe when it feels like all the surrounding variables are against us? Take control of the little things, Angels. The little things build upon each other to make the big things great. Sleep well, my sisters. May tomorrow be filled with [all good emojis].

[No Missive for Day 222…or, was there? Yes, there was; it was just a little late. Read on, dear Reader.]

[Day 223 = Guest Missive by Margaret]

So, I just realized that I failed my missive duties last night. Because - exhausted. And sometimes life is hard. I feel really bad, because that nightly missive is a big part of my daily ritual and grounding these days, and I have failed you all on that. I could try to come up with something profound, but I ain't got it in me. Instead, I leave you with this tale of a Christmas present gone horribly wrong that a friend shared. Moral of the tale (or tail in this story): You never know where an act of love will lead you. And,

we've all got our own "problems." Love you all! Happy Friday!
https://www.facebook.com/1371494841/
posts/10224564827332773/?extid=0&d=n

[No Missive for Day 224]

WEEK #33

Saturday, October 24, 2020 – Friday, October 30, 2020

"New Peak for U.S. Cases: Over 82,000 in a Single Day: 13 States Endure Their Worst Week Yet-Warnings of a Cold-Weather Surge" (Campbell Robertson, Edgar Sandoval, Lucy Tompkins and Simon Romero, *The New York Times*, October 24, 2020)

"Suspended Sheriff Pleads Guilty to Assault, Corruption" (David Travis Bland, *The State*, October 24, 2020)

"Charleston County Parks Will Sell Portions of Folly Pier as Souvenirs" (Shamira McCray, *The Post and Courier*, October 24, 2020)

[Day 222 = Guest Missive by Mel…offered up on Day 225]

MISSING MISSIVE: Yeah, that is me. Ladies, I am soooooo sorry. Murt, at least you were just late, I missed my assignment altogether! No excuse, just an apology. What day was this missive due? I shall blame it on COVID brain. These days seem to meld into each other, and time seems to be lasting three weeks for each week. I seriously thought I had the Thursday missive and woke up today thinking I am late on a Friday a.m. So proud of myself. I did at least find out it is Saturday. Oh, and the Mac says it is Sat 7:14 AM. Thanks, Mac. It owes me that at least; literally a 17-hour in-stall to get my new phone to be what my old one was. A first world problem, but one that kept me from FaceTime with my dearest friends and out of connectivity for most of yesterday. My thought, as I watched the leaves fall yesterday and reflected on how beauti-ful, but brief, this fall (haha, I get it now) experience of the chang-ing of the leaves is. Kind of what we are in right now. The leaves are letting go of what is hurting them as they head into a hard season. If they kept their leaves, it would be a lot more pain; take from their core, drain them of sustenance, and make them vulnerable when spring comes again, as their leaves would be wilted and dead and unable to bring them nourishment. Let us allow the COVID to be our fall, not our downfall. Shed these things in our lives that are not good for us to have present all of the time. The things that keep us from thriving, especially when the chips are down. May it help pluck out what is bad and unhealthy in us, and when light comes in again (aka human contact) we can be open to grow, renew, and thrive. Let us learn from nature and grow anew from this hard sea-son. I love you, ladies.

[Day 225 = Guest Missive by Leslie]

Insert day number here. I honestly can't find it and got tired looking. My kids kept me up roasting marshmallows and playing PG Cards Against Humanity. I've been wanting to do both for a while; so great to spend time with them. I'm loving seeing the way many of y'all spent this gorgeous fall day. Thank you, Angels, for beautiful pictures of children and the farm and cats trying to poop. I love sharing time with you and seeing your daily lives, spread out through three seasons now. And here comes winter! Madeleine L'Engle talks about the difference between chronos & kairos, the two Greek words for time. Chronos is chronological time, marked by calendars and clocks. Kairos is a more qualitative measurement, like how time flies or stands still when you're living in a certain moment. Here's my go at expressing something Mel's had me thinking about all day: COVID chronos sucks/But check-ins with my Angels / give me kairos time. Sleep tight, Angels, and feel a real-time hug whenever you read this.

[No Missive for Day 226]

As the sun sets on Day 227 (haha...remember that sitcom?), I return to the Nightly Missive after a much-needed week-long break. I return to you with one main feeling: Gratitude. I am grateful for each of you. I really felt your support, and it felt good! Thank you, thank you, thank you. I am so relieved to be done, and you helped me make it through a very long journey. You know, reflecting on this, I am encouraged to think that we can still help each other, even when we can't be together. Somehow, we are fumbling through this most exasperating year, and we are finding ways to bolster one another despite the ridiculousness that is 2020. Well done, all! Let's keep it up. My turn next! I hope I can support you as much as you supported me. You work and work and / work towards your goal, but you can- / not do it alone. I hope you've been sleeping well, Campers, because there is much working and much playing still to do!

As the sun sets on Day 228, I'm pondering roller coasters. Roller coasters come in several forms, of course, but since it's 2020, I refer to the emotional kind. The days and weeks immediately post-Summit are always a roller coaster. One minute, the adrenaline pumps, and I'm excited and motivated to do things like send thank-you's and review evaluations; the next minute, the cloud of exhaustion rolls in like a fog, and I'm pooped again. Brief bouts of manic excitement followed by longer bouts of slack-jawed staring. This year generally has been a roller coaster, too, of course. Manic periods of toilet paper hoarding and meme mining followed by depressed periods of mask cursing and political musings. None of this pondering is intended to wish the roller coaster away, though, for we won't escape it. Rather, we must watch that the highs don't get too high nor the lows too low. And here we are at Balance again. Feel the feels, lean into them even, but keep your car on the tracks overall. And recognize that some days will be a better ride than others. Your friends will be waiting for you on the platform to talk about the ride; then, you can go get a corn dog together. Maybe even a funnel cake. Hmmm, and here I hadn't thought I'd missed the Fair much this year. Keep your arms in, but / enjoy it. And maybe e- / ven scream a little. Dream of roller coasters, Angels, and smile in your sleep as you ride the ups and downs.

As the sun sets on Day 229 (hello, prime number), I find myself way too interested in the infomercial on TV right now. I also find myself sensing change in the air. Over the last week, people around me seem to be looking up and around with wider eyes than I have seen in a long time. It could be Fall. It could be the full moon (it's 2020, so it falls on Halloween and is also a hunter's blue moon). It could be Halloween. It could be the election. It could be a desire for something different, something to look forward to, perhaps. It could be a lotta things, but I'm going to take it as a positive. Feeling something Different is feeling pretty good. Besides sensing change, I am also tipping my hat to Yoga. Being the ridiculous human that I am, I convinced myself I was "too busy" for class the last few weeks, just when I should have gone. Stupid human. Well, I survived to stretch another day, and it was marvelous. I hope you had a marvelous moment this Hump Day, too! Sleep soundly, Campers, and welcome in some change!

As the sun sets on Day 230, I tip my hat to grocery store sushi. No, seriously. There's a lesson here. Somewhere. Oh, here it is... sometimes, the humble is enough to get you through. As in, you can't always take a big sushi break in the middle of the workday, so you figure, "Well, I guess it's no sushi for me today. That's really too bad because I could really use some." But then, you remember that your awesome local grocery store has sushi. For a moment, you think, "I could never," but then, you remember that oh, yes, you can. And you have. And it was just enough. It made me think that we often turn up our noses too soon, and we give up with a wistful, "I could never." In doing so, however, we potentially miss out on a pleasant surprise. So, don't give up so easily. Have a sense of adventure. Be curious. Be daring. But maybe also stick to the veg-etarian and cooked options. I mean, adventure is good, but food poisoning is bad. My thoughts and stomach / turned to nori and wasa- / bi. All was not lost. Dream of derring-do, Angels, and dare to do on your Friday!

As the sun sets on Day 231, we celebrate our 33rd week together! We are getting dangerously close to being at this for two-thirds of a year. We are heading into our 4th season together. And I'm still sitting here in the dark watching *Diners, Drive-Ins, and Dives* while ev-eryone else snuggles and snores. (Seriously, Walter...keep it down over there. I should probably make sure he doesn't have something stuck in his nose.) I know my attitude is evolving because I had three different Zooms today (admittedly, two were for fun, social purpos-es), and I did not want to throw my laptop out the window. Quite the contrary. I thoroughly enjoyed myself and sincerely appreciat-ed seeing my friends, learning new things, laughing, and sporting my Chewbacca mask...while wearing my Wonder Woman glasses. Another friend later dubbed the look "Wonder Wookiee." My life is complete. Life goes on. It's weirder right now, but it goes on. Zooma zooma zoo- / ma zoom. Watch out for the Won- / der Wookiee right there! Dream of fun and silliness, Campers, and wake to enjoy both this weekend; you deserve it.

WEEK #34

Saturday, October 31, 2020 – Friday, November 6, 2020

"Trump and Biden Make Final Blitz in Midwest Tour: Eye on Battlegrounds" (Thomas Kaplan and Annie Karni, *The New York Times*, October 31, 2020)

"Trump Counting on Election Day Surge by Lifelong Republicans" (Francesca Chambers, *The State*, October 31, 2020)

"2 Full Moons This Month Means a 'Blue Moon' Will Fall on Halloween" (Shamira McCray, *The Post and Courier*, October 31, 2020)

As the sun sets on Day 232, I smile remembering today's pictorial evidence of friends enjoying a spectacular Fall day…and a spooky Halloween day at that. Sunshine, costumes, candy, kids, candy chutes, beers, dogs, pizza dough spiders, salmon jerky. Good stuff, all! Strolling in the sun- / shine; look at that crystal clear / air. Pass the Reese's. Sleep soundly, Angels, and enjoy that extra hour.

As the sun sets on Day 233, I feel a sense of Great Expectation. We moved through All Hallows' Eve yesterday and All Saints' Day today, and tomorrow is All Souls' Day, with Día de los Muertos covering today and tomorrow (two days…cool!) While I do want to note these various Days for our record, I also did it to get them straight in my mind; I continue to confuse them, so maybe this will help. Now, we turn our attention to Election Day on Tuesday. Enter Expectation. I don't think it's hyperbole to say that this will be an election like none before, but hey, it's 2020, so go figure. I am anxious (and excited and nervous and all manner of other feels) to see what happens. One minute, I think it'll be one scenario; the next minute, I think it'll be another; the third minute, I pace around the room. Then, I remember we might not know for days or weeks. I just need a break, you know? Remember when you could go for days without thinking much or at all about politics? Yeah, it's been a while. I think we could all use some of that sweet relief. Here's hoping. Full moon, blue moon, hun- / ter's moon. Hallows, Saints, and Souls. / Turn back that clock now. Dream of that sweet relief, Campers, and wake to welcome it in.

As the sun sets on Day 234, I tip my hat to all you survivors. We've scratched and clawed our way here to Election Eve. Deep breaths. Gird your loins. Fix your gaze. Make or take(out) your favorite dinner. Pour your favorite drink, maybe a really stiff one. Here is yet another thing in year 2020 that we will all go through Together. No matter your outlook, your vote, your best guess, your hopes, your dreams…we all pause tomorrow to see which way our country goes next. There aren't a lot of situations where we really don't know how something is going to go and how it goes is really going to matter. I believe we're staring at one of those things. Screw your courage to the sticking place, Angels, because nothing inspires like some Shakespeare. Reach back to the 16th century, friends, and know that humans have always been faced with hard things. What will you do in response? Get ready and chan- / nel all the good advice shared / here. We can do this. Sleep, Angels, so that you are ready to face the day!

As the sun sets on Day 235, I find myself disappointed but not surprised that we are headed for Election Week (or longer) instead of Election Day. It's 12:06am Pacific Time, and the count is 220 to 213. Many states are still busy counting millions of ballots. The incumbent just announced he won the election, voting should stop, and they'll be heading to the Supreme Court. But I'll leave that there because every bit of that is BS. My feeling has been that if it wasn't a landslide, we were headed for days (weeks? months?) of trouble. Well, here we go. What to do, what to do. Well, I have good news. I just went into the dark kitchen (because everyone else here is asleep, per usual) to get some water. I was standing at the kitchen sink, and I heard clear as day, "You have to have faith." Now, I love these messages because they are non-partisan. I wasn't told WHAT I should have faith in or about; I was just told to have it. It's up to me. This reminder about Faith, in turn, makes me think of what General Leia and Xena taught us over the summer about Hope, and it makes me think of Wonder Woman's insistence that "Only Love can truly save the world." Oh, my…Faith, Hope, and Love. There they are again. No one tells you what the object of those should be. It's up to us. Whatever happens, I can still choose those, even when it feels so very hard to do so. That's our job. We try to bring those to whatever and whoever is around us, and it feels so bad when we feel others aren't doing the same. But what choice do we really have then? We must lead by example. And fortunately, actions speak louder than words, so we don't have to talk to others if we can't say something nice. Hmmm…I have always contemplated a Vow of Silence. It could be time. In fact, this missive has become so long, I should take a Vow now. Faith in yourself; Hope / for others; Love for all of/ the above. Just try. Dream of healing, Campers, and wake to see what's what.

As the sun sets on Day 236, I tip my hat to Patience. Once again, I'm sitting in the dark in the glow of the TV listening to the latest prognostications. With the exception of some small groups of supporters of the incumbent, our country is exhibiting admirable patience tonight as the votes continue to be counted. I'm actually pretty impressed. In today's "insta-grat" culture, we must wait. And people are waiting. Let's get this right, folks (especially since we are headed for some recounts). Remember the days when there was one phone in the house that everyone had to share? Remember when there was one television that everyone had to share? You had to learn to wait your turn. Now, everyone has their own phone and their own screen(s), and no one has to wait for anything ever. Well, we have to wait now. And from what I see, it's going just fine. Let's keep it that way, folks. Check the box; mail it / in; drop it off; close the polls. / Now, sit back and wait. Sleep peacefully, Angels, because tomorrow can wait. For now.

As the sun sets on Day 237, that number just doesn't look right, probably because the only numbers I can think of anymore are 253 and 214. Another day, another night in the glow of the TV. Faith, hope, love, patience. Keep repeating it. The faith message came through again tonight, loud and clear. After so many years of disappointment, including and especially 2020, my faith has been tested, but it has made a surprising comeback this week. I've had moments of uncertainty and rapid pulse rate, but ever since Wisconsin at 2am on Wednesday, my faith and hope have been solid. It's weird not to feel like the rug is going to be pulled out from under me. Now, could it still? Sure. It's 2020, plus those last 4 years on top of that. I doubt anyone alive during this period in history will ever again feel like something is absolutely locked down until it is. But we can heal. I am hoping this is the start of that. If it is, it won't come easily. January 20 is a long way off still. But perhaps 2020 and the last 4 years on top of that have prepared us for this final stretch. Perhaps there was a reason for this trial by fire. Look around. Your family and friends and neighbors have been tested, too. I think we're ready. We're going to choose our country and each other and determined optimism. We're going to face the pandemic so that we can get our lives and our economy back. Wouldn't that be something? Watch the numbers. Track / the margins. Pour another. / Let's go win this thing. Dream of imminent announcements, Campers, and wake to see if one has been made.

As the sun sets on Day 238, we celebrate our 34th week together. 34 was my college basketball number. Funny thing was, I thought it was Michael Jordan's number when I chose it, but his was actually 23. Ever feel like you are soooo close but you just never pull it off? Me, too. After the last three Nightly Missives, I feel like I owe you an apology. I did not shy away from political talk as we wait (and wait and wait some more) for the result. While I was nervous-typing and trying to offer some coping ideas to anyone who might also need some, the Missives were perhaps too political for this venue. Over here, I think we try to tell stories, observe our world, read a few books, write a few haikus, and offer some words of support to one another. So, if I strayed too far from that, I do apologize. I will take my interest in politics and my nervous-typing elsewhere. Tonight, I am excited to be on the verge of another welcome weekend. After days (and days) of clouds and rain, today was one of those glorious Fall days with bright sunshine, chilly air, and crunchy leaves. And let me tell you, it was welcome! That sunshine sure does boost the mental health. Molly and I are having a contest this weekend: who can do LESS. Our only big plan is to make popcorn. And I'm probably going to make muffins again. I like activities that result in something you can eat. I hope you, too, have a nice weekend with some things that you like, perhaps even some edible ones. Pop it, bake it, walk / it, watch it, read it, rest it. / Keep your spirits up. Sleep sweetly, Angels, and seize it!

WEEK #35

Saturday, November 7, 2020 – Friday, November 13, 2020

"Biden Vaults Ahead in Pennsylvania Which Opens Path to the White House: In the Lead in Three Other States-'We're Going to Win This'" (Alexander Burns and Jonathan Martin, *The New York Times*, November 7, 2020)

"Local Museums See Fewer Visitors, Go More Virtual As a Result of Pandemic" (Laurryn Thomas, *The State*, November 7, 2020)

"Dozens of Charleston Area Teachers Resign Amid Pandemic. Advocates Fear More Will Follow." (Jenna Schiferl, *The Post and Courier*, November 7, 2020)

As the sun sets on Day 239 (prime!), I am immediately – but briefly, I promise - going back on last night's Missive in order to tip my hat to America and Democracy. Not red or blue, but red, white, and blue, and the privilege of the Vote. Tonight, we see the celebrations. Tomorrow, we get to work (well, tomorrow, we make popcorn; Monday, we get to work!) An RBG quote as we prepare ourselves: "Real change, enduring change, happens one step at a time." Strap on your Chuck Taylors and get steppin'! I woke to the sound / of my neighbors banging pots / and pans. It begins. Sleep tight, Campers, and wake to face the future.

As the sun sets on Day 240, I sit in the glow of the TV again, but this time, I am also basking in the glow of a really great soup. Yes, Angels, Grandma said soup. We took our first delivery of a high-ly-regarded local food box, and one of the recipes was for Potato Leek Soup. Great ingredients, solid recipe, hot soup on a sunny, windy, chilly Fall day. Yes, please! I am convinced that what they say is true: the best recipes are those with simple ingredients that just go together. It doesn't have to be fancy; it just has to go togeth-er. I feel like there's a Persistent Pea Plant lesson there somewhere. Things don't always have to be complicated; sometimes, the simple answer is the best one. I've had a similar breakthrough on the work front in the wake of the Summit. As I learned nearly two decades ago: the KISS method is usually the way to go (Keep It Simple, Stupid). So, maybe we try that this week. Keep it simple. Small steps, stepped with care. One step at a time; one day at a time. Soon, you'll look up, and There you will be! Slice, dice, peel, chop, mince, / sauté, boil, simmer, blend, sea- / son, enjoy. Yum, soup! Sleep well, Angels, and you will be ready to make a small, simple step towards your goal.

As the sun sets on Day 241 (prime!), I tip my hat to Monday. Monday, you say? Yes, Monday. Why? Because it arrived, and we are all here to enjoy it, struggle with it, survive it, crush it, celebrate it, embrace it, reject it, praise it, curse it, and all other manner of actions and reactions. Aren't we lucky? That's not sarcasm; we are lucky. Life is messy and awesome and frustrating and fun, and we get to experience it. Jump in, roll around, get your hands messy. See what you can stir up. Today is the day / I usually dread, but / not this time, Monday! Dream of changing your expectations, Campers, and wake to do it.

As the sun sets on Day 242, I sit in the glow of the TV as I bridge a short gap between no *Friends* episode and the nightly news. Guess what's on? A Lifetime Christmas movie. I have succumbed. It's kind of a nice change of pace just watching two nice people stranded in a Montana town enjoying the Christmas festival as they wait for a rescheduled flight. You know the one (or one like it). I remember traveling. And other people. And festivals. I think. I've felt a bit of a time warp over the past week or so. I'm forgetting what it's like to do certain things, and I can't tell how long it's been since I did them. It's weird, although some of it is probably due to having moved through the entire pandemic with the Summit goal in mind. That certainly gave me some benchmarks. Now, a bit of a break, until we turn towards 2021 in earnest. I think this calls for more popcorn tomorrow. Flipping through the chan- / nels, a sappy story catch- / es my eye. Lifetime. Sleep well, Angels, as visions of sugar plums dance around.

As the sun sets on Day 243, I tip my hat to our Veterans, including my brother. I'm trying to do a better job of acknowledging (and sometimes even understanding) why we have certain holidays. I really only learned a few years ago that Veterans Day is on November 11 because that had been celebrated until 1954 as "Armistice Day," which was the day World War I ended at 11am on the 11th day of the 11th month in 1918. Oh, boy...unfortunately, that reminds me of the 1918 flu pandemic which I just read lasted from February 1918 to April 1920. COVID started in February. Does that mean we are looking at April 2022? I'm really going down the numerology hole tonight. Trying to fit the chaos in neat little boxes. Hopefully, we have learned some things in the last 102 years, and we can beat this thing back in less time. It's kind of amazing the havoc that microscopic thingies can wreak (I'm pretty sure I read that in the *New England Journal of Medicine*). Keep the faith and keep things safe, Campers. A little levity, perhaps: What's the best way to avoid touching your face? A glass of wine in each hand. Sleep well, Campers, and keep it between the ditches, as my Dad likes to say.

As the sun sets on Day 244, I tip my hat to our warm, dry house. We are settling in for a week or so of classic stormy November weather. It is really nasty out there tonight. I have been feeling inexpressibly grateful for our warm, dry house and our hot dinner. Meeting one's physical needs really does make it easier to face all the other challenges of being alive. The gratitude I am feeling falls on a list of self-care moments I saw today: breathe deeply; repeat your mantra; practice gratitude; sing a song. Oh my gosh, that's only one syllable short of a haiku! One more syllable: Done. Sleep snuggly, Angels, and dig out your GORE-TEX in the morning!

As the sun sets on Day 245 (and we celebrate our 35th week together), I just want to extend some care and encouragement to all you Campers out there. I have heard from several folks this week who are feeling the weight and stress of the pandemic as it grinds on and even takes a sharp turn for the worse here in the ol' U.S. of A. I just want to say that I hear you and understand, and you are not alone. I think many of us have made the mistake of trying to pretend we can live the lives we were living in the Before Times. I don't think we can. Even if we are able to work from home and keep to ourselves, it is all around us all the time, and we can't be with our family and friends in the same way as Before. It is a lot. There will be good days and bad days. We must do what we can to keep ourselves physically and mentally healthy, and we first have to learn what that even means because none of us has gone through this before. Hang in there. Just do your best. It's OK if things aren't perfect (because they never are). If things feel out of Balance, try to do what you can to find your way back. If something is frustrating you, give yourself permission to step back. I'm trying to practice that one. A dog walk or some raking of leaves or some baking of muffins can do wonders. And sometimes, it really is that simple. And other times, it's not, but again, that's OK. Deep breath. We're all humans under a lot of stress. Find something that makes you happy, and do a whole bunch of it this weekend! It's gonna be OK. We all wandered in- / to 2020, but soon / it turned on us all. OK, wait, I should balance that one out. Finding one's way in / 2020's a challenge, / but we can do it! Dream of a few of your favorite things, Campers, and wake to do your best Julie Andrews!

WEEK #36

Saturday, November 14, 2020 – Friday, November 20, 2020

"Testing Demand Strains Public Health Systems As Clinics Are Overrun: Long Lines as U.S. Faces Record Number of Virus Infections Almost Daily" (Joseph Goldstein, Shawn Hubier and Katherine J. Wu, *The New York Times*, November 14, 2020)

"McMaster Says GOP Gains Will Boost His Agenda" (Maayan Schechter, *The State* Newspaper, November 14, 2020)

"More Than 5,100 Charleston Students Return to the Classroom For the First Time Since March" (Jenna Schiferl, *The Post and Courier*, November 14, 2020)

As the sun sets on Day 246, I tip my hat to Neighbors. Our block is gearing up for a "Map Your Neighborhood" disaster training tomorrow afternoon. We did it a number of years ago, but everyone wanted to do a refresher; we also have a few new neighbors who haven't yet had the pleasure. The woman who runs our amazing neighborhood email will facilitate, and 17 households on our block will be participating. I feel very, very lucky to live on this block where we know each other and are interested in helping one another. I'm also grateful for Zoom which will let us hold this training despite the pandemic. I've heard it said that one of the top factors for surviving a disaster is knowing your neighbors. It sounds pretty simple, but it's become less common in many places, unfortunately. Despite that, I'll bet you know at least one of your neighbors. Reach out to them, and see how they're doing. Maybe drop off a treat. We need each other. With the shitstorm that is swirling around us, we can still choose to care. That's a win-win we could all use right about now. Grab that plate of cook- / ies and stroll on over to / see what's happening. Dream of surprise deliveries, Angels, and wake to make someone's day.

As the sun sets on Day 247, I'm basking in the glow of my neighbors' willingness to look after one another. It's still out there, Campers…that thing where people are decent and looking for ways to help. I'm also tipping my hat to accountants. I'm at my computer later than I was hoping due to an accounting deadline tomorrow, but I only had to do the proofing and a few bookkeeping tweaks. I did not have to know the current IRS rules for nonprofits. Now, that is something to be grateful for tonight (actually, this morning)!! Walk the dogs, rake the / leaves, do your chores, Zoom your neigh- / bors. Quite a Sunday. Sleep peacefully, Campers, and embrace all the opportunities the week will bring.

As the sun sets on Day 248, I'm up too late again. This time, though, I was cleaning. And by cleaning, I mean cleaning out the DVR. Some of the Fall shows have started up again, and I fell prey to one of my shows. And here I am again. How is it that a Zoom training can feel like it lasts years but most days don't feel like they have enough hours? Time, you tricky devil. Time can drag. Time can / fly. I'm not sure what kind of / watch to use anymore. Rest up, Angels, and see which way time flows tomorrow.

As the sun sets on Day 249, I tip my hat to researchers. I participated in a webinar today about a new report out of UW analyzing how nonprofits are responding to COVID. It was a good project with helpful information and some interesting plans for future work. The panelists did a good job presenting the data (never an easy task), and the attendees asked good questions. In a world of sound bites, it was nice to dig in a bit. Other researchers in the news: the epidemiologists working on coronavirus vaccinations. I'm rather grateful for their work, as well. So, good job data nerds! Please keep it up. We need you. Your quantitative excellence is the exact opposite of this qualitative exercise. I suppose we need both, though. There's that balance thing again. Here's a data-driven haiku in their honor: Seven syllables / makes one poem. One per night / makes seven per week. Dream of divine data, Campers, and wake to put some out into the world, quantitative or qualitative.

As the sun sets on Day 250 (that's a nice-looking number), there is really only one thing to write about: *Wonder Woman 1984* will, in fact, be released on Christmas Day in both theaters (where applicable) and in your own home on HBO Max!! I will only ask Santa for one more thing ever. (It's HBO Max. That's the thing.) Perhaps this is something that will bring some joy to fans and families. Last Christmas, it was Star Wars IX in the theater; this year, Wonder Woman at home. That really doesn't sound too bad! So many pros, actually: unlimited and nearly free popcorn; ability to pause for a bathroom break; sitting in your favorite spot; volume control; no commute; adult beverage option; the popcorn and the bathroom thing. There might, in fact, only be one con: not sporting your WW onesie in public. 37 days to go. I'm going to need an adjusted version of the Advent calendar. I hope I can sleep tonight! Sleep soundly, Angels, and dream of being a Hero.

As the sun sets on Day 251 (prime!), I tip my hat to Kale. Well, not necessarily to kale specifically, but to healthy food generally. I like to cook, and Molly and I decided from Day 1 of this string to try to stay as healthy as possible. We had already been migrating to more veggies and less meat. Now, don't get me wrong, we are still eating meat at this point. In fact, I had some leftover Chicken Tikka Masala today (recipe from our new local food box), and we love some Italian sausage on our Friday night pizzas. I also deeply appreciate the occasional BLT which results in having leftover bacon around for various applications. However, we are preferring more veggies, and our meal kit is a veggie plan. Tonight, we had leftover kidney bean burgers (really delicious), and I made a kale salad (there's the kale; Molly loves it) and roasted carrots and parsnips. Once you learn a few tricks and you find out your favorite preparation for each veggie, they are easy and fast and oh-so-yummy. Plus, I don't have to worry about killing us by contaminating the kitchen during prep. Bonus! We are both feeling much better after our veggie fests than after many of our meat meals, too, although those meatball subs from last week will be welcomed here anytime. It is really weird how our tastebuds are evolving in such a similar manner. As the primary cook around here, I am really glad about that. So, thank you, Healthy Food. I hope you, too, find some tasty treats that you like and that make you feel good. But don't skip the pie. I mean, we're not animals. I mean, we are, but even bears go for the honey when they can get it. I'd better wrap this up; it's getting weird(er). Some people say they'd / take a pill instead of eat- / ing. That makes me sad. Dream of a rainbow of foods, Campers, and wake to make yourself something nourishing.

As the sun sets on Day 252, we celebrate our 36th week together (and Murt's birthday!) 36 weeks is 69% of one year. My, my, my. The things we have learned; the stories we have told; the haikus we have tolerated. I tip my hat to all of you and to Togetherness. I am so glad we have this forum and all our text strings and our Zooms and all those ways we are trying to stay in touch. It will serve us well. The roller coaster is still there, but aren't they more fun when someone is in your car with you? I think so. Thanks for taking this ride together. It's not the one we would have chosen (I'll take Space Mountain or the Mind Bender any day), but it's the one presented to us right now. So, strap in and get ready to laugh and scream and get that fun feeling in your tummy. And then, go eat a corn dog or a funnel cake (but maybe eat your funnel cake first because it is 2020, after all). The year goes up, the / year goes down. We take the cra- / zy ride Together. Dream of roller coasters and fair food, Angels, but don't let them mix in a dangerous way.

WEEK #37
Saturday, November 21, 2020 – Friday, November 27, 2020

"Georgia and Michigan Deliver Blows to Trump's Efforts to Undo the Election" (Richard Fausset, Nick Corasaniti, and Maggie Haberman, *The New York Times*, November 21, 2020)

"McMaster Says 'Get Tested Before Turkey' For Thanksgiving" (Maayan Schechter, *The State*, November 21, 2020)

"McMaster Pushes Virus Tests Ahead of Holiday" (Maayan Schechter and Zak Koeske, *The Rock Hill Herald*, November 21, 2020)

As the sun sets on Day 253, I tip my hat to our Bellingham Wine Group. Tonight, we celebrated our 10th Anniversary of sipping wines, nibbling nibbles, and Camp Whatchamakeit Wine Group Edition (this August would have been 8 years of Camping!) I met most of these Wine-os through Molly, many of them at a fundraiser 19 years ago now! The Group typically meets monthly, so we are really missing our gatherings at this point. However, we had to agree that it was better to "see" one another on Zoom than not to see one another at all. Friends with whom you have a deep history in terms of Time are really valuable. It is quite something to ride the roller coaster together and then keep riding it together. You all know this. This group is like that, too. I'm glad to ride with you! Open, pour, enjoy, / repeat. So go the years. Thanks / for the memories! Sleep peacefully, Campers, and wake to ride (and sip) again tomorrow!

As the sun sets on Day 254, I tip my hat to short weeks. We have arrived together at the beginning of Thanksgiving week. Good grief. Also, Hooray!! Short weeks are like the Thursdays of weeks…it's all about that anticipation. If Monday or Tuesday or Wednesday get to you, you can just revel in Thursday and, hopefully, Friday. "Who cares?" you may say if irritants arise "because Thursday is a holiday!" Thanksgiving will look different this year, but it can still be great. Look for new ways to make it special. And pass the stuffing. And pie. Don't forget the pie. Monday, Tuesday, Wednes- / day and then Thursday. You can / make it until then. Dream of cozy celebrations, Angels, and wake to tackle that shopping list.

As the sun sets on Day 255, I tip my hat to the simple – and as of late extremely infrequent – joy of marking things off one's to-do list. For the first time in I-don't-know-when, I marked off 5 of the 6 things on my work list. Were most of them simple things? Yes. Was I still excited to mark them off? Yes! Was it basically a miracle that I did so? YES! Follow that up by a dog walk and a nice Zoom with a friend who recently moved, and I am feeling pretty amazed by all I did in one day (which honestly wasn't that much). Better time management has not been seen in the Pocket Office in many, many (many!) moons. And I haven't spent all night working either. Funny thing is, the motivation was clearing things off the list in the short week in anticipation of the holiday. We are one day closer to Thursday, Campers! You think you forgot, / but then you remember. This / is how you do it. Sleep well, Campers, and keep the countdown running!

As the sun sets on Day 256, I've kept the countdown running. Checked off a big work thing; started prepping some food for the big day. I'm excited! Are you excited? Time to get excited. One day to go. And if you happen to drift away from your responsibilities tomorrow a little early, I won't tell. After all this getting ready, I fell asleep while luxuriating in my favorite supported Yoga pose in front of the TV. I was awakened by a dog in my face. Time to get up and go to bed. Roast the pumpkin, boil / the cranberries, chop the pe- / cans. Find the remote. Dream of some down time, Angels, and don't forget to defrost the turkey (if applicable).

As the sun sets on Day 257, we have made it! Tomorrow is Turkey Day. Hopefully, you are all on vacation now, either for a day or two or even four. Hooray! We did it! At our house, we have huge plans for tomorrow involving relaxation, dog walks, food, shows, and gratitudes. All day long, we will shout out (or maybe just say in a normal voice) things for which we are grateful. And there are so many, including YOU. It's funny...2020 has been such a dumpster fire, but I probably feel even more grateful this year than ever. I guess you do have to have the Dark in order to see and appreciate the Light. I wish each and every one of you the very best holiday packed full of Gratitude and family and good food and happiness. It's been a long haul. You deserve it. Relish it. Have seconds. Watch another movie. Have some more pie. 2020 has taught us that, too. Dream of a warm, cozy Turkey Day, Campers, and wake with Gratitude.

As the sun sets on Day 258 (aka Thanksgiving 2020, I tip my hat to 2020. OK, is that shocking and a bit of a stretch? Yes. However, as Turkey Day approached, quite a few friends observed that they were feeling even more grateful than usual this year. So, instead of cracking on 2020 as many of these missives have done, I'm going to turn the table and say, "Thank you, 2020, for turning every darned thing on its head. Things look very different upside down, and maybe it's not always a bad thing to stand on one's head once in a while. So, while many things you have subjected us to have been a real gut punch, even a crotch kick at times, I begrudgingly tip my hat to you and your crazy ways because I assure you I have thought and done and reflected upon many, many things that I would never ever have thought, done, or reflected upon in the Before Times." And it has only taken me 258 days to realize that. Turkey burgers, stuf- / fin' muffins, mashed pots, green beans, / hand pies. Yummy! Burp. Sleep soundly, Angels, and wake for some killer leftovers.

As the sun sets on Day 259, we celebrate our 37th week together. Anyone else laze around enjoying leftovers, another movie, and more shows? Thank goodness a dog walk and Pop Shop gym time were also involved, or I would be really worried about my health. Actually, my mental health has really benefitted from this break from the routine. It feels so good to step outside the work and the home routines and to have Molly doing that at the same time, too. It's almost like a staycation! She had a summer break, but I was worrying over the Summit; so, we haven't had this kind of down time since I can't remember when. I hope you, too, have found a break from your routines. Relax. Recharge. Get ready. We have another push until the next holiday break (including the blessed turn of the calendar to 2021!) Until then, though, take a break from the routine, and do something different. When thoughts of the work / week enter your mind, grab one / more turkey sandwich. Dream of what you'd like to do tomorrow, Campers, and wake to do it!

WEEK #38
Saturday, November 28, 2020 – Friday, December 4, 2020

"No Return to 'Normal' for the Global Economy: Facing Worst Outlook Since the Depression" (Peter S. Goodman, *The New York Times*, November 28, 2020)

"SC Reports Most COVID-19 Cases Since July; 28 Deaths This Month" (Zak Koeske, *The State*, November 28, 2020)

"CDC Says US Coronavirus Death Toll Could Reach 321K by Mid-December" (Tim Darnell, *The Atlanta Journal-Constitution/ The Rock Hill Herald*, November 28, 2020)

As the sun sets on Day 260, I think I've been left alone in the dark with the remote for too long. I'm flipping between Hallmark movies, *Hot Tub Time Machine,* and *Friends.* And *Harry Potter.* And the news. Oh, wait…it's just another night for me! Time to go read (past time, really). I hope everyone is continuing to have a good break. On our dog walk down to the water today, we saw more harbor seals lying in wait for the spawning salmon, lots of diving cormorants, and huge flocks of geese winging south. The animal kingdom is on the move! While the humans hibernate, other animals are busy. I shall emulate the bear for one more day; then, it's back to loon(y) status on Monday. Strolling along the / Bay with a dog in a cart / and wildlife all 'round. Dream of winter wonderlands, Angels, and gather your blankets around you.

As the sun sets on Day 261, our Thanksgiving respite draws to a close. Rather than feeling the Sunday Blues, though, I feel gratitude tonight. I actually felt like I had time to step out of the routine and relax a bit. Perhaps all weekends should be four days long! Two days just doesn't feel like enough. I'd even take three; I'm not greedy. Next, I will play the "how long will this good feeling last" game. It often dissipates by around mid-day Monday, but I'm going to shoot for Tuesday this time. Maybe even mid-afternoon Tuesday! We'll see. It's mostly up to me. Challenge (realistically) accepted! Sleep like a bear for one more night, Campers, and wake to live like a loon!

As the sun sets on Day 262, I am wondering how my Loony Angels did today on our first day back. I did better than expected, probably due to the fact that I slept longer than usual last night. I also stuck to a question I am trying to ask more often during the workday: "What do you WANT to get done today?" I like this question because it puts my focus on wanting to do something and not feeling like I have to do something. I also like it because I can apply it to things I want to do, as well as to things that I don't really want to do but would like to mark off the list. I may not like the thing, but I still want to do it because then I don't have to worry about it anymore. It seemed to work today; I'll try it again tomorrow. If you have a list, / just try to tackle it with / determination. (I feel like that last one-word stanza is worth a Scrabble bonus or something. That's a first!) Dream of the fun you had and the fun you will have, Angels, and wake one day closer to your next holiday!

As the sun sets on Day 263 (Spicoli's birthday!!), I tip my hat to asking what you WANT to get done. I tried it again today. Turns out, I wanted to bake again. Did I do some work and walk the dogs? Yes. But smack dab in the middle of the day, I baked. Using some of the pumpkin purée I made last week, I tackled a legendary family recipe: our long-time neighbor's Harvest Loaf. Bonus: chocolate chips are involved. Double Bonus: it makes two big loaves. Thank you, long-time neighbor, and your beautiful, delicious Harvest Loaf. It is so good I suspect I will need to head to the Pop Shop Gym very soon. But it will be worth it. Work it, walk it, bake / it. Do what you want to do. / It's all on the list. Dream of your favorite loaf, Campers, and wake and bake (haha).

As the sun sets on Day 264, I am pleasantly surprised that my refreshed attitude has carried me all the way through Hump Day. We are having lots of sunshine, and I am certain that is helping. It's a little colder, too, and I like a cold, sunny day now. Gonna need all that dog walkin' and more to work off that Loaf. Gonna need all these good vibes to get through a couple more Zoom events, including one on Sunday. Better go get some sleep. As soon as I see if Harmony ends up with Luke in this Lifetime Christmas movie. I really think they're gonna end up together. And I'm pretty sure they're going to sing a duet, too. It's amazing what / some sunshine can do for your / mood. That, and some Loaf. Sleep sweetly, Angels, and wake to some sunshine, real or in your noggin.

As the sun sets on Day 265, I tip my hat to free grocery store pick-up. I'm kind of obsessed. I may never go into the store again. My brother remarked that he still likes to push the cart and browse. I admit I have enjoyed that pastime myself. However, since we used to practice the French form of grocery shopping (i.e. we went to the store almost every damn day and shopped for one or two meals at a time based on how we were feeling, plus essentials), I think I did enough cart pushing for a lifetime. Then, there were the days that we forgot stuff, so we went back a second time. One time, we were baking, and I think we went 4 times in one day between the two of us. That's not good math. Thank goodness that particular store is in walking distance. For now, I will take the pickup option every day of the week (except I only go to the store every couple of weeks now, so I'll take it once every two weeks). If you need me Sat- / urday morning, I'll be pick- / ing up an order. Dream of dancing carts, Campers, and wake to place your order.

As the sun sets on Day 266, we celebrate our 38th week together. Huh?? Yowser, that's a few weeks. 73% of one year. 99 more days, and we'll hit our year anniversary. Geez, that means we're only 99 days away from early March. Hardly seems possible. Well, let's not wish the time away! We have the winter holiday season for our entertainment and diversion, including ringing in a New Year (yay!!) Trees and lights are going up all around our neighborhood. I hear the PSL is back at Starbucks. Black Friday and Cyber Monday have come and gone. Shoppers are panicking about shipping delays. Snow is flying in many places. It's getting colder, and the sun is rising later and setting earlier. It's kind of amazing that there are many predictable things about our annual trip around the sun. I mean, what if every little thing were completely random? There is some comfort in our seasonal cycles. It's nice to pull out the hoodies and slippers and fleece and do a little hibernating. Time to rest and look inward and regroup. Not a bad tradition. Pull your blankie up / and think about where you've been / and where you're going. Sleep snuggly, Angels, and dream of your path ahead.

WEEK #39

"Hiring Tapers Off As Virus Tightens Grip on Economy: Fewer New Jobs for 5th Straight Month" (Patricia Cohen, *The New York Times*, December 5, 2020)

"For British Prime Minister, a Week to Exorcise the Year's Demons: Most Deaths in Europe, and Last Lockdowns" (Mark Landler, *The New York Times*, December 5, 2020)

"COVID-19 Pandemic Forces Closure of All State Jury Trials" (John Monk, *The State*, December 5, 2020)

As the sun sets on Day 267, I am nursing an unfortunate knee injury, as many of you know. Thank you for all the good wishes! I'm just getting this new development into the record. I am struck mainly by two things: 1) I'm amazed this was an innocent "non-contact" injury that occurred during a brisk, straight-ahead walk with Wally. No twisting; nothing stupid or risky. Just a stride and a pop in front of the next-door neighbor's house. I almost made it! In a weird way, this has made it a little easier to accept. Between a college injury, many predictable flare-ups over the years, and a recent new mystery symptom, along with a decline in Yoga and cycling around Summit time, it's not a total shock. Still hurts, though. 2) I'm kind of surprised how much it hurts. Luckily, it's OK when I'm off my feet, but it is really painful when walking around. I've had muscular and nerve stuff with my low back and shoulder over the years, but it's been a long time since I had a big joint issue. Ouch. Oh, I guess there's a third thing, too: my world had already shrunk considerably in the COVID times, and I can't believe it just shrank some more (also, "shrank" is a weird word). I'm just glad I'm not angry and depressed like my knee problems usually make me. 2020 has toughened me up, I guess! Of course this happened; it's 2020! Oh, well…I'm just going to figure out how to enjoy modified versions of the three things that keep me going: Yoga, dog walking, and cooking. Good thing we own crutches (although, that's also a clue about us, I guess). I may need to "borrow" one of those motorized scooters from the grocery store. I actually used one of those at Costco years ago after foot surgery. I whined about it until I started driving it around. I had way too much fun with it. It really parts the crowds in the toilet paper aisle! Stay safe and healthy, Campers. It's not a great time for ailments. I know some of you are dealing with similar, so I wish you well. Sometimes, you're just in- / nocently walking your pup / when something goes pop. Sleep restoratively, Campers, and wake to care for yourself.

As the sun sets on Day 268, I tip my hat to volunteer planning committee members who are willing to Zoom for 4 hours on a

Sunday. Well, that's pretty specific. How about we just tip our hats to Volunteers generally? I see lots of good being done lately; I think the holiday spirit is kicking in. The pandemic can't keep that down; maybe it's even promoting more. Yet another way 2020 is the worst and…well, maybe not the best but…different and surprising. Silver linings. Like virtual Summits. No hugs or Indian Taco trucks but more accessibility and options for introverts. I see your double edge, Sword! Also like a bum knee…hurts like a mutha but someone cooks dinner for you. Sometimes, Sunday is / for working, but the people / are so nice, it's fine. Sleep well, Angels, and wake to find the silver lining on your Monday (it's there).

As the sun sets on Day 269, I tip my hat to Curiosity. Today, I found myself thinking about turning the calendar over and stepping into the New Year. Then, I found myself feeling Curious about what lies ahead. I was pleasantly surprised to feel Curiosity and not something else, like Dread. Seems like a good sign. I haven't felt a lot of Curiosity lately. It's been more about Worry and Anxiety and Frustration. Things feel like they're shifting, though. Those other things are there, but new things are crowding them out a bit. I think we've settled more into our Next Normal; the election and the vaccines make it feel like new things may be coming. No one knows how good or bad those new things will be, but they'll be different. And I think "different from 2020" is a very good thing. Gimping around the / house thinking different thoughts. / Well, hi, there, New Year! Dream of a captivating future, Campers, because we could all use one.

As the sun sets on Day 270, I tip my hat to our neighborhood leader. She included a couple sentences that she wrote entitled "When I Cry" in today's email. I've been pondering it since I read it. I offer it up here in case you want to ponder it, too: "If, when I cry, I rigorously point my mind towards the goodness of this world, the goodness of other humans, and my own goodness, every teardrop that falls is a piece of confusion falling away forever. Crying as a victim is less helpful than crying in determination on my way out." That's it tonight. Just that to ponder. Sleep soundly, Angels, and rest your ponderer for tomorrow.

As the sun sets on Day 271, I find my mind wandering to Christmas break. Seven more school days to go. I'm ready. My work is a little slower right now – so much so that I started tackling the filing cabinet today – but Molly is still full-steam ahead. That is really cramping my holiday vibe (and hers, too, I imagine). Perhaps I will distract myself with a holiday haiku: Lifetime or Hallmark / or maybe *Home Alone*? Some- / one pass the eggnog. Dream of sugar plums, Campers, and wake another day closer.

As the sun sets on Day 272, I tip my hat to anniversaries. Today happens to be one of our (mine and Molly's) anniversaries. I say "one of" because we have several anniversaries that reflect the long road to equal marriage rights. Today's is a very important one in that series in that it was the final step, it was in our own state, and it granted us full and equal rights, including hospital visits, joint filing of Federal income tax returns, and hundreds of other things married couples too often take for granted. Eight years ago today (12.10.12), we were legally married in the great State of Washington. It came eight years and nine months after our first attempt down in Portland, Oregon (3.19.04). Long story for another time, but that one was struck down by the courts a few weeks later, and they refunded our marriage license fee. Pretty awful. Then, we went through years of baby steps at The State and federal levels (domestic partnership, etc., etc.). Pretty frustrating...but headed in the right direction. Finally, the big event we remember today. Someday, I'll show you the PowerPoint, if you're interested. And the banner. Pretty cool. So, here's to Washington State and our friends and Molly!! We celebrated with a normal work day, Door-Dash, and our programs. In fact, this is now also the anniversary of when we finished watching *Parks and Rec* in its entirety for the second time. Tonight's topical haiku is based on a cartoon Molly found during our journey down the long road: One step forward, two / steps back. Gay marriages al- / ways take forever. Haha! I like that one. It's easier to laugh now. I just hope it stays that way. Dream of your best wedding dance, Angels, and wake to cut a rug!

As the sun sets on Day 273, we celebrate our 39th week together. We have hit the 75% (of one year) mark! I'm not sure what to say about that. Instead, I shall attempt the Little Sebastian haiku that one of our gentle readers requested this morning: Bye Bye Little Se- / bastian. A great song about / a great little horse. Or, perhaps this one? People of Pawnee / know the truth: there's only one / Little Sebastian. Or, maybe third time's a charm? Short of stature but / a true giant of Pawnee: / Little Sebastian. Simple takes, but I hope you enjoy them. (I guess that's the essence of a haiku!) I'm glad to make it to this Friday night with you all. Thanks for continuing to make this journey a little bit easier. Another thing that might help? Some breaking news! The Food and Drug Administration just authorized the first COVID-19 vaccine for emergency use. Thank you, Pfizer and BioNTech who are reporting 95% efficacy in people 16 and older using new messenger RNA tech in a two-dose regimen. [Just getting this into the record since it is a(n) historic moment.] We just need CDC recommendation, likely tomorrow, and we can start sticking arms. It is nine months to the day since the WHO declared a pandemic. Thank you, scientists! Thank you, drug trial volunteers! Thank you, STEM education! I'm really glad you all exist. I have tried to do my part while you worked...by staying at home, masking up when I don't, doing grocery pickups, and watching lots of TV. You know, I guess I really am a patriot! Haha. See you in the vaccination line. Next summer or so. Dream of needles, Campers, unless you have trypanophobia.

WEEK #40

Saturday, December 12, 2020 – Friday, December 18, 2020

"A Divided and Distrustful U.S. Awaits Vaccines: Many Are Eager, But Push is On to Win Over the Wary" (Simon Romero and Miriam Jordan, *The New York Times*, December 12, 2020)

"South Carolina Reports Record 3,137 COVID-19 Cases, 42 Deaths In a Single Day" (Zak Koeske, *The State*, December 12, 2020)

"40 Charged in 'Sprawling Criminal Enterprise' In, Outside SC State Prisons" (John Monk, *The Rock Hill Herald*, December 12, 2020)

As the sun sets on Day 274, I bask in the glow of holiday movies. We don't always decorate a lot – it depends on the year – but I am embracing holiday entertainment this year (because it's a pandemic, and I'm injured; so, pass the remote, please). We are covering a wide range, from Disney to *Die Hard* and from *Elf* to Lifetime. It's fun, and who doesn't need a little fun right now? We also dipped into the HBO Max pool since they have all the *Die Hard* movies, so we're now ready – really, REALLY ready – for *Wonder Woman 1984* on Christmas Day. Twelve days to go (and today's date is 12/12, so that has to mean something, right?) I think it means I still have 12 days to go. Too bad I never implemented my Wonder Woman Advent Calendar idea. That woulda been cool. Maybe I'll just eat a chocolate a day until then and call it good. I heard tonight somewhere along the media way that our communities have become closer this year. Wouldn't it be something if our slowing down has made us more aware of and engaged with our neighbors? All those years of bemoaning the idea that no one knows their neighbors anymore. Could this be another silver lining? Let's hope! Basking in the glow / again; gotta get to bed. / French toast in the morn. Dream of Sunday breakfast, Angels, and wake to dig in.

As the sun sets on Day 275, I'm internalizing one of the main messages of *Elf*. As we all know, Santa's sleigh is powered by Christmas Spirit, but the Clausometer has been known to dip very low at times. We just need to Believe, folks (and sing loud for all to hear, of course). We believe Santa will come; we believe the animals will talk on Christmas Eve (well, I do); we believe in each other; we believe things are going to get better. And if we don't believe those things, we should try because Santa needs our help. If you're not feeling it, try singing out loud for all to hear. Even if you don't start believing, you will amuse yourself and, likely, others. Spread the Christmas cheer, Campers, and start Believin' because we could use a bunch of both this year! Sleep sweetly, Campers, and dream of reindeer and cookies.

As the sun sets on Day 276, I tip my hat, at long last, to a day truly worth celebrating (December 14, 2020). Among the highlights: delivery and administration of the first COVID-19 vaccine; members of the Electoral College cast their ballots (to be formally counted on January 6 during a joint session of Congress); Olive, our canine matriarch, celebrated her golden birthday; we mark what would have been BKS Iyengar's 102nd birthday (he founded the school of Yoga that I study and was one of *Time's* most influential people in the world). That is honestly a list worth celebrating. And you deserve it! Celebrate; feel good; believe things are improving. The day dawned with one / great thing on the calendar. / Many more followed. Sleep deeply, Angels, because this was one big day!

As the sun sets on Day 277, I reflect on the fact that some nights, I think back over my entire day to see what profound gems might be hidden among the hours; other nights, it's just the very latest shiny thing that jets out of my fingertips. Tonight, my head is decidedly experiencing the latter. Right now, I am feeling very excited for the *Wonder Woman 1984* premiere on Christmas Day. I just updated an Evite to neighbors and local friends that has been rattling around since February 19. It has gone through several updates as the release date was pushed from June 5 to August 14 to October 2 to December 25. And so went my 2020…one disappointment after another. Well, I mean, there were lots of other things mixed in there, plenty of them good, but it's been a real roller coaster for me and WW. I'm needing some of that fun and inspiration that a good '80s-style movie can provide. Remember those? Fun!! We could all use some! And even if your fun and inspiration comes in a different form on Christmas Day, go for it! No better year to lean into the holidays than this one. Sleep lots; eat, drink, and watch all your faves; snuggle all those in your bubble; believe that next Christmas will be different. Or, maybe you decide it should be the same! Silver bells; silver / linings. I can't stop grinning. / Who says I have to? Dream of your faves, Campers, and hang your stockings with care.

As the sun sets on Day 278, I tip my hat to our Farmer and our Baker. Last week, I picked up our last veggie box of the season. Our subscription started waaay back on May 20 (the day the Summit was supposed to have opened, actually). I can hardly remember May, although I do recall feeling much more stressed out and not sleeping as well. Progress. I have no doubt those veggies helped, too. Today, I picked up our last 2 loaves of bread from a baker who delivers to our neighborhood. We started our bread runs even before our veggie runs (April 1, but it ain't been no joke). This bread is the real deal and never makes me feel icky like store bread does at times. I feel so lucky to live in this decidedly non-food-desert corner of the world. At the very beginning of the pandemic, Molly and I decided our only job was to stay out of the hospital; so, we upped our nutrition game, and I am convinced it has really helped. I think we're eating better now than ever. I guess I've had more time and desire to put towards it. I wonder if some of our new habits will stick once we can poke our heads out of our caves. Things will get busy again; restaurants will beckon, both for speed and for socializing; humans tend to drift from what's good for them. Well, we'll see. For now, pass the bread and Brussels sprouts. Walk four blocks to bread; / go two more for veggies. Eat / and be well tonight. Dream of all your new habits, Angels, and wake to keep them going.

As the sun sets on Day 279, I tip my hat to Connie Thompson. Who's Connie, you might ask? She is a Seattle news reporter who retired today…after a 46-year career with the same network! I've watched her for about half of her career (and I come from a family that gets very attached to their news people), and I am so impressed by what she's accomplished. Her co-workers honored her during the 6pm newscast; one asked her what she learned over the course of her long career. I really liked her answer. She said she learned that everyone has a story and that even if you can't come up with a solution, most people just want to be heard. I thought that was a great message to share. So, congratulations and thanks, Connie! Immersed in a Zoom / training, there arose such a / clatter. Walter snores. Sleep sweetly, Campers, and wake to another freaky Friday.

As the sun sets on Day 280, we celebrate our 40th week together. Those are some nice-lookin' even numbers. And 2 times 40 is 80. I'll stop. So, a friend observed recently that the haikus don't just write themselves. Well, tonight it'll have to because I'm going to go drink eggnog and watch a holiday movie. Or *Fargo*. I haven't decided. Oh, wait...I lied. One just came to me: One week until Won- / der Woman. Wonder if I'll / be able to sleep. There! The week is done. See ya tomorrow. I'll do better. I hope. Sleep peacefully, Angels, and enjoy your long winter's nap.

WEEK #41

Saturday, December 19, 2020 – Friday, December 25, 2020

"Moderna Vaccine Is Second To Get Cleared by F.D.A.: Nearly 6 Million Doses" (Denise Grady, Abby Goodnough, and Noah Weiland, *The New York Times*, December 19, 2020)

"Suit Over Dining Ban: Restaurant Industry Pushes Baltimore City, Two Other Counties to Reopen by Christmas" (Christina Tkacik, *The Baltimore Sun*, December 19, 2020)

"Delays Abound Amid Virus, Historic Holiday Mail Volume" (Christine Condon, *The Baltimore Sun*, December 19, 2020)

As the sun sets on Day 281, I'm bummed because I had this really profound thought while vacuuming today (was it, really, though? let's just say it was for the sake of the Missive), and now, I can't remember what it was! I am devastated to cheat you out of what was surely a precious gem of insight and observation. Only one thing to do in this case…some holiday jokes! What happens if you eat Christmas decorations? You get tinselitus! Why do mummies like Christmas so much? Because of all the wrapping! What does an elf study in school? The elfabet! Where does a snowman keep his money? In a snow bank! What is every parent's favorite Christmas carol? Silent Night. What did one snowman say to the other? Do you smell carrots?! What's another name for Santa's Little Helpers? Subordinate Clauses! What falls but never gets hurt? Snow! Whew!! I hope you can breathe from all the laughing. It's always a good policy to end (or begin) the day with some laughter. Dream of great punchlines, Campers, and wake with a great big smile.

As the sun sets on Day 282, I tip my hat to the firmament above. All you NASA nerds probably know this already, but I recently learned that a truly stellar (haha) celestial event is occurring tomorrow on the Winter Solstice. Prepare yourselves for Jupiter and Saturn's GREAT CONJUNCTION!! This is literally the Christmas Star, people! EarthSky.org explains: "Jupiter-Saturn conjunctions happen every 20 years; the last one was in the year 2000. But these conjunctions aren't all created equal. *The 2020 great conjunction of Jupiter and Saturn will be the closest since 1623 and the closest observable since 1226!* 2020's extra-close Jupiter-Saturn conjunction won't be matched again until the Jupiter-Saturn conjunction of March 15, 2080." So, take your eyeballs and your telescopes if you have them, and point them towards the western/southwestern sky just after sunset for a real treat. If it's cloudy, watch online. This is a big one, people. Go outside and be Amazed! Dream of the cosmos, Angels, and wake to witness its mysteries.

As the sun sets on Day 283, we celebrate the Christmas Star and revel in the mysteries of the cosmos, whether seen with the naked eye or via the interwebs. What a day! The Great Conjunction; the Winter Solstice; torrential rain; snow; Grandma Eppard's birthday; 4 days until *Wonder Woman*. I mean, that's a big day! I hope everyone is chugging away, whether at work, at play, or at Christmas preps (or all three). If you get bogged down, just remember that the days are only getting longer now! Look to the skies and / find the Christmas spirit in / your eyes and your heart. Sleep peacefully, Campers, because the big day is coming, and anticipation is fun.

As the sun sets on Day 284, I ponder the dawning of the Age of Aquarius. A friend pointed out that some believe yesterday's Great Conjunction heralded in the Age of Aquarius. I went down a bit of a rabbit hole looking into this idea. Interestingly, no one knows exactly when this astrological age began (or will begin). I did learn, however, that an astrological age lasts for 2160 years, on average. This number is the result of dividing one "Great Year" (i.e. the Earth's 25,920-year "period of precession," or rotation of its axis) by the 12 signs of the zodiac. Some believe that with the dawning of the Age of Aquarius, the world will enter a new age of peace, love, and light unlike the current Age of Pisces. That's about all I can say about it at this point, although I can also say that the song from *Hair* is now stuck in my head, which is fine because I've always liked it. Rotate on your ax- / is, bring some peace, love, and light / into your practice. Dream of constellations and their slow but persistent march across the heavens, Angels, and wake to another sunrise as the earth keeps on spinning. (That might've been a little much, but I do love some star talk.)

As the sun sets on Day 285, the excitement grows. Work winds down, temporarily at least; cooking and wrapping and anticipation ramp up. Tomorrow is Christmas Eve. I've grown to love Christmas Eve as much or more than Christmas Day. All the preps, all the anticipation; then, after all the hubbub and maybe a holiday movie, a quiet moment before bedtime, perhaps with a small glass of Christmas cheer, gazing at the lights of the Christmas tree (this year, more specifically, the lights on the Christmas Ficus Tree... which I just learned is also called a Weeping Fig). I will also glance over at our Charlie Brown Christmas tree, complete with one red ball and Linus's blanket. It is perhaps the greatest gift Molly has ever given me, and it will forever be my favorite Christmas tree. There's simply no improving it; it is Perfect as it is. Then, there's a legend I love that says the animals speak at midnight on Christmas Eve. I shall perform my annual test again tomorrow while gazing at the lights. I'm quite certain Olive and Walter speak to me, but I'm not always smart enough or auditorily gifted enough to hear them. But, I'll try again. Let's get ready! It's time to soak up the spirit. All the preps, all the / excitement gather now at / the foot of the tree. Sleep well, Campers, and wake to a couple great days!

As the sun sets on Day 286, I tip my Christmas Tree hat to... CHRISTMAS EVE!! It's kind of like Buddy the Elf and smiling... it's my Favorite! It has been so fun reading about what family and friends have been doing today. So many brave Elves making the best of a different kind of Christmas. I tip my hat to you, too, Elves! Maybe a little more of that genuine Christmas spirit is flying around this year. Another Silver Lining. Silver Bells bring Silver Linings. Now, I must away to bed because I think some movie comes out tomorrow that we have plans to watch. Plus, I want Santa to come, although he already brought me the only thing I'll ever ask him for again (HBO Max is the thing). I may try to last another half-hour and have a quick chat with Olive and Walter. They'll probably just ask me to give them some of the roast chicken (more specifically, 2-day beer brined, spatchcock roasted, marinated pan-fried chicken sandwiches with oven fries & blistered Brussels sprouts). I imagine they'll skip the sprouts. Elves with projects; elves / cooking; elves watching movies. / Elves make me smiley. Dream of those sugar plums, Angels, because this is the actual night to do it, and wake to a day that feels just a little bit more Special.

As the sun sets on Day 287 (our 41st week together!), I tip my brand-new Wonder Woman cape (yes, you read that correctly…I said "c-a-p-e"!) to Christmas Day, COVID-style. It was a real 2020 mix of craptacular (a close friend over on my college string was part of the emergency response to the Nashville bombing) and silver-lining spectacular (two extremely-long-awaited viewings of my favorite superhero did not disappoint). We also enjoyed good food and champagne, an impromptu trip to a friend's to deliver a special surprise, and fun FaceTimes with family and friends. All you Hero Elves out there making do. I hope you, too, discovered some new fun amidst the weirdness. I think that's called Resilience, Campers. I know I stared at my phone for a few extra seconds this morning when I saw "December 25" on the screen. If you'd asked me about 250 days ago, I might not have believed Christmas would ever come. But it came. It came just the same. And I'm so glad it did. I have a feeling it was more about people than presents for many Hero Elves this year. Silver linings. Pick up the paper / and bows, and bask in the lights. / Merry Christmas, y'all. Dream of Christmases past, present, and future, Campers, and smile knowing they'll come.

WEEK #42

Saturday, December 26, 2020 – Friday, January 1, 2021

"Poorer Nations At Back of Line for The Vaccine: Unequal Distribution Is Increasing Disparity" (Peter S. Goodman, *The New York Times*, December 26, 2020)

"Nashville Blast Called Deliberate: Recorded Warning Heard From RV Before Morning Explosion; Three Injured, But None Critical, As Flights Grounded at Airport" (Kimberlee Kruesi and Thalia Beaty, *The Baltimore Sun*, December 26, 2020)

"This Is My Home: Longtime Baltimore Neighborhood Leader Among Thousands of Marylanders Facing Eviction Amid Pandemic" (Angela Roberts, *The Baltimore Sun*, December 26, 2020)

As the sun sets on Day 288, I tip my hat to Boxing Day (whatever that is). Actually, it turns out the day has many meanings. The primary two seem to be a shopping day and, on the other side of the coin (haha), a day to give to the poor and service providers (turns out that one comes from the old "alms box"). So, take your pick (or pick both), and put on your gloves; time for some Boxing (Day) spirit. Boxing Day. What is / it? No one really knows. Shop, / or give, or do both. Sleep soundly, Angels, because hopefully, you've been playing with all your presents today.

As the sun sets on Day 289, my eye is wandering over to the remote. Perhaps I will just play a little bit of the movie. Just a bit. Just to remember how good it feels to see others doing good. And to hear that voice. Maybe. Probably. We are nearing the end of our current favorite show (at least until the final season comes out, hopefully next year), and we were previewing a few new shows to see what might come next. They were all violent and depressing or just not very interesting. So, I feel dirty and need a hit of WW. I was so good yesterday, but it is calling me ever so softly but also insistently. So, I will answer. Be sure to tap in to whatever makes you feel better, and gear up for the last four days of the year. My, that sounds pretty good! Sitting here wrapping / up the day, but one thing re- / mains. Better hit Play. Sleep well, Campers, and wake with the finish line in sight.

As the sun sets on Day 290, I'm feeling Quiet. Believe it or not, it does happen, and more than you might think, my captive audience. Lots of activity lately; lots of excitement; lots of noise. So, we take a beat and exhale. Rest and regroup so that you're ready. Ebb and flow. The waves come in; the waves wash out. Sometimes, you just need / to sit quietly. Enjoy / all the benefits. Sleep peacefully, Angels, and enjoy the silence.

As the sun sets on Day 291, I tip my hat to Vitamin G. That G is for Gratitude. The woman who owns the Yoga studio I frequent shared a holiday message, and it was focused on a Ted Talk by a Sri Lankan woman who has discovered the "Magic Pill of Bliss": the words "Thank You." She says Thank You to 50-100 things or people every day, either out loud or to herself, and she finds it takes her from anxiety to bliss. My Yoga teacher has started doing this, too, and observed that there are thousands of things to be grateful for every single day. One way to look at it is that each Thank You creates a vibration or energy, and that energy of gratitude then creates a connection between you and that person or thing; enter Bliss. Science backs this up, as it has shown that gratitude strengthens our immune systems. Our minds more easily turn to negativity and worry; actively focusing on gratitude instead strengthens our ability to focus on the positive and shift our whole lives around. That's the idea anyway. Pretty cool. It's as easy as saying Thank You. A lot. And sincerely. Let's give it a shot. There's nothing to lose and Bliss to gain. Sleep blissfully, Campers, and wake to give thanks.

As the sun sets on Day 292, I tip my hat to waving good-bye to 2020 forever. Tomorrow is New Year's Eve, and I haven't been this glad about it since 1999. Let's wrap this one up and turn the page. One year that felt like / ten years. Let's toast to a new / beginning for all. Dream of fresh starts, Angels, and dust off your coupes and flutes!

As the sun sets on Day 293 (our 293rd day together…haha!), I tip my hat to friends, fun, aspirations, and the NEW YEAR!!! Hallelujah, the New Year has arrived!! While tipping my hat to all the Silver Linings of 2020 (and I admit, there were Many, friends!), I am still VERY glad to be turning the calendar. I tip my hat to friends who will watch a certain movie with me just because they know who much it means to me, and I hope they enjoy it, too! Besides giving some Thanks, though, I can't do much better than to point you to our neighborhood leader who is a guitarist and singer. Skip to 2:12 if you want to just hear the round. It goes on for a bit, but it makes sense in the end. Just enjoy, and I'll see you in the New Year! https://www.dropbox.com/s/xzstlt256ky0uor/PSGW%20 NYE%20Song.mp4?dl=0 Sleep deeply, Campers, and know that when you wake, we've been given a new beginning.

As the sun sets on Day 294, we celebrate the arrival of a New Year. Today is the first day of 2021. I always like January 1. It really does feel like a new beginning. Some years, it's about resolutions; some years, it's the Polar Plunge (not this year); other years, it's traveling home from visiting family after a busy holiday season. This year, though, I find myself less harried and less pressured because for all its innumerable frustrations, last year (oooh, it feels so good to call it that) taught me a lot about what's important and what isn't so important. There was a lot more reflecting along the way, so I feel more in tune with things I want to change, things I want to maintain, things I want to add. And I feel like I will have the time to do those things, if and when I choose. I feel like I have a clearer head than many other years (plus, I'm not sick from traveling). I'm feeling curious and ready, and I'm pacing myself. We still have many challenges ahead, but we've been tested. Now (hopefully), we're rested. So, let's enjoy every minute of this final holiday weekend before getting after it. Together. Sleep well, Angels, and wake to shape your New Year.

WEEK #43

Saturday, January 2, 2021 – Friday, January 8, 2021

"In Blow to Trump Senate Overrides Defense Bill Veto: A First as His Presidency Nears an End - Only 7 Republicans Vote No" (Catie Edmonson, *The New York Times*, January 2, 2021)

"On New Year's Day, Virus's 2nd-highest Tally" (Christine Tkacik, *The Baltimore Sun*, January 2, 2021)

"Making a Positive Out of a Negative: A Local County Offers Antibody Tests to All Its Employees" (Alison Knezevich, *The Baltimore Sun*, January 2, 2021)

As the sun sets on Day 295, I'm thinking about the phrases "work with what you've got" and "let things come to you." Last year involved quite a bit of struggle and frustration for me. Instead of fighting everything, I'm going to try some acceptance instead... and then, figure out a way around! The struggling is hard and noisy and usually not very productive. Acceptance might quiet things down so the situation can be tackled. It's easy to say right now when things are pretty quiet and we're coming off the holidays. Can I do it when things get noisy again? We'll see. Nothing's wrong with being a little aspirational. That's all heavier than I intended. How about a joke? Where can you go to practice math on New Year's Eve? Times Square! What's the best New Year's resolution? 1080p. And finally...Not to brag, but I already have a date for next New Year's Eve...December 31. Sleep with a grin on your face, Campers, if you can muster one after that round.

As the sun sets on Day 296, our holiday season draws to a close. Rather than feeling blue, though, I feel more rested than after most holidays and really ready for something different. The new year will have its challenges to be sure, but we've been taught that time can move at different rates; the long game is more apparent now. We've hibernated, played within our safe bubbles, and streamed like crazy. Time to get after it again, and as we do, we have some memories to look back on, hopefully with a smile, that will propel us into a new year. So, take the wisdom of the Warrior Women, the sparrow, the curious monkey, the persistent pea plant, and the whole Peanuts gang and draw upon it as you put something good out into the world. Just try. It's worth it. Think back fondly as / you prep for the future, but / stay in the present. Dream of the year you'd like to see, Angels, and wake to take the first step.

As the sun sets on Day 297, I tip my hat to steady rain and shakshuka (Arabic for "mixture"). The steady rain made it much, much easier to stay indoors and focus on my to-do list for the first day back at it. The shakshuka made it much, much easier to warm up afterwards. Ever since shakshuka started showing up on cooking shows and in stories about trendy brunches, I've wanted to make one. Thanks to our local box, tonight was the night. I learned that it's a very popular dish throughout the Mediterranean, particularly Israel, that involves poaching eggs in a spiced tomato and pepper sauce. Turns out it's easy and very satisfying. I love learning new tricks. Checking things off the list can be satisfying. Just add rain. Rain plus tomatoes / and eggs equals a nice way / to start the New Year. Dream of new tricks, Campers, and wake to learn one!

As the sun sets on Day 298, I reflect somewhat sheepishly on the extraordinarily high level of procrastination that occurred around here today. And by "around here" I mean my office and other environs; Molly seemed fine. Sadly but not surprisingly, my Dad's health continues to degrade, and he has to go back to the hospital on Thursday for another periodic procedure. Between his failing health and the COVID numbers there, this trip feels even more dicey than the previous ones. So, I found it hard to buckle down today, hence the procrastination. Not all was lost, though. While a significant portion of my work was left until a few hours ago, we do have clean sheets and a clean bedroom floor. And we had another good dinner from our local box (Thai Noodle Salad this time). So, rather than beat myself up, I'm going to celebrate the fact that I got anything at all done today. Sometimes, you just have to adjust your plans. Procrastination: / Avoiding your To-Do List. / Procrastination. Dream of whatever you want, Angels, because you shouldn't procrastinate on those.

As the sun sets on Day 299, some of our number have been re-thinking their Dry January aspirations; others have been re-thinking their resolution not to use the "dumpster fire" descriptor this year. Besides being the Feast of the Epiphany, today was the Electoral College certification turned Capitol riot. I found those events to be excruciatingly stressful. At the same time, my Dad's failing health has grown more acute, and he has another hospital procedure tomorrow morning. So, not a great day to say the least. Except, Campers, amidst all that, there was still a Silver Lining. What could it possibly have been? It was Y'ALL!! Thank you for all the support, past, present, and future. I feel like last year brought us together and tested us. As a result, I feel supported and more prepared. I hope that's been a two-way street. No jokes or haikus tonight; just a quiet prayer for all of us. Sleep well.

As the sun sets on Day 300, I'm just staring at that number. Not sure what to say. It's a nice rounded number; lots of curves; no sharp edges. Good grief, it's a big number when you're talking lockdowns and nightly missives! *300* is also a movie (with a sequel), but I've never seen it. I just Googled it and was reminded that it's about the Battle of Thermopylae between the Spartans and the Persians. Sounds about right. Three hundred nights to- / gether. Eighty-two percent / of a crazy year. Dream of the passage of time, Angels, and wake to have experienced it.

As the sun sets on Day 301, we welcome in a new Wine Club over on the college friends' string. This momentous occasion coincides with our 43rd week anniversary. 43, people. 43. Prime number. 43. OK, at this point, I'm not sure if I'm still shocked or just stalling. In the Wine Club book we are using, each month is a different varietal. January, to my distinct pleasure, is Champagne which I happen to love. Once Champagne and Popcorn became the official Snack Combo of our *Wonder Woman* screenings, I made an important two-stage New Year's Resolution a couple years ago: Always keep some Champagne in the fridge, and don't be afraid to open it. Those words of wisdom are offered up in the same spirit as "carpe diem" and "Life is short; eat dessert first." You don't have to save your faves for a special occasion; another way to look at it is that every day has something worth celebrating. So, what's your fave? Be sure to do it, eat it, drink it, watch it, paint it, ride it, walk it, whatever it TODAY. Nothing's guaranteed, so don't wait. It's OK to enjoy life. Dream of something that makes you happy, Campers, and wake to lay your plans.

WEEK #44
Saturday, January 9, 2021 – Friday, January 15, 2021

"House Prepares Articles of Impeachment: Pelosi Says Trump Has to Go Now - He Maintains a Defiant Tone" (Nicholas Fandos, Maggie Haberman, and Luke Broadwater, *The New York Times*, January 9, 2021)

"Dems Ramp Up Impeachment: Pelosi Asks About Curbing Trump's Power Over Nuclear Weapons" (Lisa Mascaro, Mary Clare Jalonik, and Zeke Miller, *The Baltimore Sun*, January 9, 2021)

"Slow Vaccination Rollout a Concern: Hospitals Slammed With Patient Care and Testing" (Meredith Cohn and Hallie Miller, *The Baltimore Sun*, January 9, 2021)

As the sun sets on Day 302, I realize I took the advice of last night's Missive and enjoyed life today. I don't even have that much to show for it, but I enjoyed it, which I think is OK. A little work (just a smidge), some chores, some cooking, some watching our sports team tank in the playoffs, a little walk with the canine queen, a few shows, some more chores. Really, really basic but also really nice. Feels good to do some of those little things that get pushed all week. Some days are simple. / You get stuff done, but you can't / say what exactly. Sleep restfully, Angels, and have another day tomorrow.

As the sun sets on Day 303, I'm a little restless. I want to buckle down and focus on my stuff, but there's a lot going on right now. Add that to my pandemic brain, and I am often a jumpy dither-er. A ditherer with a stress headache, or at least a sore neck and shoulders. What to do, what to do. Just keep swimming, I suppose. Sometimes, you wander up to your desk or over to the pile of laundry, make an attempt, and you look up and half an hour has gone by. I am going to hope that is how my Monday goes. One of my friends said recently that I seemed to be in a place of acceptance about things. I think she's right. If last year taught me anything, it was that the punches can just keep on coming...and coming and coming...BUT at the same time, we made it! So, I just try not to think that I know what's going to happen on any given day, and I'm fine! [Cue maniacal laughter.] Now, paired with that Acceptance is my own inclination towards Action. We must put Love out front; however, borrowing from *WW84* (because, apparently, I only understand WW advice), we must pair Love with Truth and Justice. We need all three right now in massive amounts. It's up to each of us. Sleep plentifully, Campers, and prepare yourselves to face the week ahead.

As the sun sets on Day 304, I can't believe how much did and didn't happen today. By "didn't" I mean that I had a long, some might say boring, stretch of straightforward Monday stuff; by "did"

I reference a bunch of stuff that happened this evening, some good (Roll Tide…again! *Bob's Burgers* episode I haven't seen yet) and some bad (Congressional Rep I admire testing positive for COVID after being in lockdown during the Capitol Riot with other Reps who refused to wear a mask; so many new variants across the globe it's like the freakin' COVID Olympics). I was hopeful this train was gonna slow down a little after the New Year, but I think that ship's sailed [so many transportation sayings!] Well, buckle up and, as my Dad says, keep it between the ditches. That's my goal for the next week. Doesn't have to be / perfect; use the whole road. Just / stay outta the ditch. Dream of a still pool, Angels, and wake to see one on the sidewalk because I don't think it's ever going to stop raining around here.

As the sun sets on Day 305, I'm still worked up over a Terrible Tuesday. This was a bad one. And yet, the training from last year held. We all kept going, and we are here reading the Missive now. And we'll gather for another one tomorrow night. If we have learned anything, we now know that Time keeps marching, even when we are pummeled every step of the way. Bend, don't break, Campers. Deep breaths. Believe in the many, many good people out there. Hope for enlightenment for the others. I'm sorry this was / a Terrible Tuesday. I'd / rather have tacos. Sleep, Campers, because we could all use a break from things.

As the sun sets on Day 306, I have some sad news to share. I apologize for doing this via our Nightly Missive, but at the same time, it seems fitting this year. I learned about 7pm this evening (January 13, 2021, for the record) that my Dad died at about 5pm Pacific Time. He likely had a small stroke this morning but was doing better; however, he was coughing a lot this evening, and he couldn't pull out of it. My Mom was right there with him. His initial diagnosis was back in April 2019, so he (and my Mom) really hung in there. I am so glad they had each other. As my Dad said, "We're the number one team!" I'm doing OK tonight and just remembering what a unique character my Dad was (those of you who knew him definitely know what I mean!) I'm also feeling like he's OK, and I actually feel like he's here with us. He gave me the very best of starts, and I'll carry that with me wherever I go. So, raise a glass for Al when you have a chance. He'd like that (and he would insist on "cheersing" you and clinking your glass, even when you didn't really feel like it). But it was just because he wanted you to have a good time. The stats: Alfred John Rossi, born June 30, 1936, in Ouray, Colorado; died January 13, 2021, in Huntsville, Alabama. Cheers to you, Dad!! Sleep well, Angels, and dream of stardust.

As the sun sets on Day 307 (prime!), I am reminded that one day can feel as long as a week. When I reach a "critical event," I just try to move through the day according to my mood. When I want to work, I work; when I want to walk the dog, I walk the dog; when I want to share with a friend, I share with a friend; if I want to eat, I eat; and apparently, when I want to vacuum, I vacuum. It was a slow, organic day. I did only what I wanted. And it seemed to go on and on (and on a little more). And then 3pm rolled around, just as I was thinking, "Surely, it must be midnight." But here we are now, and it really is moving towards midnight. Time marches on, even when you march in place for a while. Be sure to give your loved ones an extra squeeze or text or Zoom, Campers, and keep marching.

[Day 308 = Guest Missive by Margaret]
As the sun sets on Day 308, I tip my hat to knowing when to raise your hand and take a break. It's a marathon, after all, not a sprint - and we have to be sure to pace ourselves. One of the key frameworks for my son's classroom- which is full of kids who are learning how to understand their emotions - is the Zones of Regulation. Are you blue (tired)? Are you red (motor running)? Are you green (smooth sailing)? All of which are totally fine, but green is the best one for learning. So, take a break to help get yourself

there. Do some jumping jacks; try some breathing; take a walk. The important part is knowing when to take a break. Sleep well, my Angels, and be sure to take a break whenever you need it so you can keep on keeping on.

[Day 308 = Guest Missive by Laura]

This week we honor D. Prince's father, Alfred John Rossi, who was born on the same day that the 40-hour work week was signed into law for federal employees. I learned that what must have brought him to Huntsville, Alabama, was a career with the Army Redstone Arsenal where he worked on the Lance project and subsequent Multiple Launch Rocket Systems. I think you might have to be one of the sharper tools in the shed to be able to work on a really special, elite and secretive program like Lance – I doubt they need dumb-dumbs when you are racing against time in a Cold War arms race, creating a long range missile system that required additional thrust after launch to control trajectory, and dealing with setbacks that included liquid propulsion problems, tight schedules, ten years at least of tests after tests, and the request to add a nuclear warhead option for the missiles with the danger that brings to the equation. It took about four years from concept (1958) to naming "Missile B" the "Lance" missile (1962), and three more to successful flight tests, and another ten or so years with multiple challenges, until orders could be filled. The reason for the Lance name came from "the cultural traditions of North American Native Americans. Only the experienced warriors were allowed to carry a lance" (History.army.redstone.mil). It was able to deliver nuclear warheads a distance of 75 miles (!!!) and conventional warheads for 45 miles. Wow, the STEM we had at one time in this country. Also, the real, lasting impacts of the Cold War and the arms and space races. With pride we can say that the Lance missile system was "never launched in anger"—what an interesting phrase—and that after the treaty with the USSR, nuclear tactical missiles were dismantled, but multiple Lance units were stationed around the world secretively for decades before the last Lance battalion stood down in 1992. Beyond just the real life-and-death, fast-paced but critical and sober responsibilities this all must have required, we have to remember that they really, really didn't know how the story would turn out! We can be clinical and removed from this now, but it must have been Tense. Tense for Years. All of my respect to your father, who without doubt, had many, many more accomplishments than his time working at Redstone, and chief among them, the love he so clearly shared with his family and the commitment he had to his community and church. His energy is in his family and the light behind their eyes, and his memory will carry on in the stories that they share, as well as the small smiles, the private jokes, the vibrations of his Love that travel now without sound, to reverberate and then join the chorus of the Great Symphony. Safe travels. Sweet dreams, Campers. Love is the only thing that matters.

WEEK #45

Saturday, January 16, 2021 – Friday, January 22, 2021

"Biden Plans Blitz for Inoculations In First Three Months: Surging Variant May Dominate U.S." (Apoorva Mandavilli and Roni Caryn Rabin, *The New York Times*, January 16, 2021)

"Nashville Mayor: 'We Need More Vaccine': Federal Reserve May Already Be Gone" (Brett Kelman, *The Tennessean*, January 16, 2021)

"Why Tennessee Colleges Might Add New Winter Terms" (Monica Kast, *The Tennessean*, January 16, 2021)

[Day 309 = Guest Missive by Cameron]

As the sun sets on day 309 (OK, Lasso of Truth, it is clearly the morning of Day 310, but we need some stability in this time), I tip my hat to the gracious passing of time. No matter what we do, the minutes, hours, and days keep going. Instead of this being a problem, which sometimes it seems like it is, right now it seems like a gift. Moving forward, the chance for a new day, the chance for healing, the chance for a change in an attitude...my attitude. A chance to soak in the graciousness of getting to live a life and celebrate and stand with those around us. So, wherever you are today, Angels, may you have a moment to relish in, and may you have a moment of being thankful that we are pressing on. Hope you are all awake by now.

[Day 309 = Guest Missive by Laura] Oooh, boy, I fell asleep on the job, Campers! I hope you are having peaceful, sweet dreams right now. I'm going to share a short video that really spoke to me (https://twitter.com/lesdoggg/status/1350671786287927296?s=10), and we will have to wait for an insightful commentary from me for tomorrow evening. Love, love, love, sending radiating waves of love out to infinity. I learned today that the number one less than infinity, is also called infinity. I was contemplating this when I woke up and realized I had been sleeping. Now wondering how imaginary numbers fit in. Will have to look that up tomorrow.

[Day 310 = Guest Missive by Leslie]

As the sun sets on Day 310, I tip my hat to the bed. Not just any bed, your bed, with your favorite mattress selected to give you just the right support at the end of the day; your favorite sheets that are warm in winter and cool in summer; and, if you're very lucky, the perfect pillow, which, once you finally found it in your forties, gave you hope that your neck wouldn't hurt every day for the rest of your life. The right bed, and I hope you've all found yours, Angels, is like a warm hug at the end of a long day, a sacred space away from it all, where you can read, snuggle, watch TV (if you have one in your bedroom), drink wine, and even Zoom with your very closest friends. It is a haven and a sanctuary and is, come to think of it, where I was asked to marry my husband. (Not in a TMI sort of way; we just have always talked a lot in bed, and he asked me on a Saturday morning when we woke up. But I digress.) So, take the plunge tonight, Angels; let out a deep sigh and snuggle in, for you've made it through another day. And for now, that is enough. Enjoy your bed and / Snuggle in, for morning time/ Will come again-sigh.

[Day 310 = Guest Missive by Laura] Oops! Foiled again by a comfy bed and a good book. I simply do not know how you do it every night without falling asleep, D. Prince! At any rate, if you are reading this, I haven't gone dark or down a QAnon rabbit hole. On the contrary, I have discovered the most delightful children's book series which I got for my son for Xmas: *The Mysterious Benedict Society*. We are enjoying it so much. I can't tell you much about it because we just started it this weekend, but a group of gifted kids has to go undercover to outsmart a mad scientist. As they solve clues, you get to do so, too. I tell you what, Campers, not only is a good book a lip balm for the soul, but it allows the jaw to unclench long enough for sleep to come up and overtake you. I know you knew that, but I needed to be reminded. I truly hope that all of you can have a little extra relaxation tomorrow/today and reflect on the life and legacy of Dr. Martin Luther King, but I'm afraid that any deep or artful words at this time of abrupt awakening would be beyond my capabilities. I will share my son's words of wisdom, however bleak they sound. He said if they shot Lincoln in the 1860's and they shot Martin Luther King in the 1960's, we better hope they don't shoot anyone in the 2060's and that by that time, we can all get along. We were talking about his great MLK drawing from school last year. He said they mostly focused on making a drawing. I said we would address this topic tomorrow/today, and now, I'm looking forward to it. But I'm not prepared with any curriculum. I'm sure my education is lacking on the subject, but I have been to a church where MLK preached in Montgomery many times. I've hung out at the fountain downtown where Rosa Parks and the bus boycott happened. I tell you something, if the Southern Poverty Law Center had not moved into downtown Montgomery, you would not have seen a public memorial to MLK when I was growing up. As it was, the SPLC building was designed super modern with a great MLK quote on a big fountain out front. But you can't go inside, as they have massive security and cameras all over the building. This is, as you can imagine, from the constant threats. You have to be invited to go in. At least this is my memory from when I lived there. Now that I look on the website it seems that they have added more interpretation and more to the Memorial itself since I was there. I think that's where my son and I will start tomorrow. Ooof, the richness of our lives and the colossal waste of lives that hate and intolerance brings. The South is so beautiful in so many ways, but there is blood in the red clay. We will not be satisfied "until justice rolls down like waters and righteousness like a mighty stream." Let's just get 'er dun before 2060.

[Day 311 = Guest Missive by Catherine]
As the sun sets on Day 311 (a prime number!), I am thankful for another trip around the sun, and that I have spent so much of it with such an amazing group of Angels. You guys really do help me get through it all. It has been such a crazy year. I'm so hopeful for exciting things to come. Dare I believe that we really could be on the verge of a time when Dr. King's dream may come true? Is that insane? I'm trying to think positively and hope that certain factions have finally gone too far…that sanity and goodness and light and love will prevail. That's my birthday wish, anyway. So tonight I'll blow out the candles / and dream that wishes come true / for peace, light, and love. Good night, Angels! Sleep well!

[Day 311 = Guest Missive by Spicoli] We use words like diversity and inclusion all the time, and as anthropologists, we all understand that a diverse gene pool is a strong gene pool, but I really appreciate those moments when the true power of diversity shows itself in more than just an academic way. Like when you realize that a team who are all great swimmers won't win a relay. You must have a variety of skills and challenges to really be strong. It isn't just theoretical.

[Day 312 = Guest Missive by Cameron]
As the sun sets on Day 312 (just for argument's sake), I tip my hat to good people. There are lots of them out there, who share what they have, who are kind, and who do incredible things, even for strangers. Keep believing that, Angels, and keep being that. On this day of inauguration, let us believe the best of others and love our neighbors as ourselves. Wake to be the Angels that you are!

[Day 312 = Guest Missive by Spicoli] I want to say tonight that life is better with friends. I know that we know and celebrate this regularly, but I also think it is worth remembering that friends help fill in an empty chair, both figuratively and literally. They reflect, they are honest when that is what you need. So, dear friends, turn and look at those around you who make this life we have more real and worth celebrating.

[Day 313 = Guest Missive by Cameron]
As the sun sets on Day 313 (prime!), I tip my hat to grief in its many stages. A friend wrote a poem reframing grief not as an emotion or reaction, but as a faithful, gentle companion on the way with us when life gets tough. And we all grieve. And the great news is that, eventually, we all heal. In time, with care, walking with companions, we heal. So, I also tip my hat to healing. And, believe it or not, I tip my hat a third time tonight to women in general, whether grieving or healing or somewhere in between! There have been so many brave, intelligent, pioneering women that have gone ahead of us and have made it seem as though glass ceilings don't really exist. Sadly they do, but how wonderful to get to celebrate an intelligent, brave and pioneering woman today!! Awake, my Angels, to a day full of possibilities!

[Day 313 = Guest Missive by Spicoli]

Day 313. Inauguration Day 2021. Ding-dong, the witch is dead. Well, not really…pouty fallen dictator runs to his hideaway. We are living, feeling and breathing history. The power of this moment will hold like a long wave rolling towards our collective future. All the feelings today were surprising and huge. It felt like a familiar friend or a favorite blanket or opening a box of beloved clothes that you forgot you had. Like your heart was going to burst. This is the energy we need to move the needle on sharing resources, removing barriers, lifting others so we can all rise; the thing is, what can each of us do tomorrow to help bring down a racist system that we currently allow to happen? What hate can we counteract with love tomorrow before we say we are done for the day? How can we take all these feeling and turn them into action? Sleep on all this opportunity.

As the sun sets on Day 314, I return to the tradition that is the Nightly Missive. First and foremost, I extend to each and every one of you Angels the most heartfelt Thank You, both for your words and deeds of genuine kindness and for your Guest Missives. I am extremely touched and grateful. I felt your support, and I enjoyed hearing your voices and thoughts in the Missives and the conversations sparked by them. Thank you so much! Friendship is a two-way street, so please know that I've got your backs, too. My mind and my emotions have been swirling and twirling (like the sea of gumdrops traversed by Buddy the Elf), so a cohesive Missive might be beyond my reach tonight. Instead, some random observations about our 314th day together: we are now in the 300's, which will bring us to the one-year mark; 3+14=17 which is my birthdate; 14 is Molly's favorite number; 3+1=4; (4 x 3)+1=Lucky 13. Yikes. In terms of the date itself (Thursday, January 21, 2021 or 1.21.21): that's a lot of "one's"; today marks 4 years since the Women's March; it also marks one year since the first COVID case was reported in the US (right here in WA State); it's Thursday, my favorite day of the week! Finally, a non-numerological observation:

I was thinking today about the importance of "curiosity" (back to that cheeky little monkey from last Spring). Curiosity about one's journey; curiosity about what comes next; curiosity about others; curiosity about what's possible. If we can remain curious about the world, those in it, and our role in making it better, then we can better tackle any challenge. If we cultivate curiosity, we will be open to solutions from any source. This is the thinking we will need to heal and to move forward. And that can be as an individual or a country or a planet. That's all we've got to do. No biggie. I had to step a- / way for a bit, but with the / help of friends, I'm back. Dream of curious possibilities, Angels, and wake to explore them.

As the sun sets on Day 315 (3x5=15), I tip my hat to Curiosity, Part Deux. Tonight, as I settle in after movie night (*The High Note* on HBO Max; really enjoyed it) and catch up on some earlier breaking news, I am curious about what makes someone do the right thing or the wrong thing. And yes, I realize right and wrong are sometimes subjective, but I'm talking about the more objective times (e.g. committing election fraud or not committing election fraud). It is very easy to do the right thing when your basic needs are met. My basic needs are met and then some, so I can sit here in the glow of the TV night after night, safe from COVID, safe from hunger, safe from danger, and pontificate on all manner of pithy observations about life (at least as I'm experiencing it) and exhortations to "just keep swimming." It's easy to spend time pondering such things, keeping a mostly optimistic attitude, and offering such pearls when I am warm and dry and safe from COVID. But what if I wasn't all those things? What if I was down at the homeless camp outside City Hall? Or the one over in Fairhaven? Or any of the ones around Seattle? Without any food or dry clothing or a door to lock or countless channels to flip through while fretting that "I've seen all those" or "Most of this is crap." What vastly different lives we lead. Which makes me wonder, would it be different if we tried to level the playing field? What if everyone's basic needs were met? Maybe it would be easier to do the right thing instead of the wrong thing. I'm not sure, but boy, I'd be willing to find out. There's a whole lotta talk about "equity" right now. I hope we keep at it. There have been many riffs on this quote (e.g. "Everybody does better when everybody does better" by Jim Hightower... well, his father, actually), but leave it to a woman to get there first: "When it's better for everyone, it's better for everyone" said one Eleanor Roosevelt. No haiku tonight, Campers... I've already used all the words. Sleep tight! [Holy crap, those last 2 sentences make a haiku!!]

WEEK #46

Saturday, January 23, 2021 – Friday, January 29, 2021

"President Takes Two Quick Actions to Aid the Poor – 'Economic Imperative' – Urges Lawmakers to Pass $1.9 Trillion Package for Broad Relief" (Jim Tankersley and Alan Rappeport, *The New York Times*, January 23, 2021)

"Tenn. Lawmakers Approve $160M Schools Package: Stagnant Literacy Rates, COVID-related Learning Loss Are Among Targets" (Meghan Mangrum and Natalie Allison, *The Tennessean*, January 23, 2021)

"Hank Aaron Dies at 86: Hall of Famer Broke MLB Home Run Record" (Steve Gardner and Bob Nightengale, *The Tennessean*, January 23, 2021)

As the sun sets on Day 316, I tip my hat to…Warrior Women, what else?? As I might have mentioned somewhere along the way, *Wonder Woman 1984* leaves HBO Max this weekend [cue sad music]. So, I had to sneak in one more viewing tonight (number five, if anyone is counting). Once the sun sets tomorrow (Sunday), I will most likely have to wait until the Blu-ray release later this year for number six. Sigh. I think President Biden's speech writers must have watched the movie, too. One of the main themes on Inauguration Day was the importance of the Truth. *WW84* opens with a lesson about Truth; then, the climactic scene includes a plea from Wonder Woman to all of us mortals to realize the price of our selfish wishes; she says, "You cannot have it all. You can only have the Truth. And the Truth is enough." We've all seen the importance of Truth lately. There's a lot of gray area in the world, but some things aren't debatable. We need a common starting line. Which I will think about more tomorrow because now, I'm tired, and the Truth is, I need some sleep. "No true hero is / born from lies." Those Amazons / can lay down some Truth. Dream of being a hero, Angels, and wake to give it a try.

As the sun sets on Day 317 (prime!), I'm experiencing a little Sunday Resistance. And by "little" I mean a fair amount. I try not to sink into the Sunday Blues as we call them around here, and this isn't exactly that, but I am resisting the Truth that the weekend is coming to a close and Monday is just around the corner. Truthfully, I'm not in the mood. Work sounds very unimportant right about now; well, not so much unimportant as unappealing. Perhaps it would be better suited to Tuesday! No? Well, I just devised a plan. I'm going to channel my Dad. Talk about a worker bee! He and my Mom both. And they very rarely complain about it. I need a little more of that outlook right about now. So, tomorrow, I will deploy the elephant approach: How do you survive your Monday? One task, one step at a time. Sometimes, simple is best. And a low bar. I think I'm going to need a low bar. And that's OK. Grasping at the week- / end, Sunday still slips through my / fingers. Nice try, though. Sleep restfully, Campers, and get ready to roll…or, at least to step steadily.

As the sun sets on Day 318, I tip my hat to Bedtime. It seems we've made it! I had the type of Monday anticipated, but I worked hard to channel Al and just trudge right on through it. It wasn't pretty, but some things were checked off, the sun set, and it's time to wind down. Thank you, Dad! I've also been thinking about a quote I recently heard on one of our shows: "We are all broken. That's how the light gets in." I really like that. I did a little Googling, and the quote is often attributed to either Ernest Hemingway or Leonard Cohen. However, it appears to be a combination of two quotes. Leonard Cohen writes this in the song "Anthem": "Ring the bells that can still ring / Forget your perfect offering / There is a crack, a crack in everything / That's how the light gets in." Pretty awesome. In *A Farewell to Arms*, Hemingway writes: "If people bring so much courage to this world the world has to kill them to break them, so of course it kills them. The world breaks every one and afterward many are strong at the broken places. But those that will not break it kills. It kills the very good and the very gentle and the very brave impartially. If you are none of these you can be sure it will kill you too but there will be no special hurry." My, there are some good thinkers and some good writers out there. They really distill this Life thing down, don't they? I'm glad they're out there. Find your inspira- / tion where you are able, e- / ven on a Monday. Dream of letting the light in, Angels, and wake to celebrate your broken places.

As the sun sets on Day 319, I am reflecting on my first MRI (that's "magnetic resonance imaging" for anyone curious). First, I have to admit up front that I got off as easily as you probably can where this test is concerned: I only had to be in the tube for 15 minutes, and my head remained outside the tube the whole time. Plus, I was able to listen to music, which included Lady Gaga and Journey, so that was a definite win. However, the machine was definitely as noisy as I'd been warned. I mean, Geez!! When all was said and done, I decided that I feel about MRIs the way I feel about drywalling: the end result is nice, but the process is Truly Ridiculous. Now, for something perhaps a little more profound and useful. Some of you may be familiar with this already, but I was recently introduced to the "ring theory" of helping people with grief, including the idea of a "Kvetching Order" which I love because "kvetching" is a great word (https://medium.com/@GeralynBMurray/ring-theory-pandemic-edition-comfort-in-dump-out-switch-ef402d7c2e94). Being the recipient of so much kindness and comfort lately has made me think of all the other people who would benefit from the same (there is a pandemic on, after all). Take a look and see where you are in the rings; see where others are; reach out (or in) accordingly. The article ends like this: "Perhaps by allowing our individual suffering to be heard and comforted, our collective global grief will be eased bit by bit. Comfort in, dump out." Hey, that inspires me: Comfort in, dump out. / Sometimes you're in the middle. / Comfort in, dump out. Dream of rings, Campers, and know that you are covered wherever you land.

As the sun sets on Day 320, I reflect in stunned silence on a very hectic Hump Day. An exhausting day trying to juggle too many things on too many fronts. The saving grace? A fresh batch of homemade chocolate cupcakes for Molly's birthday tomorrow. Grandma Eppard's recipe can save even a maddening Hump Day and soothe the knowledge that tomorrow is probably going to be even busier. Cupcake therapy to the rescue. Today was busy; / tomorrow will be, too. Cup- / cakes to the rescue. Hey, look at that…the haiku told you all you need to know. Not sure why all those words preceding it were necessary. Dream of homemade cupcakes, Angels, and wake 'n bake.

As the sun sets on Day 321, I reflect upon the busiest day I've had in ages, as well as one of the best days. The victories: 1) cupcakes (see last night's Missive); 2) Molly's 50th birthday (much fun was sprinkled throughout the day, as well as some howling at the full moon down by the Bay); and 3) a positive MRI, as in positively showing a tear of the medial meniscus, which might sound counter-intuitive to describe as a victory but which, in fact, is one because the test was conclusive, and we know what we need to do now. I've watched Molly deal with inconclusive tests and the resulting frustration and uncertainty, and I'm so grateful my path is obvious. Next up is scheduling a 'scope to clean things up in there, things that have been brewing since I was a college sophomore...last century. Relief! I thought about rubbing a cupcake on my knee, but I wisely realized my stomach needed a victory, too. I hope each of you was able to recognize some victories here and there today, even if that victory is just that you are reading this Missive. All that noise was worth / it. If only cupcakes were / allowed in the tube. Dream of victory, Campers, and wake to know you can achieve one (or more) today.

As the sun sets on Day 322 (our 46th week together...shout out to our 46th President!), I tip my hat to red wine and chocolate (cupcakes). That should give you a glimpse into our evening. After getting after it on the work front, I wrapped a little early and joined Molly who took a couple personal days at the end of the week, which is basically unheard of. I'm not sure I can recall her ever taking personal days except to help at the Summit. She is a true work horse. Late afternoon melded into an early evening of pizza, a really good bottle of red wine created one neighborhood over, and those irresistible chocolate cupcakes (and really, why would anyone try to resist them??) Add a Masterpiece Mystery, and I honestly can't imagine wanting anything more. Which is good because we both fell sound asleep under our blankies around 8:30. Quoting Joey from *Friends* who, now that I think of it, actually had chocolate all over his face when he said this, "I'm not even sorry!" Three-ring circus? No, thank you. Give me the simple stuff that just goes together. And a nice warm blankie. If I had any / profound thoughts today, wine and / cake washed them away. Sleep peacefully, Angels, because you have tried hard this week.

WEEK #47

Saturday, January 30, 2021 – Friday, February 5, 2021

"One-Dose Vaccine Proved Effective to Fight COVID-19 – Red Flags on Variants – Johnson & Johnson Says Shot Adds Protection in Most Cases" (Carl Zimmer, Noah Weiland, and Sharon LaFraniere, *The New York Times*, January 30, 2021)

"MNPS Says Reopening Possible Soon: District Likely Will Announce Plan Monday if COVID-19 Risk Score Remains Below 7" (Meghan Mangrum, *The Tennessean*, January 30, 2021)

"Glad to Have Each Other: Nashville Couple in Their 80s Gets COVID-19 Vaccinations After Tying Knot in October" (Rachel Wegner, *The Tennessean*, January 30, 2021)

As the sun sets on Day 323, I hear the cupcakes calling me from the kitchen, but I am trying to resist (having another one). I mentioned a special bottle of red wine last night, and I want to share a little bit more about that. The vintner (a.k.a. winemaker) is a truly lovely man from Lithuania. He makes very special Cabernet Sauvignon and Syrah. Some of the wines are bestowed with special names, always with a great backstory. Last night's bottle was a 2017 Cab Sauv made with grapes from the Yakima Valley AVA (or, "American Viticultural Area," which is a wine grape-growing region with geographic or climatic features distinct enough to distinguish it from surrounding regions and affecting how the grapes are grown; WA State now boasts 16 AVAs) [FYI, 3 more AVAs were added in 2021 for a total of 19]. This particular Cab's name is "Conchie." Who or what is a Conchie, you may ask? Well, here's what the label says: "This bottle represents a 'conscientious objector,' one who boldly stands alone against many." I grinned when I read that. I like it. As I happily quaffed the Conchie, I recalled that 2017 was the year the first *Wonder Woman* movie saved me from the political climate. Looks like my friend, the vintner, was in a similar place then. Lucky me! It seems good things really do come to those who wait, even in the realms of wine and politics. At times, it's neces- / sary to object, but not / to wine or cupcakes. Dream of Conchie, Campers, and wake to wine with a spine.

As the sun sets on Day 324, I sit in the glow of the TV doing some tax stuff (blech!) and reflecting on the weekend that is winding down. I'm sad to see it go, but it has been a good one. What did I do? Who knows? I remember spending most of yesterday making Gumbo. I remember cupcakes. I remember a lovely FaceTime with friends this morning. I remember a lot of rain today. I remember a nice dog walk yesterday, complete with some pushing of Olive in her cart. I remember some TV (never the specifics, of course). I remember that I have to get up for an early phone call tomorrow, so I'm going to remember myself all the way to bed now. I hope everyone had a chance to rest and relax and do a few things they enjoy. It's time for another week. Try to carry some of that Weekend Cupcake feeling into it. Your fellow Miniature Cake Aficionados are with you. Dream of the weekend, Angels, and wake to know it will come again.

As the sun sets on Day 325, I reflect on a day of Learning, some expected and some unexpected. Expected learning included two webinars, one expected but almost forgotten and one basically unexpected, although it should have been expected and was only remembered thanks to a kind friend. (All of that should give you an idea of my mental state today, too; yikes.) Unexpected learning included more family business calls in the wake of my Dad's departure and post-webinar musings on what a learning curve we (i.e. our country, our species) seem to be on lately. Specifically, conversations in my profession, including those at recent Summits, are expanding and merging with larger societal conversations about big and important things like equity and diversity and how to integrate scientific ecological knowledge (SEK) and traditional ecological knowledge (TEK) into Biocultural Restoration, which is "the science and practice of restoring not only ecosystems, but human and cultural relationships to place, so that cultures are strengthened and revitalized along with the lands to which they are inextricably linked." As one whose academic training in Anthropology included an emphasis on holistic approaches to problem solving and the benefits of interdisciplinary collaboration, this approach makes so much sense to me. It's been backed up by lessons learned working in Indian Country, too. I feel very lucky to have been exposed to both social and natural sciences. Concepts like "ecosystem" itself and the idea that these systems include the land and the people and the practices make sense to me. When you look around you, what are your values? What is your relationship to your place? What do you think your role in it is? These outlooks will likely determine your actions. Then, there are group decisions on the city, county, state, national, and even planetary levels. How do we (singular and plural) see ourselves in this place (local and even universal)? As one of the speakers also observed, I don't have The Answer with all this, just a way, hopefully, to start asking more illuminating questions. That was a lot, but / pondering your place is al- / ways valuable. Sleep on it, Campers, and know your place here is secure.

As the sun sets on Day 326, I tip my hat to all the adventurers out there. Friends in the Galapagos, friends sledding in the snow zone, friends who conquered Taco Tuesday. I love it! My day, in contrast, was super vanilla, so much so that it even included tax stuff. I'm trying to salvage it with a little TV and reading tonight. So, straight to the haikus (we have 2 tonight): Some nights, you wait a / little too long to start the / Missive. Time for bed. I don't think the An- / gels will mind because I've used / lots of words lately. Those are borderline, so a few snow jokes to even things out: What do you get from sitting on the ice too long? Polaroids! What's it called when a snowman has a temper tantrum? A meltdown! What do you call a snowman with a six pack? An abdominal snowman! There, that's the stuff! Dream of your next adventure, Angels, and smile at the possibilities!

As the sun sets on Day 327, I'm thinking a lot about my Mom. My sister headed home early this morning, so my Mom is now in an empty house, at least until the next visit. Last night, in anticipation, I invited her to "Elevenses" today. So, she had her lunch, I had my toast and jam, and we chatted. It was nice. Then, we made a pact to take afternoon walks and report back at dinnertime, which we did. Baby steps. One day at a time. All those things. I was also working with the beautiful flowers and plants sent by friends and feeling very grateful for all the support I've received on this end. Sadness can be big; / toast is fairly small. They are / not exclusive, though. Dream of whatever makes you happy, Campers, because you deserve a smile.

As the sun sets on Day 328, I'm wondering how the sun is setting on yet another Thursday. It was one of those days where I got things done, but almost none of those things were on The List (because I successfully avoided most of those!) Now, I'm looking around a dark house wondering how I filled all those hours. It felt very roller-coastery. You'd think by going straight up and then straight down again you would stay in the same spot, but here it is, Night once again. I am just never going to figure out this Time thing. I am watching Olive for attitude advice, though. Her Old Dog Syndrome has really hit her hind end this time. Regardless of where that part of her is going, she just tilts her head and lurches up the stairs or around the corner. Inconvenient, yes. Surprising, I would think so. Frustrating, most likely. But no matter...on she goes. And so, I shall go on, too, right into Friday. And we shall see. Please keep your hands in- / side the car at all times. It / will be a fast ride. Dream of roller coasters, Angels, and ride it right on into your weekend.

As the sun sets on Day 329, we celebrate our 47th week together. In terms of the percentage of one year together, we have hit the 90s. Speaking of the 90s, I miss the '90s. Things seemed simpler then. As is evidenced in these Missives, I'm fond of the show *Friends*. It came out in September 1994 when I was 21 (and, if anyone's wondering, ran until May 2004, just shy of my 31st birthday). I associate the show with my senior year in college, my first full year in the workforce, grad school, and my first real job. That's a rather big decade for most folks in terms of figuring out how to make it on your own, having important relationships, and so on (you were around, too, so you know). During recent re-runs, I noticed how the focus is on their relationships with one another...not screens or social media or "gotcha" moments. They met at Central Perk in person and drank coffee together (and ate muffins and crullers). They had bagel brunch together. The boys watched *Baywatch*. The girls shopped together. They (well, three of them) went to see Hootie & the Blowfish for Ross's birthday. They lived in the Big City, so no one had a car (well, Ross had one for a bit, and then Phoebe bought a cab; oh, and Joey pretended a Porsche parked near Central Perk was his, but you know what I mean). Cell phones showed up, but only to make a phone call. OK, I could go on, but I won't (and I'm not even watching it right now!) My point is: Relationships. Hanging out together in person and talking without a single screen around (except the TV screen, which is completely acceptable to a child of the '80s). Remember that? I do. But it's been 90% of a year, so it's a little fuzzy. But I remember, and I look forward to having that option again. Ya feel me? I'm thinkin' ya might. Friday makes me think / about hanging out. Party; / Movie; Options. Yeah. Dream of options, Campers, and believe that they will come again.

WEEK #48

Saturday, February 6, 2021 – Friday, February 12, 2021

"Amid Poor Jobs Report, Biden Calls for Fast Aid With or Without G.O.P. – Seeks a Substantial Package in Weeks" (Jim Tankersley and Luke Broadwater, *The New York Times*, February 6, 2021)

"Nashville's Expanded 'Sidewalk Cafe' Permit Gets 1-year Extension" (Yihyun Jeong, *The Tennessean*, February 6, 2021)

"Daughter of Man Executed for Murder Appeals for DNA Testing" (Mariah Timms, *The Tennessean*, February 6, 2021)

As the sun sets on Day 330 (30/3=10 and 10 is my fave number), I'm sitting in the dark giggling by myself while watching *SNL* hosted by Dan Levy (David on *Schitt'$ Creek*). And friends, Giggling is Good. This is a strange sentence, perhaps, but Molly and I were laughing earlier…as we worked on our Last Will and Testament. We've procrastinated on this important task for ages, and we were ready to get things done; so, we started off in a very matter-of-fact manner. Soon, I was laughing at how we were saying, "If you croak first, then…" and "If I kick the bucket first, then…" and "If we've both signed off and so have our siblings…" (well, they might not laugh if they read this). Laughter is good medicine; find it wherever you can. I hear there's some football game tomorrow, so…Why was the tiny ghost asked to join the Super Bowl football team? They needed a little team spirit! Why do field goal kickers bring string to the Super Bowl? Just in case they need to tie the score! Why do the best field goal kickers take ballet lessons? To learn how to split the uprights! What did the receiver say to the football before the big game? Catch you later.

As the sun sets on Day 331, I tip my hat to food and football. Even if you're not really into the Super Bowl, it's kind of fun to experience a live event along with much of the country and even many parts of the world. Those kinds of events aren't that common anymore in the era of on-demand entertainment. That's another thing I miss: everybody watching the same TV shows on the same night (*Facts of Life* anyone?) and seeing the big blockbusters when they're in the theater (*Raiders of the Lost Ark* was a biggie and even provided some important career advice). Now, my head spins with all the platforms and options and binging, and it never seems to end. No wonder FOMO is a thing for some people…our knowledge of Pop Culture has become hard to maintain. All those screens keeping us from all those other things. This all seems like a good reminder of that wise saying: "All things in Moderation." Unless everyone's binging some awesome show on Prime because then, you'd better grab the popcorn and a seat because you don't want to miss out. Perhaps those pretzels / and poppers went to my head. / Say no to FOMO. Sleep well, Campers, for you are victorious tonight!

As the sun sets on Day 332, I tip my hat to Cookies. Turns out, my Mom (and Molly, for that matter!) is a real Cookie Monster. Last week, while bemoaning my avoidance of a particular work task, I asked her how she makes herself do things she doesn't want to do, and I mentioned I might have to bribe myself at this point. Her answer: "I bribe myself with Cookies!" I don't have a huge sweet tooth, so I've always been a bit neutral about cookies. I mean, don't get me wrong, I like them; I just don't live for them. However, we had a cookie jar on the kitchen counter growing up, and my Mom always had homemade cookies in there. She might've been the most frequent customer. The lid of jar made a very distinctive sound, even when one was trying to be quiet and sneaky, so we were always busting each other late at night. Or, mid-afternoon. Or, around Elevenses. She always made cookies for the first day of school, too, and we'd munch on them while telling her about our day when we got home. We knew it was a stereotype, but we all played along. I'm not always great about doing things for holidays, but I have been determined to do something for my Mom for Valentine's Day this year, which she loves. So, no brainer...I decided to make her some cookies. Tonight, I made these really great Peanut Butter & Chocolate Chip cookies (double batch!), and I'm trying not to go in there and have one...and by "one" I mean "another." ... Well, an update: my laptop battery gave out, so what the heck was I supposed to do while it charged up? That's right... munch a cookie. Peanut butter. Choc- / olate chip. Oatmeal. Molas- / ses. Snickerdoodle. Dream of cookies, Angels, and wake to treat yourself to one...or some.

As the sun sets on Day 333 (so many threes; a trio of them, in fact; three cubed), I find myself still thinking about...Cookies. We had an unexpected mid-day interruption around here, so those cookies did not make it into today's mail, unfortunately. However, after a smidge more sampling…you know, just to make sure they're still good (also a good thing I made a double batch!), my Mom's portion of the bounty is now wrapped tightly in plastic wrap in anticipation of their long journey that should start sometime tomorrow. I read that a good way to ship cookies is to put them back-to-back in an inverted cookie sandwich of sorts, and wrap each one of those little gems. Pop them in a container, and then pop that into your flat-rate box (well, that's my postal jam, anyway). I'm pretty excited. I hate to admit it, especially after the countless boxes my Mom's sent me over my 47 years, but I've never sent her homemade cookies. Well, there's a first time for everything, and that time is Now. Just like in the Yoga Sutras, the first one of which says, "Now begins the study of Yoga." Doesn't matter what you've never done or started or accomplished or procrastinated; you can start Now, and Now is the thing that matters. I like the forgiveness and the opportunity in that. Now is the right time / to sample cookies and send / some to a loved one. Dream of cookies again, Campers, and if you didn't have any today, Now is the time!

As the sun sets on Day 334, why break the streak…let's talk Cookies again. Actually, I'll give you a break. I'll just confirm that the cookies are now in the mail, along with two handwritten recipe cards and a handmade Valentine. Godspeed, care package. On a more serious note, our family wrote a detailed obituary for my Dad for publication in his hometown (Ouray, Colorado) newspaper, *The Plaindealer*. Dad always sent us a gift subscription for Christmas so that we could keep up on the happenings there. If any of you Angels are interested in some more stories about Al, you can read our tribute here: https://www.ouraynews.com/index.php/obituaries/alfred-john-rossi My siblings did the bulk of the writing, but I provided some edits and a little research on a few of the stories I remembered a bit differently. I hope you enjoy it. Bake, color, tape, mail. / Valentine's Day is coming. / Cookies are going. Sleep well, Angels, and think about your legacy (in a good way, not a paralyzing way).

As the sun sets on Day 335, I'm bonking, as we call it around here (the tired meaning, not the other meaning I just discovered). I've been wandering around all day on about 4 hours of sleep be-caaaaaase...we were extremely rudely awakened early this morning by three of our smoke alarms, which we now know merely need new batteries. Our smoke alarms are hard-wired, so we had to take the battery out AND disconnect them from the wiring. This work was poorly performed while they were shrieking in our tender ears, dogs were fleeing the scene, and we were still half-asleep in our jammies as the wind chill outside hit single digits. I couldn't even think straight. My heart still hasn't fully recovered. Afterwards, I managed - somehow - to finish a work task I've procrastinated over for about a week and a half, and then, I eventually gave up. Showered and made soup. And ate two cookies. And maybe a chocolate from the box my brother sent us. Lasso of Truth: I ate a chocolate from the box my brother sent us. On the plus side, I shared this story with my Mom and siblings, and we all had fun laughing at the classic *I Love Lucy* episode at the chocolate factory. You should, too: https://www.youtube.com/watch?v=NkQ58I53mjk Take a deep breath, Campers, and get some sleep; tomorrow, change your smoke alarm batteries.

As the sun sets on Day 336 (3+3=6 and that 6 plus the other 6=12), I celebrate the close of our 48th week together (4+8=12 and there's that 12 again). I'm also giggling because my typing is a bit off right now. Could it be my hot toddy? Perhabz. Could it be my hot toddy and two very poor nights of sleep in a row? Also pozzibull. It's sad to giggle alone; characteristically, everyone else is asleep already, including Walter who is curled up on the other end of the couch blissfully unaware of my poor typing. Last night's poor sleeping involved a bitterly cold wind storm that woke Olive; her hearing is not so great anymore, and the sounds were scaring her. So, after listening for a while to see if she could settle down, I arose after three whole hours of sleep and moved out to the couch where I hung over the side petting her with one sleepy hand. It worked, and we both feel asleep…for half an hour when Molly got up for work. Olive and I retreated to the bedroom again as the winds had eased a bit, and I did get some more sleep; however, it did not feel that way when I awoke for good. I know…poor me. We muddled through our day, and now, we are waiting for some snow. Well, I am. Everyone else is dreaming about it at this point. I am going to bed on a good note, though. We held our first Summit "Flash Contest" today, and I asked folks to send a brief account of a simple act of kindness that they performed or received or witnessed over the last few months. I just read them over and sent them to the planning committee so that we can pick two "winners" who will get one of two fabulous prizes. We received four great stories, so I have a sneaking suspicion that four prizes may actually be awarded. I definitely don't want to squelch any enthusiasm for future acts of kindness! What better use of funds could there be anyway, I ask you? So many random / acts of kindness happen eve- / ry day. Thank goodness! Dream of kindness, Angels, and maybe hot toddeeeez, too!

WEEK #49

Saturday, February 13, 2021 – Friday, February 19, 2021

"New Way to Qualify for a Shot: Take a 75-Year-Old to Get One" (Ellen Barry, *The New York Times*, February 13, 2021)

"CDC Urges Reopening of Schools; Here's the Blueprint" (Apoorva Mandavilli, Kate Taylor, and Dana Goldstein, *The Seattle Times*, February 13, 2021)

"(Governor) Inslee: 5 Regions to Move to Phase 2; More Aid on the Way" (Sara Gentzler, *The Bellingham Herald*, February 13, 2021)

As the sun sets on Day 337 (prime!), I tip my hat to SNOW! It snowed here all day long. Last time I measured, we had 6 inches, but it kept on a-snowin'. So pretty (when you have a warm house and you are baking). I always love a snow day. It's pretty and peaceful and quiet and exciting and bright and there's often baking. That's a pretty good package. I didn't really venture out today due to my bum knee, but tomorrow, I shall venture forth to complete my Sunday chores and toss a few snowballs. And once again, I shall take a cue from Olive whose head is really tilting but whose love for snow is strong as ever, even if she needs a little help from the belly sling right now. And then there's Wally, jumping around happily and hoping she'll play with him, and if she doesn't, then where's that new Snoopy toy from the Bark Box his friends sent him? Or, a treat. Or, a bone. Or, "Oh boy, oh boy, oh boy, isn't this fun??" Yes, it is! And pretty. And quiet. And frankly, kind of amazing. Unless you are from the Arctic; then, it's pretty much just another Saturday. But we're not from the Arctic, so around here, it's pretty amazing. When the snow flies, grab / the flour and the sugar. White / outside; white inside. Dream of snow people, Campers, and wake to greet some!

As the sun sets on Day 338, I wish you (including, or maybe especially, any cynics out there) a very Happy Valentine's Day. In the midst of a pandemic winter, a day devoted to love (and chocolate) is welcome, indeed. Wikipedia reveals the origins of the modern cliché poem; it can be found in a collection of English nursery rhymes entitled *Gammer Gurton's Garland* from 1784: "The rose is red, the violet's blue, / The honey's sweet, and so are you. / Thou art my love and I am thine; / I drew thee to my Valentine. / The lot was cast and then I drew, / And Fortune said it shou'd be you." Hopefully, we all showed another being some love today. Tomorrow would be good, too. Let's start the week off right. A card, a flower, / a chocolate, a poem, / a smile, all for you. Dream of sweet treats given with love, Angels, and wake to pass them on.

As the sun sets on Day 339, I bear witness to Slush Fest 2021. Over the weekend, we welcomed over 6 inches of snow. Good ol' snowball-packin' snow. Beautiful. A nice change of pace. Lovely to observe from one's cozy home. Well, let me tell ya…the temperature rose last night, and I went to bed listening to the drip, drip, drip of our rapidly melting white stuff. Today, a whole lot more dripping. A stroll with Walter confirmed the sloppy slush fest that is now the sections of sidewalk that were not shoveled. Luckily, Molly shoveled the majority of our side of the block, and it was delightful; otherwise, I was glad to have Gore-Tex shoes. Meanwhile, a true deep freeze settles across a wide swath of the South right on up to the Northeast. Rolling blackouts and everything. Not fun. I hope for electrical service, warm blankets, and lots of baking for as many as possible. Sometimes, a storm can / lead to cozy pastimes. Some- / times, it's not as fun. Sleep well, Campers, so that you are ready for what comes next!

As the sun sets on Day 340, I I am am seeing seeing double double. [That's kinda trippy trippy!] Another night assisting Olive. However, we now have some nerve/pain meds for her, and she seems calmer. The Old Dog Syndrome is so much worse at night. Poor girl. I can't even think straight at this point, so I'm heading to bed realllllllly early for me. Happily, I have a work thing in the morning I'm really looking forward to tackling. It's a service I've pondered for years, and I finally figured out how it might work. Another pandemic/Zoom Silver Lining, actually. The intended audience was willing, so here we go! Feels nice to work on something new. Also, feeling thankful – yet again – for coffee. A lack of sleep makes / one's mind do weird things. There are / also the dry eyes. Sleep deeply, Angels, because there really ain't nothin' like it.

As the sun sets on Day 341, I am feeling extremely (extremely!) grateful to have power and heat and water. The situation in many parts of Texas looks very (very!) different. I really feel for our friends down there. It's one thing to ride out a storm; it's a completely different thing to ride it out without any of the comforts of home. It's one thing to do that when you are relatively healthy, too; just think if you weren't. It's probably time for another Red Cross donation. It reminds me of the April 2011 Super Outbreak (tornadoes) that knocked out my parents' power for a week. In their typically nonplussed way, they politely declined our offer to put them up out here, and they iced down all their coolers and had a cookout every night. They also warmed water on the camp stove for washing, charged their phones in their truck, and listened to the radio for the latest news, updates, and tips (like which stores had ice). They wanted to be at home to keep an eye on things and to be there when the power was restored. Now, keep in mind that they were 72 and 74 years old in April 2011. I can only hope I am cut of the same cloth. We shall see. Olive update: nerve/pain meds are helping. She's more comfortable, although her back end still gives her a lot of trouble. Her stomach, however, is just fine; her face was practically in my bowl of Pumpkin Alfredo tonight. She makes it seem like it's partially due to her vicious head tilt, but I wonder. She's sneaky like that. But do I care? I do not. Enjoy every mo- / ment of your creature comforts; / it's hard when they're gone. Dream of heat and warm water, Campers, and wake never to take them for granted.

As the sun sets on Day 342, I ponder Reciprocity. One definition reads thusly: "the practice of exchanging things with others for mutual benefit." I'm reading about how we might extend that practice to include how humans interact with the natural world. I think we often forget that we are part of Kingdom Animalia (i.e. we're animals); we didn't always have homes and electricity and Netflix. We are part of Nature and not separated from it or masters of it. Reciprocity can result in more for all; commodification, in contrast, typically leads to more for only a few. I'm not sure we have the courage to believe this and then act on it, though. Perhaps my reading has merged with last night's Missive on creature comforts. Those comforts can be taken away (did anyone watch the TV drama *Revolution*?) Would I be able to survive without them? I don't know. Even my folks "only" had to make it a week. Well, here's hoping I don't have to find out. And here's hoping for some Reciprocity if I do. If I could only / truly live in the moment, / I'd know I'm OK. Sleep peacefully, Angels, despite this perplexing Missive.

As the sun sets on Day 343, we immediately join our haiku in progress: Cabernet Sauvi- / gnon. Pour, swirl, sniff, quaff, smile, ex- / hale, repeat. Good night. Dream of the weekend, Campers, because you've made it!

WEEK #50

Saturday, February 20, 2021 – Friday, February 26, 2021

"Brutal Cold Kills Texans in Beds, Yards and Cars: Carbon Monoxide, Fire and Exposure Raise Toll of Power Crisis" (Giulia McDonell Nieto del Rio, Richard Fausset, and Johnny Diaz, *The New York Times*, February 20, 2021)

"Single Shot of Pfizer Vaccine Is Effective" (Katie Thomas, *The Seattle Times*, February 20, 2021)

"Car with Washington Plates Vandalized in Canada" (David Rasbach, *The Bellingham Herald*, February 20, 2021)

As the sun sets on Day 344, I tip my hat to fresh air and thinking about others. Today, we all loaded Olive into the cart and aired ourselves out. We walked down to "the tree" at a lookout on the edge of the neighborhood where we can survey the Bay. A breeze was coming up, and it was starting to sprinkle. I needed that shot of fresh air to wake my mind; I've been feeling a little flat. Even tweaking my knee twice and listening to Olive bark approximately every 6 seconds all the way home could not dampen my spirits. The thinking about others part refers to tomorrow's "Archaeology Camp Baking Exchange" wherein all four Campers will bake a mystery item, divide it four ways, and send it on its way on Monday. Then, next weekend, we will have a tasting of all four items, only one of which we had to bake ourselves. I cannot wait to partake in this seeming Ponzi scheme or pyramid scheme or chain letter of baked goods! It seems almost too good to be true; rather, it's just a few friends thinking of others. My stomach thanks them already. Airing oneself out / from time to time is wise. Oth- / erwise, you get stale. Dream of dancing delights, Angels, and wake to locate your measuring cups.

As the sun sets on Day 345, I mark one year since my last haircut. No lie. Over the last 366 days (2020 was a leap year), I've grown to like my longer locks. Reminds me of when I was young. Growing up, I had long hair, parted in the middle, two barrettes, thank you very much. You know the look. I hated having my hair combed. Tackling those tangles was so annoying. At some point, I'd hit my wall and go running outside to hide up in the magnolia. I never did learn much about hair (said Captain Obvious). Thankfully, Molly has successfully mastered cutting her own hair, and she's offered to try to learn how to cut mine. Now, that is an exemplary spouse! Sunday winds down. The / weekend slips away. I'm glad / weekends are a thing. Sleep soundly, Campers, and wake to the promise of a new week and maybe even a haircut.

As the sun sets on Day 346, I tip my hat to citizen advocates everywhere. All manner of citizens were busy today advocating to save our democracy. It was inspiring. Just as showing gratitude improves your mood and outlook, so does pitching in to work on a common cause together. Find something that matters to you, and get to work. And also get some sleep; you can't save the world without a good night's rest. If you work a week's / worth Monday, can you start your / weekend on Tuesday? Dream of democracy, Angels, and wake to exercise your considerable rights!

As the sun sets on Day 347 (prime!), I wonder if I'll be able to sleep tonight. Tomorrow is my appointment with the knee surgeon! I'm hoping it'll serve as the pre-op, and I will leave with a date for the surgery. I'm excited to get this show on the road! The December 4 injury feels like a long time ago. I've been trying to walk Walter, but it feels crummy. It's not impossible, but it's crummy. Even standing at my standing desk for more than an hour or so doesn't feel good. I'm ready to get things fixed up and get back to my dog walking and Yoga. I'm pretty sure I've never been this excited for a medical appointment. Bring it! I made myself feel better this evening by sampling the first box received in the Archaeology Camper Baking Exchange. Deeeeee-licious!! It (they) brought a smile. The chain letter of baked goods really pays off! The harness and leash / come out when the sun appears. / Get your dog walk on! Sleep sweetly, Campers, for tomorrow brings new opportunities!

As the sun sets on Day 348, the plot thickens re: the ol' trick knee. The surgeon won't know for sure if the medial meniscus can be repaired until he gets in there. If it can't repair it, he'll just clean it up, and recovery will be a couple weeks. Pretty straightforward and common (just ask Molly). If, on the other hand, he can repair it, he will do the more complicated procedure, and recovery will be...wait for it...two MONTHS. As in, non-weight-bearing for two months. Eeek. That sounds like a long time, even though

Time moves at a different rate now. Still, the more cushioning I can retain, the better. Short-term vs. long-term benefits. I guess we haven't talked about Balance in a while. We're a little out of balance over here. Olive is dealing with her syndrome. Molly is trying to get to the bottom of some significant health problems, too. I guess Walter's the only one on his game (and he weighed in heavy at the vet the other day, so he may be headed for a reduction in his daily treat allotment). How am I supposed to practice Patience when I can't practice my Yoga, I ask you? I suppose I should be able to lean into those 19.5 years of prior practice. No excuses! I shall just focus on all the future dog walks and down dogs and hikes. Those sure sound good right about now. Well, on a more positive note, the second box in the Archaeology Camper Baking Exchange arrived, and it, too, was marvelous! Seriously, get yourself into one of these chain letters of baked goods stat! Imagining two / months on crutches was not on / my mind this morning. Chin up, Angels, because you just never know.

As the sun sets on Day 349, I lament the fact that so much is going on right now, my brain has been too busy to notice the little magical things very often. I love the little magical things (I'm thinkin' about you, persistent pea plant). I miss them. Perhaps that shall be my goal for the weekend: try to take a few quiet moments and look around for some of those little magical things that are still there, even if my over-taxed system doesn't notice them. And now, instead of a joke, a deep thought (of sorts), as seen on the Interwebs: "Sometimes, I feel useless, but then I remember I breathe out carbon dioxide for plants." So, there. Even if I walk / past them, the little magi- / cal things still exist. Dream of little magical things, Campers, and wake to enjoy them.

As the sun sets on Day 350, we celebrate our 50th week together! The big 5-0! Will wonders never cease. (No. No, they will not.) How are you feeling on this big milestone? I had a couple friend Zooms today, and some cracks are showing, including in my general direction. We've been doing this a long time now, my friends. I mean, I know it could (and still might) be longer, but let's give ourselves a break. This has been a lot. And we need to keep it together for a bit longer. Get those shots in arms. (I'm waving mine wildly over here. Stick me! Stick me!) Together, we will trudge forward and see what comes next. I sit in the dark / a bit stunned. It's become a / familiar feeling. Dream of peaceful pursuits, Angels, and wake to be kind to yourself.

WEEK #51
Saturday, February 27, 2021 – Friday, March 5, 2021

"States Itching to Open Up, to Dismay of C.D.C.: Issuing Warning Even as 3rd Vaccine Is Set to be Authorized" (Sheryl Gay Stolberg, *The New York Times*, February 27, 2021)

"FDA Says It Will 'Rapidly Work' to Approve J&J's One-Dose Vaccine" (Laurie McGinley and Carolyn Y. Johnson, *The Seattle Times*, February 27, 2021)

"Vaccine Demand Still Far Exceeds Supply, But State Expects More Doses" (Kie Relyea, *The Bellingham Herald*, February 27, 2021)

As the sun sets on Day 351, we howl at another full moon. One of our best friends turned 60 today, and like Molly when celebrating her 50th on the full moon last month, she's howling at the moon with her friends. We also burned some things in the fire (memories, regrets, experiences, baggage). While I'm not the first one to propose such rituals, I've participated willingly the last couple of months, and I have to admit, they have been really rewarding. I really liked the burning tonight. Time to let some [poop emoji] go. Our country doesn't have a whole lot of rituals, at least of a certain kind, and during the pandemic, we are missing out on so many of the ones we do have. Rituals are important, though, and there are still ways to hold them. Don't neglect your rituals and your marking of the passage of time. They may not seem that important, but you might really enjoy them, especially now. Campfires are nice to / build and watch and even burn / some stuff to cinders. Dream of crackling campfires, Campers, and wake to renew your rituals.

As the sun sets on Day 352, we celebrate another birthday: Molly's Mom turned 78 today. We had a family Wine and Cheese Zoom complete with cheeses from Murray's in New York City shipped to us by Molly's sister. It was really fun and so good to "see" everyone. It's been a long time since we've hung out with all the Minnesota and Indiana crews. Trying to stick to some semblance of the birthday ritual during pandemic times. We also wind down another weekend and look ahead to the unknown. I see people all around just trying to do their thing. The worry still lurks, but the desire to live and think about other things is there. So many things swirl / around us all the time. Fo- / cus on one and Go! Sleep well, Angels, and wake to a new month!

As the sun sets on Day 353, I grow weary. Weary of waiting. Weary of the status quo. I'm ready for a happy knee, a vaccination, wrapping a second virtual Summit, and sitting on the back deck in my lawn chair. For a very long, quiet, uninterrupted time. Do I think any of these things are going to happen, at least any time soon? No, I do not. But I think I'll focus on them instead of my weariness. It's time to shift the outlook, even if that feels harder to do right now. I'm not sure where to look for inspiration. I am, instead, focusing on getting my work ship-shape before surgery so that I can muddle through the brain fog without too much impact. Since this Missive has been sort of a downer thus far, I looked up some knee jokes. They are pretty bad: No matter what treatment I did on my knee, it still complained; I have never seen such a whi-knee! I recently went fishing with my friend, and we were surprised to catch something with two knees; it turned out to be a two-knee fish! My friend had a weird disease where she couldn't remember that she had knees; the doctors diagnosed it as a case of am-knee-sia! During the game, my friend was injured; it looked like ago-knee! I once met a man who had many knees; he was from the country of Poly-Knee-Sia! Boy, those are painful. I kneed a break. However, I have been distracted and can move on. I hope they have moved you, too! Sleep well, Campers, and don't worry…no jokes tomorrow.

As the sun sets on Day 354, I celebrate a surgery date! I am booked for Thursday, March 11, which happens to be the one-year anniversary of the World Health Organization declaring the pandemic. The 12th will be one year since I went inside our local grocery store (I realize that's extreme, but I became enamored with grocery pickup); the 13th will be one year since the Bellingham School District closed; and the 14th will be one year of Missives! I like to think, therefore, that as we hit these anniversaries, my surgery will mark a New Beginning. I'll get fixed up; we'll throw a 2nd Virtual Summit; and perhaps I shall get my vaccination by the end of May as the President predicted today. Then, it's off to Huntsville for the big celebration of my Dad. Could that be a teensy glimmer of light at the end of a very long tunnel? It's been a very long tunnel, indeed, but I often think about how much longer it could have been if we didn't have such brilliant scientists who came up with a vaccine in a mind-blowingly short amount of time. Thank goodness for them!! Add to this the fact that Olive is snoozing away on her first dose of Melatonin after a few ruff nights and Spring will arrive on the 20th, and things appear to be looking up. Weariness can some- / times be followed by a re- / newed optimism. Sleep soundly, Angels, with the assurance that things always change.

As the sun sets on Day 355, I tip my hat to a sense of purpose. Work, work, work; tidy up; dial in doggie meds; rest up; clean out your Inbox; change your sheets; pick up some groceries. Get ready for your next normal. Every so often, one comes around the bend. I'll be bringing mine in on crutches but with that bigger, better goal in mind. In addition to all the readying, this week has proven a little Zoomy again, so it'll be nice to hit Pause on that for a bit. Remember days off and vacations? I almost don't, but I like to try. Break up the monotony, folks. Step back and do something you like, even if it's just for a short time. Humans cannot live on work alone. Ginger miso ra- / men is something that I learned / I like. A whole lot. Dream of something you like to do, Campers, and wake to chart your course.

As the sun sets on Day 356, I eagerly await tomorrow's third Wine Club meeting. Per our guidebook, March is Syrah/Shiraz. It's one of my faves. Big, bold, juicy, spicy. Goes with pizza. Yes, please, and pour me another. Remember: step back and do something you like. Also: having something to look forward to can be pleasant. So many things we have learned here together over the past 356 days! I'm very grateful. I mean, not for the pandemic, of course, but for this most unique opportunity to spend all this quality time together. Well, maybe "quality" is giving it too much credit when you consider things like silly jokes and questionable haikus, but even those seem to have brought some smiles; so, I guess those count, too. The time spent here to- / gether has not been wasted. / I'm very grateful. Sleep sweetly, Angels, because you are heroes.

As the sun sets on Day 357, we celebrate our 51st week together.

Hmmm…now, how many weeks are in a year? 52! We are one week from our year anniversary! That will fall specifically on Sunday, March 14. One week from this Sunday. (I just keep typing variations on this theme because, frankly, I'm in shock.) Microsoft Word tells me I'm on page 100. I'm nearly certain I've never written 100 pages before, even with my thesis (I think…I mean, who ever looks at their thesis again?) What does this all mean? I don't know. Probably that you are very patient people. No matter what's go- / ing on, Time keeps on marching. / Just look at you now! Dream of your ideal year, Campers, and wake to get started!

WEEK #52
Saturday, March 6, 2021 – Friday, March 12, 2021

"Surprise Jump In Job Growth Stirs Optimism: Biggest Gain Since Fall Is Led by Restaurants" (Patricia Cohen, *The New York Times*, March 6, 2021)

"Senate Democrats Reach Accord On Relief Bill's Jobless Benefits" (Erica Werner, Jeff Stein, and Tony Romm, *The Seattle Times*, March 6, 2021)

"(Governor) Inslee Expands Next Group Eligible for Vaccination to Include All Critical Workers" (Sara Gentzler, *The Bellingham Herald*, March 6, 2021)

As the sun sets on Day 358, we wrap our final week before our final week. Haha…I'm still just typing because I'm in shock at these numbers. Tonight, I tip my hat to buds. Now, talk about a word with some homonyms. I was primarily thinking about all the beautiful, delicate, promising BUDS out there preparing for Spring's arrival on the 20th, as well as the ones my neighbors dropped off at our door (right off the plum tree whose fruits I will turn into jam in a few months). Think of allllllll we've been through together since the last Spring Equinox. And you know, at the same time, our friends in the Southern Hemisphere will be welcoming Fall. The Earth keeps on moving. Then, there are the BUDS down at the pot shop. Something tells me those shops have seen an increase in business since the last Spring Equinox. Then, there are the BUDS that are you all. My buds. Each other's buds. Beautiful plant buds; beautiful human buds. A fun, short word full of potential. Warning: silly joke ahead…What do you call flowers who are BFFs? Buds. I should have said "jokes" plural because I can't omit these: What do you say when you want a flower to drive faster? Floret! What do flowers study in college? Stem. You're welcome, buds! Dream of fields of gold, Angels, and wake to be one day closer.

As the sun sets on Day 359, we say night-night to another weekend. Anyone else think those 48 hours move faster than others? Ah, well…that's how it goes. It's good to break out of the weekday routine and do something different for a little while, if you are able. We also welcome in International Women's Day tomorrow. I wish all my Warrior Women a very happy Day. I, for one, am glad to be a woman, even with all the BS that comes with it at times. I'm excited to hear some stories tomorrow about amazing women and all the ground-breaking things they have done. Women rule the world. / We all know it. Let's be glad / and get on with it. [OK, I know I'm not supposed to weigh in, but that might be one of the best haikus yet!] Dream of your strengths and your gifts, Campers, because they are many and mighty.

As the sun sets on Day 360 [that's a nice number to play around with!], I tip my hat to Women, particularly the Heroic Woman who mothers Olive with me. Part of Olive's new behaviors involves pestering Molly relentlessly from about 6am until 8am. Molly is innocently trying to drink her coffee, read her news, and have some "me" time before work, all while Olive pesters her for food, runs her in and out of the backyard, and grumbles and barks at her. We are extremely good at reading Olive, and we cannot figure out what she needs. I swear every one of her needs is being met, from food to pain relief to potty time to treats to thunder shirts to you name it. And still, she pesters on. While this is happening, I'm in the bedroom with the covers over my head trying to sleep, and it can all be maddening. I feel like yelling at her at times, and Molly just ignores her and then takes her out and then talks to her and then sits on the floor with her and almost never gets flustered. I mean, once in a while I hear her tell Olive to hush, but it's not mean; then, a few minutes later, I hear her apologizing to Olive for not being able to understand what she needs. This morning, Olive continued to pester Molly when she went to shower; so, I dragged myself out of bed, explained to Olive that she was driving Molly crazy when all she was doing was trying to help her, and herded her into her bed. She settled down after a while, and when Molly snuck out of the house around 8am, Olive got up once to look around, came back to her bed, and promptly fell sound asleep. And then, my alarm went off. (It's possible I re-set it. Lasso of Truth: I re-set it so fast.) So, Molly wins my Heroic Woman award today. May I aspire to be like my dog…nope, like my dog's mommy. Sometimes, you try eve- / rything, and you still can't fig- /ure out what they want. Sleep, Angels; that's it…just Sleep.

As the sun sets on Day 361, I tip my hat to dark, quiet homes full of sleeping bodies, human and canine. Is there a sweeter setting? If so, I do not know it (further proof, perhaps, that I need to get out a lot more often). I am glad this day is a wrap. It was one of those ridiculous work days where one thing followed the last with hardly a break to be seen. Made it kind of hard to prep for Thursday. Oh, yeah…and the day started with my first COVID test in advance of surgery. Speaking of, I must send up a Missive flare once again: would any Campers like to cover Thursday and Friday nights? I have a sneaking suspicion I will be mentally Very Unavailable. Jump in, if you wish! The Seattle news is now showing some beautiful pictures of tonight's sunset. It is time for me to throttle back and smell some roses. I've barely made it outside this week, and the Spring sunshine is here. I encourage you all to go out, look up, breathe in, sit down. Don't miss what Mother Nature is offering us. It's better than what's on our screens! Busy days happen, / but don't let them cause you to / miss out on Springtime. Dream of flowers and warmer days, Campers, and wake to notice them.

As the sun sets on Day 362 (why, yes…3 times 2 does equal 6…and so on), a hush settles over our home base. A hush tinged with the scent of antibacterial soap and a final piece of toast. Time to get one's game face on. Actually, time to get one's compliant face on and do exactly what they tell you. Hopefully, at this time tomorrow, I will be nestled into my couch bed clutching the remote, and recovery will be underway. I wonder what it's like to be the surgeon right now. I mean, he's (hopefully) done hundreds of these (he has), so this might be just a regular ol' night. Or not. I mean, if it were me, I don't think I'd ever feel like it was old hat. Well, who knows? As long as he's not drinking heavily tonight, we are good. Thank you to any Guest Missivers who step in the next couple of nights. I will be back on Saturday (Day 365), which might be kinda funny. Or weird. We'll see. Then, our big One Year Anniversary on Sunday. Good grief. Who would have thought? (Well, maybe an epidemiologist would have thought.) Stop your eating, wash / your bod, drink your water, get / some sleep. It's Go Time. Sleep well, Angels, and show some gratitude for your good health, warts and all.

[Day 363 = Guest Missive by Mel]

As the moon rises on Day 363, our thoughts are on Mary as the sun sets on her surgery day. Molly's initial report is the knee gave up the ghost, but it'll make the recovery period quicker. So, hope returns that the persistent peas may have their day in the sun this summer after all.

The amazing thought of the evening is we are once again together talking about peas. Which means it's been a year already. Reflect a moment on what you've endured in the past year. And by the grace of God, we are all still here to process it together. That is a blessing. We cannot go back and change time, but we can reflect on lessons learned through difficult experiences and how to carry those forward to honor what we've collectively been through. Personally or vicariously, we've endured it together and that is true friendship.

Lessons learned – reply with your top three. For mine:

1) Being in the presence of another human. Living alone has made this past year interesting when no one wants to be near another. I suspect it may feel the opposite when you are locked in with folks you can't escape. Perspective.

2) Pushing pause on life long enough to slow down and realize ALL I was missing by living on warp speed. And promising myself not to return to that. When I can control the pace, that is.

3) Time is fleeting and precious. While this year may have felt longer than any other, the time with those we lost during it can't ever be reclaimed. So appreciating every interaction, even very small ones, as the bigger picture is vaster than we can begin to imagine. Sleep well, Angels; we need our strength to share with Mary and to keep our pace up in this marathon of unscripted and unprecedented times. List your three lessons to share below.

[Mel's excellent Missive solicited a number of responses]
Mary:

Mmmmm...a wonderful Missive! It is so nice to hear another Angel's voice. Thank you!

Three Lessons From the Past Year:

1) This is a VERY special group of Angels. They listen and support and encourage. They show up. They drink down. They persist. They are inquisitive. They are generous. They are Warrior Women.

2) We can do hard things. Take your pick this year! Isolate. Persevere. Worry. Exercise. Work. School. Family. Sickness. Death. Animals. Dinners. Travel. Wait. Surgery. Politics. Movie releases. Tragedies. Isolate. Yes, that one again. All of these things are part of Life, but living in Isolation is a harder thing.

3) Time keeps marching. Here we are, almost at our one-year anniversary. Time can move slowly (isolation, inoculation, politics, real change). Time can move quickly (weekends, one year in retrospect, a lifetime in review, weekends). We are here. We are making it. We are Warrior Women. But only Together.

(And now, we are tired again. Have a great day, Angels!!)

Cathy:

1) Everyone deserves grace (especially yourself).

2) How to let go that which I cannot control (learning to let go of worry, anxiety or stress).

3) Random acts of kindness make me happy and spread love.

Margaret:

1) We truly have no idea what the next hour, day, month, or year may bring. Just gotta roll with it.

2) There's always more than one way to get something done (i.e. we CAN toss out old habits.)

3) The world needs a lot more listening and a lot less talking.

BONUS: There are some really good TV shows out there.

Elizabeth:

1) You can only pour out what you've been poured into.

2) If you can't run, walk; can't walk, crawl; can't crawl, roll; can't roll, float...just keep moving forward, even if reliant on the current.

3) I feel all things deeply, and when healthy, I send to my brain quickly; when exhausted, I just feeeeeeel...and that's not productive.

4) Bonus 1: Even introverts need in-person community.

5) Bonus 2: Thankful beyond words and feelings for you Angels!

Cameron:

Lessons for the year...great idea and discipline, Mel. Thank you. I started weeping this morning when my son's third grade teacher shared a thought about the year anniversary of school closing (for us it is today, March 12). What a scary time it was and is, but we have made it this far, and there have been some good learnings and even silver linings. For me they are:

1) I really enjoy my family and am really thankful for them and that.

2) My emotional happiness depends greatly on (among other things) getting to work in my strengths. I can work not in my strengths all day, but it makes me grumpy. Working in my strengths makes me happy.

3) It is hard to know what someone is else is thinking/feeling/ how they are dealing with the emotional stress of a pandemic, but it is important to remember that we are all. I guess it is that grace thing that Murt was talking about.

Bonus 1: I cannot control much of the world, but I can do my best to control the 10 square inches that is my brain. It makes all the difference.

Bonus 2: I don't like meal planning and cooking, but I can do hard things!

Leslie:

1) I tend to put important things on the back burner when work gets busy, and sometimes they fall off the stove. I apologize for being late with this and the missive.

2) There really is something to knowing friends through decades of life that transcends every other type of friendship.

3) I am grateful, as Cam said, for my family and the people they all are. I love spending time with them.

Bonus 1: Individuals and families go through phases. My son has turned a corner, reaching for more independence, and that's normal and healthy and hard as hell.

Bonus 2: The people I'm closest to in my life are amazing, strong individuals whom I admire and learn from every day.

[Day 364 = Guest Missive by Phoenix]

Wow, look who fell asleep on the couch. Did I say I would do a missive? Lol, too much vivid vision to cram into a text, but I'll lay the first scene on you. But first, if I've never said it out loud before, I'd like to raise a glass to the strong women business owners in my life; truly, all of you guys, it hit me, own your own business (yes, even you, Symbol, you boss). I guess I've always wanted to own my own business, so this is probably where this dream is coming from.

So, what if the systems we set up can mostly self-perpetuate and can help people and can share the spirit of Camp and can allow us to do more Camping? This is the problem I've been noodling. I don't have all the answers, but I'm ready to share some ideas. The first idea is a pop-up store that sells Camp crates, t-shirts and merch, and flowers. I have drawn what goes in the crates, but I'm sure you can improve it. Proceeds go to rotating charities. I'm interested in real estate, so next started plotting how to have a free space, e.g. if you bought a commercial building and rented out part of it to pay for the whole thing or something like that. It's too bad we are so far apart. We will just have to pop up everywhere. That will be part of our charm. I have many more thoughts about all of this, but it's so late that it's early now, so I'll sign off with my rough crate sketch.

[Phoenix's excellent Missive solicited some responses]
Spicoli:

Camp craft: homemade tiki torch. Directions: drink bottle of gin, insert wick and wick holder, fill with torch fluid, and Magic.

D. Prince:

You are all AMAZING!! So Good and Creative and Generous.

Update: I feel my knee a little more today, but I get to shower, so that should help. It's just nice to be able to get to the bathroom on my own! Simple pleasures. Gonna get up for some breakfast now. Love you!

[Day 364 = Guest Missive by Leslie]

As the sun rises on day 365, I tip my hat to our friend, the Missive. I didn't leave my writing until this morning on purpose, but forgetting last night (and no more wine was consumed after dinner, which pulled me off Zoom, I just flat-out forgot) at the end of what I can only describe as a postmodern week gave me such appreciation for the dedication and discipline of Mary, our Missive Creator. How many mornings have we all reached for our phones or laptops, perhaps after reading a more obliquely religious devotional but before facing the secular news of the day, and spent time with our friend, the Missive? How many times have the various and sundry metaphors and childhood character friends and words of Rossi wisdom reassured us that yes, this would be another COVID day, but like that persistent pea plant, like that Amazon warrior (from whom Rosie the riveter surely drew inspiration) together we could do it?! If the Missive has helped you navigate work full of Zoom and lacking human interaction, kids and animals and contractors and husbands and wives who're tired of you and just want to go play with their friends or needy for you when you get a bit tired of them, guilt that you have all you need but are still on empty because, let's face it, pandemics suck— if our friend the Missive has helped you, then raise an early morning glass in Her honor (the Missive is surely female, am I right?) Cheers to the guiding star, the bringer of kairos time to our chronos-burdened days, the persistent pea plant, best joke, and secret piece of Dove chocolate all rolled into one: to the Missive! Thank you, Mary, for bringing her to us so faithfully for what will tonight be a full year.

[Leslie's sweet Missive prompted a response from Mary]

Whoa. So, I was just making sure to copy/paste the Guest Missives into my Master Word doc, and I re-read Leslie's from this morning. Thank YOU for noticing (dedication and discipline) and for toasting (coffee, donuts, toast, whatever). I REALLY appreciate that. I'm not gonna lie...some nights, it was a grind. I was tired; you were tired; the world was tired. But I did not want to let you down. I had the late-night energy (almost all the time), and I wanted to do it for you. I suspected it became a small but important part of the day so that you didn't feel alone; so that you knew others were with you; so that you knew we could do it Together; so that you knew that you, too, are Warrior Women. Thank you for loving the Missive. We owe Her a lot, including me, because, Angels, the secret is...I'm not always sure where She came from. Most nights, I was as surprised as you. I'm gonna miss Her, but She'll show up here and there. I do think that's the light at the end of the tunnel that we are seeing, so it's time for Her to get some down-time, too. I'm excited for when She does show up, though. I can always use a new silly joke or haiku. So, stay tuned....

FINAL TWO DAYS
Saturday, March 13, 2021 – Sunday, March 14, 2021

Saturday, March 13, 2021

"U.S. Takes Step To Use Vaccine For Diplomacy" (Sheryl Gay Stolberg and Michael Crowley, *The New York Times*, March 13, 2021)

"(Governor) Inslee Orders Some In-Person Learning For All K-12 Students" (Hannah Furfaro, Joseph O'Sullivan, and Dahlia Bazzaz, *The Seattle Times*, March 13, 2021)

"(Governor) Inslee to Issue Order Requiring Option of In-person Classes for All Students" (Sara Gentzler, *The Bellingham Herald*, March 13, 2021)

[Day 365 = Guest Missive by Cameron]

As the sun sets on Day #XXX (I'm not sure what the exact number count is, and will leave that to Mary, the number-keeper), I tip my hat to a firm foundation. This summer, when we went to the beach right after our bout with COVID, we got to take a boat tour of a mangrove thicket. We got to explore a barrier island/sandbar that separated the thicket from the open sea. It was beautiful; a long swath of white sand beach and clear water lapping the beach. When we disembarked, it was funny that we unexpectedly sank shin-deep (knee deep on my daughter) into the sand. It was fun for about 10 steps, and then became really frustrating. One could not predict if you would sink an inch or 12 inches on any given step, nor how long it would take to dislodge said foot for the next step. When I stumbled upon a patch of firm sand, it was such a relief and a joy and an A-ha! Firm foundations make all the difference...I think I read that in a book about building on sand or something. Anyway, for this purpose I tip my hat to the firm foundation of friendship, of routine, of missives, and of our angels. Thank you for being / a firm foundation of love / and sharing this life. Night-night!

[Cameron's Missive prompted another response from Mary]

Whoa. So, another great Guest Missive! That is quite the haiku, Cam, as well as a great reminder about firm foundations. How true. I think a lot about that parable, too (house on sand; house on rock). I was lucky: my parents gave me the firmest of foundations. When I grew up, most of that held, but some of it changed because I'm my own person. But I hope the stones I traded out kept the overall foundation intact. And then I added others of my own choosing...like you Angels. And now, I have a freakin' castle!! It gives me the strength and confidence to get up in the morning. To try to do something Good each day (or just something, if that's all I can muster). To survive a pandemic for a year. To not give up. To keep going. You are stones in my foundation. I hope I'm the same in yours. Bring it. Cuz you know the Universe will. But you've learned this year that you can do it. The Universe also taught us that. So, get out there and do it. If the pea can, you can.

Sunday, March 14, 2021

"Focusing on the Bright Side in the Sunshine State" (Patricia Mazzei, *The New York Times*, March 14, 2021)

"U.S. Thinks Big, Achieves Much, Neglects Basics" (Griff Witte, Abigail Hauslohner, and Emily Wax-Thibodeaux, *The Seattle Times*, March 14, 2021)

"Business Owners Excited for 50% Capacity" (Dave Gallagher, *The Bellingham Herald*, March 14, 2021)

As the sun sets on Day 366 [Sunday, March 14, 2021], I'm smiling, once again, in the glow of the TV while the household slumbers because Campers, We Made It. Together. A full year of Nightly Missives. What in the world?? Among other things, I think the Missive has taught us that we are still standing, now with new strengths and understanding. Each of you has made this possible.

Spicoli with her wisdom and integrity and mother-wisdom (you know what I mean).

Symbol with her care and adventure and knowledge (of all things, professional and pop).

Phoenix with her inquisitiveness and creativity and deep feeling (for family and others).

Cameron (Margarita) with her service and dinner preps and family beach adventures.

Catherine (Hoyden) with her nursing and car camping and expanding family.

Cathy (Ring Leader) with her enviro stewardship and family hikes and Chick-Fil-A.

Elizabeth (Aunt Button) with her leadership and loooooong bike rides and tiny humans.

Leslie (Grocery Warrior) with her love of lit and air fryer and wordsmithing.

Margaret (Murt) with her creativity and justice and knowledge of all the good shows.

Mel with her farm skills and determination and four-legged charges.

I'm certainly not doing you Campers and Angels justice, but I thought it important to mention each of you on this important anniversary. Kipling was correct: "For the strength of the Pack is the Wolf, and the strength of the Wolf is the Pack." What a prescient lesson for 2020-21. I tip my hat deeply to my Wolves and my Pack. You are important to me. Thanks for listening to me for a year. We'll have some more Missives here and there, but it's time to get to work and time to get to living. I'm excited to do some of that Together again, too! So, how about a "final" haiku? I wrote this one a few weeks ago and thought it might be a good one for tonight. Sometimes, you find the / haiku; sometimes it finds you; / all these were for You. Dream of a world that models the Missives, Campers and Angels, and know that you can wake to make it so.

♥♥♥♥♥

And just like that, an entire year of Nightly Missives came to a close. She did not abandon us entirely, however. As promised, She made an appearance a few more times….

As the sun sets on Day 385 [Friday, April 2, 2021…Good Friday…our 55th week together!], I return again to the keyboard… in the glow of the TV, of course, while all but Olive are snoozling (Olive is talking to me, but I'm not sure what she wants; maybe her Melatonin). I have missed you all! I intended to offer up a Missive at the fortnight mark, but we can all see how that worked out. I have been busy recovering from the knee surgery, finishing a big work project (the first phase, anyway), and exploring health issues (Molly and Olive). Except for a minor setback last Sunday, my knee is healing up well; Olive is having her spleen out next Friday; and Molly is having several tests done with an eye on what I think will prove to be the cause. Over on the COVID front, Molly will be considered "fully vaccinated" on the 10th with me following on the 24th. Progress!! Tomorrow, we will enjoy a very extravagant outing to the movies where we will be treated to our own private screening of *Wonder Woman 1984*. Next week is Spring Break in our school district. The experts say the tulips will bloom sometime during that week. We are less than 6 weeks from the 14th Annual and 2nd Virtual Summit.

Besides reading all these things into the record, I also wanted to point them out because, as we have learned here, Time continues marching on; some things are good, some not so good. [FYI, Olive didn't need the Melatonin; she needed a potty break and a few treats.] But the world keeps spinning. And you can spin right out of a not-so-good time and find yourself smack dab in the middle of another good time. Or vice versa…but that's OK because then the other better thing happens again. I've been thinking again about these sorts of things as my already narrow world became even narrower post-op. I have spent most of my time icing in my couch bed. Thankfully (maybe), I have been able to work comfortably from said couch bed, so it has become my little universe. Ice, work, eat, rest, work, eat, TV, work, TV. One afternoon seems to drag on to infinity, and then all of a sudden, you hit your three-week post-op mark (yesterday). All these "Time keeps marching" lessons convince me to just keep going. Don't like where you are today? That's likely going to change in the next few days (or maybe a week or so, but it probably won't be too awfully long). I think that's why the saying "Time heals all wounds" keeps floating around. While the wounds don't heal exactly, they do change. Hopefully, they change in a way that makes them easier to carry around. They may still be painful, but maybe you're not in pain all the time. I dunno… just some thoughts from the couch bed. Maybe you've had some thoughts from your own couch bed recently. I hope they have been good ones. Time is marching. Spring / is springing. We move through this / life with each other. Sleep well, Angels, because I have learned how important sleep really is (see how early this was posted?)

As the sun sets on Day 386, a haiku: Watching a movie / in your own private thea- / ter is pretty rad. Dream of saving the day, Angels, because you are the Hero of your story.

As the sun sets on Day 483 [Friday, July 9, 2021…our 69th week together! Yes, I was just counting by hand], I am thrilled to announce that the Missive has returned! Well, for one day, at least. I thought she would have appeared again before Day 483, but she became extremely distracted by the 14th Annual and 2nd Virtual Summit and her Dad's Celebration of Life. Well, those are now a wrap, and she felt like checking in with you Angels once again.

She writes to you not from the glow of the TV this time but from the glow of the early morning sunshine streaming in the window of Row 29 on Alaska Flight 1415 from Nashville to Seattle (although, she is now posting to you from…the glow of the TV!) We are both somewhere over Montana, I believe.

I am winging home from my Dad's Celebration, which we held on Wednesday, June 30. It would have been his 85th birthday. My Mom designed the whole affair herself (including the centerpieces) and worked on it for months. It involved a funeral Mass (that my Dad designed) followed by a picnic lunch in the Parish Hall (my Dad loooooved a good picnic). It was well-attended as my folks are "VIPs" at their Church, and the mood was wonderful. My Mom asked us kids (me, my brother, and my sister) to read some "Thank-You's" that she wanted to extend publicly. My bro and sis were reluctant to take on the public speaking, so they stood with me while I channeled some of that Summit Zoom hosting experience I've garnered over the past 483 days. I hope I made my Dad proud by practicing in advance the pronunciation of names, trying to project and enunciate, and working in a few jokes here and there…he was in Toastmasters for years (I'm even coming home with his Past President pin for the shadow box of mementos). After our picnic, we cleaned up and headed to the columbarium as a family (9 of us total). Several of us, including me, hadn't even had the chance yet to visit my Dad there in person. What a wonderful place! He is in a great niche with trees overhead and birds and dragonflies zipping about; geckos, too! It's very peaceful there, and my Mom goes often to sit on the bench and visit. I was a bit sad for sure, but mainly because I just wished he could be there with us. He would have loved it. Then, home for family time…and because it's the South, friend and neighbor time, too…with lots of food! By Sunday morning, our party of 9 had dwindled to 2: me and my Mom. We spent the 4th of July sitting on the patio for the entire day and reminiscing. It was wonderful! Monday and Tuesday, we went on picnics (and then sat on the patio until it got dark). Wednesday was for visits from high school friends and packing. Thursday was for Nashville friends and heading for the airport. Friday…well, that's today. It's for flying and hugging spouse and doggies and sitting on the deck.

After wrapping knee surgery, Olive surgery, Molly to Mayo, the Summit, and the Celebration, I am finally starting to breathe more freely again. Having these things in the rearview mirror is such a relief. I know you, too, have been through so much, as has the entire world. I, for one, strongly feel that the entire planet should get the summer off. We all need some deep rest and recuperation. However, as we have learned over the past 483 days, the world keeps spinning, and people are anxious to get back to their busy lives (as is evident by the full flight). I am now tracking news of the Delta variant with some concern, but I'm hoping our shots and our masks might get us through this new wrinkle, as well. The Missive and I think of you every single day, even if we don't always write. I hope you are feeling stronger and more optimistic with each day that passes. That, I hope, is the Legacy of the Missive. Stronger Together and such. Winging over the / U.S. I start to exhale. / All good things to y'all. Well, we haven't been practicing our haikus lately, but I hope you like that one. Sleep soundly, Angels, and know that the Missive marches on, no matter what.

Afterword

Thank you, again, to the Campfire Girls, the College Angels, Molly, Olive, Walter, and my entire family, especially my Mom who encouraged me to put the Missives out into the wider world. Y'all helped me get through a whole lotta days!

A heartfelt extra thank-you to Olive who had to leave us on September 7, 2021, for that very special place where all good dogs go. We are certain she gave us some extra time to help us through a very difficult stretch. We miss her every single day. In the spirit of the Missive, we try to find solace in this anonymous dedication:

"It came to me that every time I lose a dog, they take a piece of my heart with them. Yet, every new dog who comes into my life gifts me with a piece of their heart. If I live long enough, all the components of my heart will be dog, and I will become as generous and loving as they are."

Here's hoping, Campers and Angels!